ON YOUR MARK

On Your Mark

*Reading Mark
in the Shadow of the Cross*

M<small>EGAN</small> M<small>C</small>K<small>ENNA</small>

ORBIS BOOKS

Maryknoll, New York 10545

Founded in 1970, Orbis Books endeavors to publish works that enlighten the mind, nourish the spirit, and challenge the conscience. The publishing arm of the Maryknoll Fathers and Brothers, Orbis seeks to explore the global dimensions of the Christian faith and mission, to invite dialogue with diverse cultures and religious traditions, and to serve the cause of reconciliation and peace. The books published reflect the views of their authors and do not represent the official position of the Maryknoll Society. To learn more about Maryknoll and Orbis Books, please visit our website at www.maryknoll.org.

The primary source of quotations from scripture is the *Christian Community Bible*, 31st edition (Quezon City/Manila, Philippines: Claretians/St. Pauls, 2000) and is used with permission. A few citations come from the *New American Bible* (© 1986 by the Confraternity of Christian Doctrine) and occasionally passages come from older editions of the *NAB*.

Library of Congress Cataloging-in-Publication Data

McKenna, Megan.
    On your Mark : reading Mark in the shadow of the cross / Megan McKenna.
        p. cm.
    Includes bibliographical references.
    ISBN-13: 978-1-57075-634-4 (pbk.)
    1. Bible. N.T. Mark—Criticism, interpretation, etc. I. Title.

BS2585.52.M35 2006
226.3'06—dc22
                                    2005031848

With gratitude and love for my family in Singapore,
Bernard and Ying Thio and their children,
Jonathan, Justin, Joel, Marie, Michelle, and Jerome

and the Lau family, Bobby, James, and Valerie Lau

For my dear friends Catherine and José deVinck

For Grace Curran,
whose love for Hebrew and Greek inspired me again

Contents

Introduction

On Your Mark, the title I have chosen for this study of the Gospel of Mark, is the beginning of that well-known phrase "On your mark! Get set! Go!" —that familiar summons that calls us to be attentive because a race is about to begin. The endeavor at hand here is the call to discipleship in the Gospel of Mark, the call to follow Jesus and to learn the art of catching men and women for the kingdom of God, as did the prophets and John the Baptist and Jesus himself.

The gospel begins with the initial burst of energy, enthusiasm, and wild hope that is present at the beginning of any race or challenge or serious commitment. The following chapters of the gospel describe in detail Jesus' words and actions as many begin to hear of the dream envisioned by Jesus and as many also reject him as the bearer of the good news of God because it conflicts with their own agendas and plans. Those who reject him run the gamut from the mighty of government and commerce and the leaders of Jesus' own religion to his own family and his disciples. By chapter 8 of Mark, the halfway point of the gospel, Jesus must turn on Peter and his own followers to get them back in line. They must learn to follow him in all things, instead of rejecting the hard part of his teaching, including the reality of who he is and what is going to happen to him as he moves toward Jerusalem and death. That hard part of Jesus' teaching is reflected in the subtitle *Reading Mark in the Shadow of the Cross*.

Chapter 8, truly the hinge of the gospel, is the moment of confrontation, of being assailed by fear and insecurity when faced with the call of conversion to the cross. This is the cost of discipleship. Jesus, the Son of Man, obedient and truthful, has sought to reconcile and bind together in one body men and women, Jews and Gentiles, and those considered unclean or impure and those accepted as ritually and religiously pure and clean.

This second call to conversion is harder by far than the initial call. This is the call to "get set and face the cross," to deny oneself so as not to deny the Lord. It is a call to pick up the cross and follow Jesus all the way to execution and death. Sadly, the disciples begin to avert their eyes and ignore what is developing around them. They refuse to listen to Jesus' warnings and exhortations to stay awake and be attentive.

The reality of "missing the mark" surfaces. Sin becomes a force to be faced as it leads to the final betrayal and abandonment of Jesus by those he called, healed, forgave, and invited to live the good news of God. They appear to be "marking time" as they travel with Jesus, but in reality they are no longer with him in heart and soul. As Jesus admonishes them to "mark my words," they do not listen, growing more and more fearful as they approach Jerusalem.

The last chapter of Mark lays out the disciples' orders to "go," to return to Galilee where they were first chosen and called, to recapture their initial enthusiasm and obedience in light of the resurrection, which demonstrated the truth and power of Jesus' words. They are commanded to go once again and to listen and, this time, to mark Jesus' words and take them to heart, searing them into their minds and souls. They are not to forget that while the shadow of the cross will always be present, it will be dwarfed and engulfed by the light of the resurrection. They and we are summoned to obey and deepen our knowledge of this Jesus who is the suffering servant of Isaiah, the fullness of the Word made flesh among us, and the beloved Son of God who draws us within the Trinity through our baptisms. This Son of Man suffered, died, and rose to judge all peoples and nations with the justice born of the cross and obedience. As we turn from the darkened tomb and rise from the waters of baptism, we should turn again and again to Mark's account of Jesus Christ, the Son of God appearing in the world, remaining in the world, and observing us as we live. It is Jesus who accompanies us, sharing his life, death, and resurrection with us. His dwelling place with God is ours as we become ever more truly the body of Christ in the world.

Mark's gospel is a way to be walked over and over, in our hearts and with other followers. In a preaching class on the Gospel of Mark, one of my students tried to deal with chapter 8, the heart of Mark's gospel. In a moving homily, she connected Jesus' call to Peter and the other disciples to join him at the cross of discipleship with his call to us as Christians today. These short excerpts describe her ministry with students at the University of San Diego.

I spent five days with forty students from San Diego in Tijuana right before Holy Week this year. The University Ministry sponsors this immersion and service trip. . . . At the only place where the first and third worlds share a border, we stood on the Mexican side of the metal fence with barbed wire laced over it. Through the cracks in the wall we could see idyllic, plush San Diego, where the median price of a home is between $400,000 and $600,000. On our side, we were surrounded by the crowded, dusty hills of Tijuana. Here, men earn just fifty cents an hour at work in factories owned by American and European corporations. Here, large families live in shacks made out of old garage doors or in the garbage dumps, literally.

The border fence extends well out into the Pacific Ocean. A tool of the 1994 Operation Gatekeeper designed to keep thousands of illegal immigrants out of the U.S., it has been battered by unrelenting waves smashing up against it for eleven years. One of the young men on the trip said of the peeling and rusting wall: "It's like God is literally spitting in our faces. It's like God is saying, 'Uh-uh. There are no walls in MY house.' "

For the rest of the week, as we traveled throughout Tijuana, I heard a lot of questions: "Why this suffering?" "Why this injustice?" "What can we do?" In the gospels, we hear a lot of questions from Jesus, such as "Who do you say that I am?" The disciples, including Peter, don't really get it, but Jesus does say who he is. He is the "Son of Man." To be his disciple is to follow him "along the way," hearing and responding to the cry of the poor at all cost. The way of discipleship is the way of the cross. It is paved not just with compassion, mercy, and justice. It is ultimately paved with the willing acceptance of cruelty, persecution, suffering, and death—all for the sake of the gospel. So, then, a question: What does it mean to "take up your cross" and follow Jesus "along the way?"

The forty students who came home from Tijuana immediately organized to write letters to their Congressional representatives, to speak at the university about their experiences, to plan return trips to Tijuana to serve in whatever ways they could, and to talk about the parts of their personal lives they needed to change. To "take up your cross" means to act in love and take up the crosses of anguish, oppression, and injustice of the people with whom we share this earth. In God's house, there is no Jew or Gentile, no American or Mexican. Just as Jesus acts on both sides of the lake throughout the Gospel of Mark, we need to stand up for what we believe on all sides of all borders so that we all may rise out of the water and live in justice. Now, the final question: How will each of us rise to the challenge?

Through her struggle with the words of Mark's gospel and the stories of the resurrection during a summer program of theology, Heather Kinney found that the word of God in Mark leads us to cross borders, to straddle fences and to stand in waters we would never think to enter. The gospel reminded her that the reality in which she dwells and ministers might as well have been Galilee at the time of Jesus. The cross and the way are found in divides like the Palestinian West Bank of Israel or a fence strung across an arbitrary piece of land and out into the Pacific Ocean, or in the sand of Iraq or the Sudan or the mountainous terrain of Afghanistan. The cross and the way are also found in urban centers on all the continents of the earth. We are told simply to "go" back to all the places we left, to all the words we rejected and the people we ignored, and to find that our God, Jesus the Christ crucified and risen, is waiting for us and observing us in our lives day by day.

This book seeks to look anew at Mark's account of Jesus' good news of God under the shadow of the cross. The early church reminded those about to be baptized that "they were already saved, on their knees and under the shadow of the cross." This referred to their obedience to the

God of Life and Truth and to the service they would provide to those most in need. It is the cross of Jesus that lifts us from slavery and fear to stand in the light of Jesus' invitation to dwell in the Trinity. Our baptisms draw us into the life Jesus knew with God the Father in the power of the Spirit, into the same relationship of intimacy and power. It is the sign of the Trinity, the sign of the cross, that saves us and makes us ever more true to our calling as the beloved children of God, brothers and sisters of Jesus who listen and are obedient to God's word.

When we are signed with the cross, we promise that we will live not under signs of power but solely under the sign of the cross. In the words of the German pastor Dietrich Bonhoeffer, "When Christ bids us come and follow him, he bids us come and die." This is true, but Jesus also bids us to rise with him and live this risen life together in hope as light to those seeking a way to dwell with others as human beings, blessing God and honoring earth. Mark's gospel is a circle, a spiral that returns again and again to the source, drawing us further into the mystery that is the incarnation and indwelling of God.

When speaking of the cyclic telling of Mark's account of the cross and resurrection of Jesus, I often recall these words of the American writer Henry David Thoreau in his book *Walden*.

> The life in us is like the water in the river. It may rise this year higher than man has ever known it, and flood the parched uplands; even this may be the eventful year, which will drown out all our muskrats. It was not always dry land where we dwell. I see far inland the banks which the stream anciently washed, before science began to record its freshets.
>
> Everyone has heard the story which has gone the rounds of New England, of a strong and beautiful bug which came out of the dry leaf of an old table of apple-tree wood, which had stood in a farmer's kitchen for sixty years, first in Connecticut, and afterwards in Massachusetts, from an egg deposited in the living tree many years earlier still, as appeared by counting the annual layers beyond it; which was heard gnawing out for several weeks, hatched perchance by the heat of an urn. Who does not feel his faith in a resurrection and immortality strengthened by hearing of this? Who knows what beautiful and winged life, whose egg had been buried for ages under many concentric layers of woodenness in the dead dry life of society, deposited at first in the laburnum of the green and living tree, which has been gradually converted into the semblance of its well seasoned tomb,—heard perchance gnawing out now for years by the astonished family of man, as they sat round the festive board,—may unexpectedly come forth from amidst society's most trivial and handselled furniture, to enjoy its perfect summer life at last!

What is it that has been seeded in us in our baptisms, as it has in so many believers, from the time of Jesus' presence upon earth, in Mark's community and two thousand years later in those of us who live far from Palestine and Rome? This seed, this good news of God that buried us in the tomb of Jesus, has been blown open and emptied. Jesus, raised from the dead by the love of the Father and the power of the Spirit, reaches into our bodies and souls and lifts us up. Jesus transforms us into new creatures as the body of the crucified and risen Christ dwelling in the world.

When we stretch out our arms to embrace one another in the world, the form of our bodies carries the shadow of the cross. But it is the light of the resurrection that outlines and marks us as the children of life. We are marked forever by the love of God for us. Now it is our time and our turn to mark the world with the touch of incarnation and inclusion, with compassion and dignity. We begin with the mark that saves us: "In the name of the Father, and of the Son and of the Spirit. Amen."

CHAPTER 1

Reading the Gospel of Mark in the Shadow of the Cross

WE BEGIN AT THE VERY BEGINNING. Mark is commonly accepted as our earliest source of a complete gospel. It is thought to have been written in the first century, around the early to mid sixties, during a time of heightened conflict for the early church. In the face of violent persecution by the Romans, there was increasing pressure from the Jewish community to participate in the resistance against the Romans. This would eventually lead to demands to fight against the Romans to protect the temple in Jerusalem and its practices and worship as the center and heart of Jewish religion and life.

The Beginnings of the Church

Just thirty years after the death of Jesus, the Roman Empire was engaged in a massive persecution of the young Christian churches. The fledging church, powered by the Spirit, had surged into the Mediterranean world. The formerly frightened apostles, all Jews, grew increasingly stronger in their faith and obedience to their Master's command to preach the good news and to pursue his ministry of hope for the poor, of justice and forgiveness for all, and of the arrival of God's kingdom of abiding peace on earth in the person of Jesus of Nazareth who had been crucified as the "King of the Jews." As missionaries and evangelists poured out from Jerusalem and Galilee into the Greek and Roman world along the trade routes and to the centers of learning, the church's growth was phenomenal. Because its practice and message were literally "good news for the poor of the earth," it was among the poor, in particular, that the church flourished.

The movement had begun as an offshoot of Judaism, calling Jews to deeper conversion and to prophetic nonviolent resistance to evil and the influence of Roman imperialism. The growing movement became a new religion with its adherents dubbed the followers of the "Way" (Acts 24). As the church made more and more converts among non-Jews, it became

7

increasingly universal in its membership, including the many peoples of the Roman Empire and beyond.

This expansion brought freshness and enthusiasm among new believers, along with tension among the original followers and their Jewish companions and adherents. Tension arose when the church sought to define itself as not primarily Jewish but as the kingdom of God on earth, a gathering of the companions of the crucified and now risen Jesus. The awareness of Jesus as the beloved Son of God grew and was expressed liturgically through prayer and ritual, including baptism, confirmation, the laying on of hands, and the Eucharist, the breaking of bread together. The faith of the church was being learned, articulated, lived, and passed on by word of mouth in phrases and through the repetition of stories told by Jesus and those who witnessed to him.

But problems arose within the church communities and also because of political, social, and religious factors in the surrounding societies. By the year 60 C.E. both major leaders of the church, Peter in Jerusalem and Rome, and Paul in the missionary areas, had been killed in the persecution. The loss of Peter and Paul is described accurately in the famous quotation that "the blood of martyrs is the seed of Christians." The valor, courage, and witness of the martyrs brought the followers of Jesus closer together and strengthened the faith and purpose of the church. Hundreds, if not thousands, died proclaiming Jesus as Lord and refusing to bow to the Roman emperor as god.

Although there were many martyrs, there were also many apostates, who gave up their faith, dragging the community down in despair and loss. Christians today often tend to look at the early church as an impossible utopian concept or a marvelous time when Christians were intent on becoming martyrs for the faith and were unfamiliar with human weakness or the obvious fears of torture or the loss of life and property that would result from imprisonment. Many succumbed, however, and gave up their faith; others waited until the persecution died down and then returned to the church, seeking forgiveness from the community, soberly aware of their failings, their sin, and how their actions contributed to the loss of faith in others.

The primary teaching of Jesus is forgiveness—for everything, for everyone, in all circumstances and deeds. The early church communities were soon faced with what to do with public sinners who failed miserably to live up to their baptismal promises, with those who reneged on their vows and betrayed their communities. Were they to be allowed to return? Were they to be welcomed back to the intimacies of the breaking of the Word and bread? How were they to be reconciled with those who had been betrayed by their fellow believers? Obedience to Jesus' commands during this time of persecution demanded of the church a maturity that came through the presence and power of the Spirit of God abiding in the community.

Thirty years after the death and resurrection of Jesus, his followers were considered traitors and subversives by the empire of Rome, which was far-reaching and capable of systematic and brutal torture and execution. Peter and Paul had both died at the hands of its killing machine. Although legal according to Roman standards, their deaths were unjust and viciously self-serving. Church leaders and those who defended their relationship to Jesus as Lord publicly paid the ultimate price of witness—martyrdom.

Even the towering figures we know as Peter and Paul confronted this conflict: obedience to the words and person of Jesus the Lord or obedience to the Roman authorities. Peter died by crucifixion. Tradition says that he deemed himself unworthy to die in the same manner as his Lord whom he had betrayed so fiercely and savagely and so pleaded with the soldiers to be crucified upside down; they obliged him. This man who had been fearful and disloyal as a follower was totally converted to the good news and to the following of Jesus, even though it was long and arduous, with failures and abysmal moments of humiliation and betrayal. It was Peter who sinned, vehemently denying any association with his Lord and cursing his name. By the power of the Spirit, it was Peter who repented, confessing his own weakness and God's goodness and mercy. It was also Peter who became the leader of the church universal.

Paul, the great orator, preacher, and missionary, was also a famed Jewish rabbi trained under Gamaliel. While he lived under house arrest in Rome for nearly two years, he continued to write letters and teach. He was called to crucifixion for his teaching and also for being a Christian. In the end, though, the great Paul fell back upon his Roman citizenship and declared that he would not be subject to the degradation and humiliation of crucifixion. As a Roman, he was accorded the privilege of beheading— a swift execution without the public brutality and shame that were part of the ritual of crucifixion.

Paul's decision must have been devastating and demoralizing for his fellow Christians. In the end, to save himself from suffering and death, Paul claimed his Roman citizenship rather than his citizenship in the kingdom of God. This has rarely been alluded to throughout history or even today. Somehow, in the end, Paul betrayed his belief in the Master and the downtrodden; he shamed Jesus by using his position in the world to protect himself. Yet this reveals much about the daily struggles of the early church—the actions of its own members, who could be courageous, but also calculating when it came to their own lives and deaths.

It is Peter, not Paul, who is the image of a believer in the Gospel of Mark. Peter is the model for those who sin again and again because of personal weakness or fear, for those who do not understand or give priority to their own ideas and agendas. Peter is also a model for those who only slowly and painstakingly come to understand the meaning of Jesus, the poor and crucified one, risen from the dead. Peter is the one who, when called, follows, stumbles, and then becomes a stumbling block for others as he betrays Jesus. Peter is slow to realize that he must repent and that he needs massive forgiveness. In the end, after Jesus' resurrection, he finally "gets it," thanks to the power of the Spirit.

The Themes of Mark's Gospel

In the sixties, as the church continued to grow both in spite of and because of the Roman persecution, the Spirit led Mark to pen an account of Jesus, the good news of God, and his teachings. The gospel is often referred to as an account of the passion, with an introductory set of questions and answers: If Jesus is who he claims to be, then why did he have to die and suffer as he did? And the corollary follows: If we are going to be followers of this Jesus, will we also suffer and die as he did? While this is a valid approach to the Gospel of Mark, it seems to blunt the terror of the actual times and the hard choices that had to be made.

While the account of the passion is often seen as overarching, Jesus' deliberate and clear invitation in chapter 8 to "deny yourself, pick up your cross and come after me" makes it much more than a passion account. Chapter 8 is key. It marks the turning toward Jerusalem, the place where the prophets met rejection and death, and the place of Jesus' own rejection and death. Thus, Mark's gospel is about more than just a set of theological propositions about the nature and person of Jesus Christ, Son of God and Son of Man. It should be read, studied, and reflected upon as a text to prepare for baptism and as essential reading for those seeking to be true to their baptismal promises. The first century was an age and time when to be baptized was an act of faith and courage that placed believers' very lives in jeopardy, including the lives of those whom they loved and to whom they were bound. Mark's gospel is really a primer on the cross that tells of suffering, rejection, and being faithful. It demonstrates how to "deny one's very self to save one's soul" and how to forgive those who betray you or fail you or deliver you over to death. It tells of how to follow Jesus, literally, to Jerusalem and the mount of Calvary and then on to resurrection glory.

Mark's gospel is also about making a community strong and free. The early church communities were at the bottom of the heap in the Roman Empire. Regarded as subversive and dangerous by the ruling authorities, the followers of Jesus could evoke hatred and inordinate fear that translated into vicious torture and a prolonged agony of dying. Mark's gospel is a declaration of faith in the power of the good news to the poor and in the forgiveness and mercy of God. It is a call to proclaim the incarnation with our bodies and souls.

And so, in Mark's gospel, it is Peter who reminds the community of new and older believers what will be demanded of them by the very fact of their baptism into Jesus Christ crucified and risen. Peter will speak the communities' fears and thoughts that conflict with the teachings of Jesus. Peter will resist Jesus' call to the cross and obedience and his instructions about forgiveness as a way of life. And it is Peter who betrays Jesus, from his initial misunderstanding at the beginning of the gospel, to his later rejection when he perceives that Jesus is not what he expected or wanted, and then to his outright betrayal, cursing and showing shame at even being associated with Jesus. Peter is the disciple who leads, sometimes leading the other disciples away from Jesus or keeping at a safe distance to protect his own safety.

This is also the story of the internal life of the church as its members struggled with persecution by the Roman Empire. Their refusal to acknowledge the emperor as god, the only one worthy of worship and obedience, was viewed as a supreme insult. The church as a whole was also under enormous pressure from the leadership of the Jewish community who had often been in collusion with the Romans and the Roman procurator in Jerusalem in exchange for the right to continue worshiping in the temple. Some factions within Judaism sought to engage in massive protests and violently resist the rule of Rome, reclaiming their sacred ground for worship after it had been defiled by the presence of the Roman soldiers and working to rebuild Israel as a nation. By the sixties, the time of Mark's writing, these zealots and rebel forces, who were becoming better organized, were demanding that the followers of the Way, still seen as Jewish or connected to Judaism, join them and fight against the Romans to secure the temple grounds and reinstate Israel as a free nation, neither occupied nor controlled by Rome. They had had enough of being despised and humiliated in their own country.

So the church as a whole had to decide if it would fight with the Jews to defend the temple against the Romans. A clear line was drawn. The Gospel of Mark delineates the meaning of that line: What is demanded in lifestyle, personally and communally, by a follower of Jesus the crucified and risen one? It is a choice, sadly, that will separate the people into two religions and begin a time of hostility that will fester and grow for millennia.

It is decided that because a Christian cannot kill and be a follower of Jesus, these members of the early church will not align themselves with the Jews to fight against the Romans in defense of the temple. For them, the new temple is the body of Christ. Followers of Jesus and the cross are not to kill—not for any reason or anyone or to defend anything. One may lay down one's life for what one believes but one may not take up arms or kill as a believer. This stance is written large into the Gospel of Mark as part and parcel of what defines one as a Christian baptized into the body and blood of Jesus. This decision and its ramifications, as outlined in Mark, became the teaching and practice of the first 350 years of the church—no member of an army or anyone willing to kill can be admitted to baptism. They may be enrolled in the catechumenate but they cannot be baptized since they are lacking in the primary "mark," if you will, of a follower of Jesus—one who lives by love, even love unto death and love for enemies as friends, in imitation of Jesus, who loves all of us this way.

The Challenge of the Way

This is the historical and religious backdrop of the Gospel of Mark. It tells the story of the communities of followers of Jesus, a movement that traveled from Jerusalem through Galilee and along the Roman trade routes to the heart of the Roman Empire, lodging there as the church of Rome, which, in time, would become the center of the one, holy, catholic, and apostolic church. It was not an easy or a smooth beginning. At times the church stumbled and fell upon its own rocks. It has also been a stumbling block for others as surely as it seeks to be a sanctuary and hope for the poor, the lost, the despairing, and the outcast. It is a very human community spurred on by the Spirit of Jesus hovering over his disciples, accompanying them, walking ahead of them and sharing their sufferings, their failures, and their fears. But the Spirit never abandoned them. Jesus, the Son of the Father, baptized in the Spirit, merciful and faithful unto death, loving and forgiving even as he dies, is with them. After the resurrection, Jesus goes before them into Galilee, leading them out into the world to preach his word and live it in their own bodies and communities.

This is the shadow of history behind this reading of Mark's gospel, the shortest of the texts of the good news. These are the questions we must ask ourselves today: What would our Christian communities, our parishes and churches, be like if we responded as the early church did to the demands of the Spirit of God in Jesus the crucified? Would we have the faith and courage in our time to resist persecution, refusing to kill even under pressure from the authorities and even under threat of loss and death?

And we should not forget the specter of Paul's last act that lingers and hovers. Do we resort to our place in society to protect us or shield us from the consequences of preaching the gospel? Or worse, have we learned to use our position of power in our culture or nation (with the United States often seen by others as a "new" Roman Empire) to betray our faith, to twist it and accommodate it to our political, economic, or social agendas while we ignore the poor and oppressed? Would our claim to be Christians be recognizable by our Lord and teacher Jesus the crucified one?

We must read the Gospel of Mark in its context and then apply it to our time. As we walk with the companions of Jesus, with Peter, James, John, and the others, men and women like us, and listen to the word of God in Jesus, we must let the gospel convict us, convert us, confirm us, and call us to repentance and the practice of being the good news to the poor in today's world. If this brings persecution or if we find ourselves considered subversive and dangerous to the powers that be, then it should be our privilege and grace to rejoice, for this is how Jesus was seen. Perhaps we are beginning to act like our Master and Lord, Jesus the crucified and risen one.

"Come and follow me!" The journey to Jerusalem and to the cross begins. What we were signed with at our baptisms, we now pick up and shoulder as walk together in glory. As Catherine of Siena once said, "If you believe that Jesus is Lord to the glory of God the Father, in the power of the Spirit, then all the way home to heaven, is heaven."

In the tradition of Jesus, a master storyteller, a story is a good way to begin.

Once upon a time there was a man who was seeking meaning in his life. He and his friend had been searching for a way to live that was graceful, freeing, and respectful of others. His friend would encourage him, and he would sustain her in their seeking. One day they heard of a teacher and were fascinated by the stories others told of him. They decided together to seek the teacher out to ask to be allowed to become apprentices, disciples of his way.

He happened to pass by the village where they were staying and along with the crowds they listened to his words. Later they sought out his company, presenting themselves and asking to be initiated into his following. It was the custom at that time to be interviewed by the teacher and then, when he had asked them a question and listened to their answer, he would decide, right there and then, on the spot, whether they would be suitable for his teaching and company.

Of course, they were nervous as both wanted to be accepted. They began in earnest: "Master, we wish to join you and follow you and learn to live as you do, according to your words." And the Master looked at them kindly but spoke realistically. "How do you know that you want to follow me, or what you are getting yourselves into?"

They were quick to reply: "Your words, Master, they stir us. This is what we have always believed and wanted and now we have found it in you!" The Master was silent a moment, as though he were praying. "Are you sure?" he queried them. "Do you have any idea what you are asking in wanting to belong to my disciples?" "Yes, we're sure," they both declared. The Master shook his head slowly and looking at them, said, "You may come and follow me, but believe me, you will lose everything you think you know, including your surety. Do you still want to join me?" "Yes, yes," they declared again. And so, they were permitted, even welcomed to his band of followers.

From that night forward there was a foreboding, a sense of unease that both of them, along with all the others—who had been asked the very same questions, sought to smother and ignore, in spite of all that would happen to them. The unease grew and festered, and sometimes in the group, when they didn't understand, they would pick at it, like a scab newly formed on a sore, until it was red and raw and bleeding.

But they had left everything for this. It had to be what they were looking for—it had to be. They would make it so. They were sure they could do it. But the Master's refrain, which he spoke like a mantra, whispering almost continuously, never failed to stir up both their hopes and their fears. "Do you want to lose everything—do you want only me? Are you sure?"

Do we want to lose everything? Or, at least, are we willing to lose everything and be left with only Jesus? Are we sure? This is the place where we must start losing everything, bit by bit, piece by piece. What will we lay aside first?

In the early church one of the primary means of teaching catechumens and deepening the faith of the baptized was to share the psalms together, praying in the Spirit with Jesus to the Father. So, in light of this tradition, each chapter will end with a psalm to add another dimension to the gospel text. We are summoned to believe in Jesus and to worship the God of Jesus, Father and Spirit, even in the face of public disdain and pressure, as a people that belongs to God alone. We pray.

> Keep me safe, O God,
> for in you I take refuge,
> I say to the Lord,
> "You are my Lord, my only good."
> The gods of the earth are but nothing,
> cursed be those who delight in them.
> Those who run after foreign gods
> only have their sorrows multiplied.
> Let me not shed blood for them,
> nor their names be heard on my lips.
> O Lord, my inheritance and my cup,
> my chosen portion—hold secure my lot.
>
> The best part has been allotted to me.
> Delightful indeed is my inheritance!
> I bless the Lord who counsels me;
> even at night my inmost self instructs me.
> I keep the Lord always before me;
> for with him at my hand, I will never be shaken.
>
> My heart, therefore, exults, my soul rejoices;
> my body too will rest assured.
> For you will not abandon
> my soul to the grave,
> Nor will you suffer your holy one
> to see decay in the land of the dead.
> You will show me the path of life,
> in your presence the fullness of joy,
> at your right hand happiness forever.
>
> (Psalm 16/15)

CHAPTER 2

On Your Mark

"Here Begins the Gospel . . ."

Mark 1

THE GOSPEL BEGINS VERY STRANGELY. In the Greek, Mark doesn't even begin with an actual sentence but rather with an announcement that appears as an interruption or a shift in perspective. It seems as if history is lurching forward from what *is* to what *will be* because of this moment, this coming into the world of a certain person. The words do not explain so much as declare; they are a proclamation that demands our undivided attention. The New American Bible (NAB) translation reads: "The beginning of the gospel" as though it was *the* defining moment, the time when a reality was set in motion that continues unabated even to this moment in our place and history.

Beginnings are crucial, and Mark's gospel is the first account we have in its entirety of what was believed about this yet unnamed person. Before Mark's writings, bits and pieces, fragments of stories, statements of belief, and oral traditions were found in liturgical forms of blessings and praise but nothing substantial and reliable existed to read.

Mark's account is about "Jesus Christ [the Son of God]." The naming is blunt and abrupt, encompassing a statement of belief. While the beginning, "according to Mark," appears to focus more on the author than on the person it speaks about as Jesus the Christ, the Son of God, Mark disappears thoroughly into the text and surfaces only once toward the very end, when he is not presented in a positive light (see the account of the young man running from the garden in Mark 15). The title Jesus Christ the Son of God will be uncovered layer by layer throughout the text, but by around thirty years after Jesus' life, death, and resurrection, the title referred to "the Crucified One, this Jesus of Nazareth who is not here, but is risen from the dead" (Mk 16:6). This is the heart of the identity of Jesus for those who believe in him. This is the beginning, the "genesis" that suggests that a process is under way, a movement like water or air, generating energy and carrying along anything and anyone lying in its path. It moves with focus, with concentration, slowly accelerating, intent on revealing this Jesus, the one who is the Son of God existing in a specific time and place and continuing to live in those who are drawn into the story.

Just as all stories are true at their deepest core, all stories are also about us and not only the characters and persons in the account. They are intent on telling us the truth about ourselves, especially if we proclaim that we are followers of Jesus the Christ, the Son of God. The Gospel of Mark is also our story, and so this is about our beginnings as believers, as followers and disciples. This is our "glad tidings" (Is 61:1), our hearing of the good news of God. This is a play on the word "gospel," which was originally the good news, a birth announcement of imperial Rome, repeated as Rome's version of what was going on in the world dominated by the emperor, who often claimed to be the savior of the realm and a god in his own right.

When Gandhi was asked if he had any message for the world, his reply was simple: "My life is my message." Similarly, the preaching, teaching, and stories in Mark are the message and the life of Jesus the Christ, the "anointed" one beloved of God. The following sixteen chapters of the gospel will show forth the truth of this description, revealing ever more clearly that this Jesus, whose name means "savior," is the Holy One of God. Indeed, the gospel is a creed in story form inviting belief, drawing all who hear these words into obedience to Jesus. It is how we begin to see, to hear, to believe, to understand, and how we begin to respond.

As abruptly as Mark begins to draw us in, he immediately flips back in time to the prophet Isaiah. The second sentence tells of Isaiah's words about a person who will come to herald Another, who will bring "comfort to my people," and "speak tenderly to Jerusalem, and proclaim to her that her service is at an end, her guilt is expiated" (Is 40:1-2a). And Isaiah introduces us—if one can be introduced to a prophet by a prophet—to John the Baptizer, the "voice" that utters with surety what was written hundreds of years before. The prophet announces the reality that is arriving now, here, among *us*. These are the words of Isaiah that begin each Advent, each new year of the Lord:

> I am sending my messenger ahead of you to prepare your way. Let the people hear the voice calling in the desert: Prepare the way of the Lord, level his paths. (Mk 1:2a-3)

This ancient image is found as far back in the tradition as the Book of Exodus, when Yahweh tells his people,

> See, I am sending an angel before you, to guard you on the way and bring you to the place I have prepared. Be attentive to him and heed his voice. Do not rebel against him, for he will not forgive your sin. My authority resides in him. If you heed his voice and carry out all I

tell you, I will be an enemy to your enemies and a foe to your foes. (Ex 23:20-22)

God speaks in the form of an angel, a messenger, or a prophet. This is the tradition of the Jewish nation and people, who were called apart from the other nations into a covenant to witness to the one God. The image runs through the earlier testament like a thread, or a stream growing ever stronger, until it appears again in the last book, the prophecy of Malachi.

Lo, I am sending my messenger
 to prepare the way before me;
And suddenly there will come to the temple
 the Lord whom you seek,
and the messenger of the covenant whom you desire.
 Yes, he is coming, says the Lord of hosts.
But who will endure the day of his coming?
 And who can stand when he appears?
For he is like the refiner's fire,
 or like the fuller's lye.
He will sit refining and purifying [silver],
 and he will purify the sons of Levi,
Refining them like gold or like silver
 that they may offer due sacrifice to the Lord. (Mal 3:1-3)

John the Baptizer

The messenger is here to open the way for us, but before we can begin to see the one who is coming we must prepare. We must be shaken to our core and change. We must have our eyes and hearts washed out with the waters of baptism and publicly declare our repentance, which will lead to the forgiveness of our sins. The good news begins with a rousing call to change that goes out to individuals, to groups of people, and to the whole nation so the way can open up before us and so we can see the one who is at the heart of John's preaching: "After me comes one who is more powerful than I am; I have baptized you with water, but he will baptize you in the Holy Spirit. As for me, I am not worthy to bend down and untie his sandals" (1:7b).

  Even in these opening lines tensions run through the gospel. There was Jerusalem, the center of sacrifice and the priesthood, theologically understood by Jews to be the center of the whole world, where one day all the nations of the earth would gather to hear the word of God. Those in Jerusalem were all suspected of being in collusion with the authorities in Rome. Then there was the Judean countryside, those from the edges of Israel who came to be baptized by John in the Jordan River. It was time to turn around, literally, and face away from the center of religious, economic, political, and military power to the borders and distant places.

There is also the tension between those who will confess their sins and acknowledge their need for conversion and those who will steadfastly refuse to be included in the group that sins or is known for being public recalcitrants in regard to the laws and customs of institutional religion. John has arrived to open our eyes and turn us around, to turn inside out or upside down all our ideas and illusions of what is coming. Malachi's words echo in the background:

> Have we not all the one Father?
>   Has not the one God created us?
> Why then do we break faith with each other,
>   violating the covenant of our fathers? (Mal 2:10)

John comes from a long line of prophets with the same refrain on their lips: "Surely I, the Lord, do not change, nor do you cease to be the sons of Jacob. Since the days of your fathers you have turned aside from my statutes, and have not kept them. Return to me, and I will return to you, says the Lord of hosts" (Mal 3:6-7). Since Moses and Elijah, Isaiah and Malachi and all the other prophets, the word of the Lord has gone forth though it has often fallen on deaf ears and hard hearts. The prophets were rejected, insulted, humiliated, and sometimes exiled or murdered, many of them in Jerusalem. This is how it has always been, this is how it is, and this is how it will continue. The last words of Malachi and the long story of the prophets resound in the voice of John crying out in the desert: "Prepare the way of the Lord." We are warned. This is the day and here is the place we may enter into the way of the Lord.

> Lo, I will send you
>   Elijah, the prophet,
> Before the day of the Lord comes,
>   the great and terrible day. (Mal 3:24b)

We are summoned to listen to the messenger, to confess our sins, and to stand with the nation that needs refining and purifying. We are to look for the one who comes after this wild prophet of the desert, this prophet dressed in camel's rough hair with a leather belt around his waist signifying that he is a slave, bound to the word of God. Like the Hebrew people who went out of Egypt to walk the desert in freedom, he lives on what is there—grasshoppers and wild honey, food that is sharp and sweet. And this man, although he is a prophet and preacher, isn't worthy to serve, even in the lowliest of ways, the one who bears such power of the Spirit of God. Are we in need of purification and refining by fire? Are we in need of repentance and baptism before we can be led to the forgiveness of our sins?

Do we realize that we are not fit to stoop and untie his sandal straps? Do we understand that while John baptized with water, this one is baptizing in the Holy Spirit? What does this mean for us?

The story is told of a group of people studying the scriptures who were reading the book of the prophet Malachi.

> When they got to the image of the refiner's fire, they talked about what it might mean. One of the group who had friends who were jewelers arranged for them to see how a silversmith worked and what this process might entail. They spent a day entranced with the workman and the process and the painstakingly careful attention to detail. The jeweler was drenched in sweat, hunched over the metal and the fire, barely glancing up when he was asked a question.
>
> After hours, someone finally asked him: "Sir, how long do you sit there watching what's happening?" The man smiled, but did not look up, answering: "The whole time, as long as the silver is in the fire. I watch the furnace, the level of the heat and how the silver is responding. If it is in too long it will be damaged and unworkable, and if it is taken out before it is refined it will not endure the engraving or etching marks after it cools."
>
> A question was inevitable: "How do you know when it's finished?" The man waited until the refining was finished and lifted his head to answer. "That's the easiest part of the process. I hold it in the fire until I can see my own image reflected in the silver."

Here begins the gospel, the life of Jesus the Christ who baptizes in the Holy Spirit.

The Baptism of Jesus

So Jesus comes from Nazareth in Galilee to be baptized in the Jordan by John. It is as though he appears out of nowhere, literally. Nazareth is a town in the far north of Israel, along the borders with the pagan Gentile nations. The story and the way and the good news all begin with baptism: for Jesus and for us. Mark's description is terse and dense: "On coming up out of the water he saw the heavens being torn apart and the Spirit descending on him like a dove. And a voice came from the heavens, 'You are my beloved Son; with you I am well pleased'" (1:10-11 NAB).

In the Greek, the adverb "immediately" appears at the beginning of verse 10. It will be repeated up to seven times in the rest of the chapter and almost become a refrain throughout the gospel. The story will develop at an ever-increasing pace. There will be no stopping this person, this Word coming into the world. There is no delay in the text of Mark, no in-betweens, the next event starts right away, the next place, the next person, the next experience, the next teaching or insight—things occur in such rapid succession that everything seems to be happening at once. Jesus is baptized, and as he rises up out of the river waters, he sees the sky above him rent in two and the air moves down on him in waves of wind or breath and there is a movement of light in the sky. This resembles a dove hovering in midair, motionless and yet at the same time containing energy and power.

The language of the story of Jesus' baptism has strong connections with the original story of Genesis.

> In the beginning, when God began to create the heavens and the earth, the earth had no form and was void; darkness was over the deep and the Spirit of God hovered over the waters.
> God said, "Let there be light"; and there was light. (Gn 1:1-2)

This is the overture to the gospel. God, who creates in Spirit and in Word from the beginning, is continuing with this amazing work of instilling life and light into all that exists. And baptism creates us by water and Word and Spirit. This image of the heavens being torn asunder has long been part of the prayer of Israel to Yahweh: "O that you would tear open the heavens and come down" (Is 63:19b), and then a voice comes from the heavens saying, "You are my beloved Son. On you my favor rests" (Mk 1:11 prayerful trans.). This is both witness and validation; it is the giving of an identity, a revelation of intimacy and of a relationship sourced in the power, the justice, and the compassion of God. Whole chapters of Isaiah, especially 42, 63, and 64 are the backdrop of these words. They are the foundation of God's relationship with Israel, showing how God's judgment and love remain close to them, taking them back again and again and pleading with them for faithfulness. God is offering them mercy and a hope for one that will be given to them as God's own servant, willing, suffering, faithful and true, gathering them in as a shepherd gathers sheep. It is this servant of God who will bear the brunt of rejection that God himself bears when his people turn aside from him.

> Here is my servant whom I uphold,
> my chosen one in whom I delight.
> I have put my spirit upon him,
> and he will bring justice to the nations. (Is 42:1-2)

For the Jewish community of believers and for the early Christians these texts of Isaiah would be pivotal in describing how Jesus acted, why he suffered, and what he knew of God. The intervention in Mark 1:11 appears to be for Jesus' eyes only. This is also his confirmation. This is the Trinity: Jesus of Nazareth in Galilee, the Spirit of God descending upon him in power and the Voice that declares the relationship of servant beloved and son beloved, and it is so. The words of the psalmist resound: "I will proclaim the decree of the Lord. He said to me, 'You are my son. This day I have begotten you'" (Ps 2:7).

But this is also our baptism, and so the declaration is for us. This day, the day of our baptism and our hearing of the voice of God in the Word of Jesus' own Spirit, we are drawn into this arrangement, this relationship with God as Trinity. Those words are for each of us to take to heart: "You are my beloved, my son, my daughter, my child. This day I have begotten you. This day I have chosen you and upon you my favor rests. In you I find my delight!"

Baptism gives us the same access, the same relationship of intimacy and knowing of God the Father that Jesus knew on earth, in the power of the Spirit. This is the initiation into the way. This is God's declaration to us when we accept repentance, forgiveness, and reconciliation with others and with God in Jesus. The Spirit that descended on Jesus is the first gift given to believers (Fourth Eucharistic Prayer).

The Greek word used to describe the heavens being "rent" is used only one more time in Mark, at the end, when Jesus dies and the curtain in the temple sanctuary is rent in two from top to bottom (15:38). There are many allusions at the beginning and end of Mark's gospel that are meant to be picked up as parallels by his hearers. This is baptism into the Trinity and also baptism into the passion of the Christ. This is the beginning of a lifelong struggle with powers, with authorities, and with ways of living in the world. Our hearts and minds are meant to be rent every time we read the text, and hear the good news of God proclaimed to us.

Immediately, it is this Spirit of God that drives Jesus into the wilderness of the desert for forty days to be tempted by Satan. Before Jesus opens his mouth to preach, before he appears in Galilee proclaiming the good news of God let loose upon the earth, he struggles, as did all God's people before him, to define what God wants and desires of him. He must be clear about how he will face those who ignore him, reject him, or oppose him outright and, inevitably, as with all those who went before him as prophets, kill him.

It took forty years in the desert to become a people. Forty years was the span of a person's life, and forty days were required to lay the foundation of self-knowledge, knowledge of God, Yahweh and Father, and knowledge of what lies ahead. The Spirit dwells with Jesus, in God the Father, and we are told that "he was with the wild animals, but angels ministered to him" (Mk 1:13). The word "Satan" means hinderer, one who blocks or seeks to stop progress, one who stands in the way of. Jesus must deal with everything that will seek to hinder him from living as the beloved son and servant of God, the one who brings the favor of God to all who listen and take it upon them as grace and the way of life. This description is to be seen not only as a time frame but as a backdrop, a shadow that will preside over all of Jesus' life—and over our lives. This is a continual call to conversion—to repentance, to forgiveness, and to being transformed to dwell with Jesus in the Spirit, with God the Father.

Jesus begins by searching into the root causes of Israel's idolatry and unfaithfulness and its collusion with the empire of Rome and other idols. In the desert of the exodus the tribes had to learn to "go out" from the slavery and bondage of Egypt to stand before the face of God to receive the gift of the Law and the covenant that would bind them into a people belonging to God alone.

The language of Jesus' struggles with Satan are reminiscent of the book of the prophet Daniel, who also struggled with the powers of evil and violence on behalf of the people. Daniel's visions included beasts that roamed and devoured the earth and its inhabitants, but he also witnessed the beast destroyed. And then he saw

> One like a son of man came on the clouds of heaven. He faced the One of Great Age and was brought into his presence.
>
> Dominion, honor and kingship were given him, and all the peoples and nations of every language served him. His dominion is eternal and will never pass away; his kingdom will never be destroyed. (Dn 7:13b-14)

Just as the way of God begins on earth in the person of Jesus, so the struggle begins between the way of God and the rulers of the world, those who devour and destroy humanity and the earth. With Jesus, we are driven into the struggle. In the beginning the lines are drawn and the decisions are made—for God and the way of the suffering servant of Yahweh (reflected in the Isaiah's teachings) over and against the violence, evil, and threatening ways of the powers of nations and those who will not forgive, nor do justice, nor serve as peacemakers.

The First Call to Discipleship

And now the account begins in earnest, with the foreboding words: "After John was arrested, Jesus appeared in Galilee proclaiming the good news of God." In Mark's gospel, anything of import often begins with a phrase that alludes to a previous event that involved violence, the intrusion of the state and nation brutally into the lives of people, or, in some way, the shadow of evil and death. John has done his work, the stage is set, and he exits. Jesus moves to center stage and begins immediately to oppose the "good news of Rome, the Pax Romana," with the good news of God, the Pax Christi. The lines are drawn. There must be no mistaking that a decision to follow Jesus implies far more than a simple acceptance of his words. In accepting baptism, which will lead to forgiveness and the refining of the Spirit of God, following Jesus will put one at odds with all the other powers of heaven and earth that are not steeped in the word of God, in the hopes of liberation and freedom of the Passover, in the psalms and the ways of the suffering servant of God.

Jesus' message is short and simple, yet simply devastating and demanding! Although we may know the words by heart, have we really taken them to heart and written them on our hearts? There are two versions of the call that loom before us—a warning and an insistence: "The time has come; the kingdom of God is at hand. Change your ways and believe the good news" (Mk 1:15). The TIME—*kairos*—has come. The time of waiting is over. If time can ever be "ripe," then that time is now! The moment is one of opportunity and inbreaking, both upsetting and hopeful. It is a moment of fulfillment when all the promises, even beyond anyone's wildest imaginings, are coming true. Time is shifting forever, as we move into the presence of God-with-us time. This moment of Jesus' presence in the world is the fulcrum that balances all time and history, backwards and forwards, since the beginning and until the end of all time. This will be an eternal yet present reality that will interpret all that has gone before and will determine and call to account all that will follow.

"The kingdom of God is at hand." The phrase "the kingdom of God," which we take for granted as central to the teaching of Jesus, appears only once in the older testament, in Wisdom 10:10. It is helpful to read the reference there for it reveals much about Jesus and how wisdom will be associated with his person and be rejected or accepted.

> But Wisdom delivered from tribulations those who served her.
> She, when the just man fled from his brother's anger,
> 　　guided him in direct ways,
> Showed him the kingdom of God
> 　　and gave him knowledge of holy things;
> She prospered him in his labors
> 　　and made abundant the fruit of his works,
> Stood by him against the greed of his defrauders,
> 　　and enriched him;
> She preserved him from foes,
> 　　and secured him against ambush.
> And she gave him the prize for his stern struggle
> 　　that he might know that devotion to God is mightier
> 　　　　than all else.
> She did not abandon the just man when he was sold,
> 　　but delivered him from sin.
> She went down with him into the dungeon,
> 　　and did not desert him in his bonds,
> Until she brought him the scepter of royalty
> 　　and authority over his oppressors.
> Showed those who had defamed him false,
> 　　and gave him eternal glory. (Wis 10:9-14 NAB)

"She," a traditional description of the Holy Spirit who came upon Jesus at his baptism to dwell with him, shows him the kingdom of God and gives him knowledge of holy things. Now, having struggled with the demons that will resist him and all that he brings, Jesus returns from his desert time and turns to the work and the good news of the kingdom of God. One could write a book, or many of them, on what, precisely, is the "kingdom of God." In a sense the Gospel of Mark is a fragmentary account of what believers were beginning to realize about this kingdom and about what it meant to actually dwell within it, which would make it firmly and deeply a part of their world.

The Aramaic for this phrase, *malkutha di elaha*, is best rendered as the rule of God or the reign of God, for it implies a vibrant, intimate, and immediate relationship. That is why in other translations Jesus' proclamation reads: "This is the time of fulfillment. The reign of God is close at hand! Repent, and believe in the gospel" (though the word "close" is often omitted from more recent translations, such as the NAB). Suddenly this power, this authority, this awesomeness of God is very near. It is "at hand."

Look at your hand. How close is it to you? It cannot be separated from you; it is part and parcel of your being. The blood from our hearts runs through the veins into our hands. The muscles and nerves, wrapped in skin, are all connected around bones. When I proclaim this line aloud, I instinctively stretch out my hand to people and afterwards I have them stretch out their hands, asking how close is the kingdom of God to you. Invariably, every hand goes straight out in front of them. I tell them "No!" I stretch out my hand again, to the side, touching the person closest to me. That is where the kingdom is—as close as the first person you can grasp by the hand. This power of God is found in the connection between human beings, bound now in Jesus, in the Spirit of God.

But this reign or rule of God is bound to the imperious command that follows: "Repent and believe in the gospel!" Other translations read, "change your ways" or "reform your lives." Somehow responding to the person of Jesus and his words draws this kingdom more into reality or into being. The rest of the gospel will tell how Jesus' presence is the doorway into this reality and how his words and actions seed it in the world for all time. And Jesus' body, his being in the world, is God's power moving among us, shifting history and opening up the world to grace and to the Spirit.

"Kingdom" is a difficult word for many people because of the history of actual kingdoms on earth that have been and still are based on violence, war, economic inequality, and power that is more often than not destructive. But if we concentrate on the relationships that are primary within the word and think of it as "kin-dom," then it is a bit more expressive of what Jesus is speaking about: the rule of God brings new relationships that override and overrule all other relationships. The relationships of family, nation, people, gender, and dominance—personal, political, or economic—

are now to be radically transformed. Jesus was born into a nation and a people long oppressed by the dominant Roman Empire and, while Christianity has often concentrated on the more personal aspects of belief, Jesus' words and actions formed a community that became an alternative of hope and an affront to institutions in society that were not based on the gospel—the good news of God. The word is about power and its use, both as the world sees it and as God uses it, inviting us to share in that expression of power in Jesus, beloved son, servant and crucified one.

The word "reign" is often interchangeable with "kingdom," and it suffers from the same negative associations. But that applies primarily to the written word and not necessarily to the word as it is heard. Then the word has three possible meanings: the *reign* of God, the *rein* of God, and the *rain* of God. It can mean the authority or power of one over another, individually or within a larger context, when one party exerts one's will over another or wills something to happen. It can also be a hold or check, as reins as used to discipline a horse, holding it in or setting it free. And, third, it can be like rain coming down upon the earth in all its myriad forms: hard or soft rain, driving rain, drizzle, rain accompanied by thunder and lightning, or rain in the midst of blinding sunlight creating rainbows in profusion. Some native peoples understand two kinds of rain: male and female. Male rain comes most often in spring when it is needed after planting to drive the seed into the ground and initiate the growth process; it tends to be cold and often short-lived—enough for what it is meant to do. The other rain comes more often in late summer when the ground is parched and the grass and crops are desperate for moisture. It comes almost daily in late afternoon; it can be short-lived and thunderous or it can come soft, barely touching the ground and hanging in the air to bring the needed bit of moisture to cool the earth and air and keep the plants alive. This rich image is echoed in the Book of Isaiah when the prophet describes Yahweh God in relation to the people, if only they would take his words and ways to heart. And this piece of Isaiah's urgings sounds like an echo of Jesus' own opening words of Mark's gospel.

> Seek Yahweh while he may be found;
> call to him while he is still near.
> Let the wicked abandon his way,
> let him forsake his thoughts,
> let him turn to Yahweh for he will have mercy,
> for our God is generous in forgiving.
>
> For my thoughts are not your thoughts,
> my ways are not your ways, says Yahweh.
> For as the heavens are above the earth,
> so are my ways higher than your ways,
> and my thoughts above your thoughts.

> As the rain and the snow come down
> from the heavens and do not return
> till they have watered the earth,
> making it yield seed for the sower
> and food for others to eat,
> so is my word that goes forth out of my mouth:
> it will not return to me idle,
> but it shall accomplish my will,
> the purpose for which it has been sent. (Is 55:6-11)

These words could have been in Jesus' own heart and mind as he called all creation to listen to his words and imitate his ways. Jesus is the word of God made flesh; his ways are not like our ways and thoughts, but he does the will of God. Sent into the world to love and to serve us, Jesus draws us into that relationship of beloved children to the Father God and beloved servants obedient to God's will, even unto death on a cross. Baptism, the good news, the Holy Trinity, and the kingdom of God overlap as concepts and as experiences, but each draws us more deeply into the new reality that is in our midst. The proclamation that will come true in Jesus and that is meant to come true in each of us calls us.

The First Calling

The story of the first calling is probably one of the most often told from Mark's gospel. Jesus, "appearing in Galilee," walks along the shore of the lake and observes two fishermen who are brothers. He calls them to leave their nets (or abandon them in earlier translations) and follow him, for he wants to make them fishers of men and women. So Jesus goes fishing and, amazingly, catches four fish at once. While this story is often used to talk about vocations—primarily to the priesthood or religious life—it was never intended for that purpose. It is the first of three stories of calling, initially of those men and women who would become Jesus' first followers or disciples, and then later of some disciples who would become apostles. "Calling" stories are found in this account of meeting the fishermen, in chapter 2 with Matthew the tax collector, and then in the calling or naming of the Twelve in chapter 3. There will be other calling stories as well, directed at all those who hear Jesus' words and are invited to take up his way of living.

The story is laced with references to prophets' warnings and challenges. In Mark's opening chapter Jesus is seen as a prophet in the tradition of Isaiah and of others before and after him, including John the Baptist. So Jesus employs that same prophetic tradition to call people to follow him, to join with him as companions. Exegetes rarely allude to this when this text is used as a summons to think about one's vocation. The primary vocation in Mark's gospel is that of discipleship now, in the company of others under the rule/reign/rain/rein of God in Jesus. Discipleship means following Jesus all the way along his way to God as Father, in the power of the Spirit, even to the cross and to the glory of the resurrection life, here and now. These disciples may have differing levels or uses of power, whether apostles, preachers, healers, reconcilers, teachers, peacemakers, leaders of prayer, or deacons, but all are first and last disciples of Jesus.

We must listen to the call! We are each being called now, along with others in our families, doing whatever it is we are already doing in our world. And God in Jesus is there, close at hand, observing us, knowing us intimately before we are summoned as we hear the words of the gospel ringing in our ears.

> As he made his way along the Sea of Galilee, he observed Simon and his brother Andrew casting their nets into the sea; they were fishermen. Jesus said to them, "Come after me: I will make you fishers of men." They immediately abandoned their nets and became his followers. Proceeding a little further along, he caught sight of James, Zebedee's son, and his brother John. They too were in their boat, putting their nets in order. He summoned them on the spot. They abandoned their father Zebedee, who was in the boat with the hired men, and went off in his company. (Mk 1:16-20)

We are summoned, on the spot, now! We are called to be with Jesus in his company, with others whom he calls, and we are called to do whatever we are doing, but passionately and with grace, in the kingdom of God. This is the first step in being invited to a radical overturning of our lives. Indeed, it isn't really all that unusual, but it can grow on you! This is what William Reiser has to say about being called this first time in his book *Jesus in Solidarity with His People: A Theologian Looks at Mark:*

> Jesus' calling ordinary working people to follow him (as in the case of Simon and Andrew, James and John and Levi) occurred far more frequently than we usually think. If Jesus lured the brothers by telling them that they would soon be fishing for people, what image might he have used in calling farmers, or shepherds, or artisans, or housewives, or even tax gatherers? Would he have told villagers from the Galilean countryside that he would teach them how to harvest people, or shepherds that they would learn how to pastor men and women, or tax gatherers how to collect human lives, or bakers how to make living bread? Indeed, if Jesus could invite a married man like Simon to discipleship and expect that he readily would follow him, what would have prevented him from calling a married woman? (pp. 60-61)

Teachers, students, accountants, engineers, computer analysts, reporters, writers, doctors, lawyers, farmers, day laborers, street people, those married, widowed, single, in families and in every occupation—all are summoned, invited to come and live a new way, under the rule of God. The two sets of brothers (Simon and Andrew, and James and John) are called to follow after Jesus. With the latter set of brothers, the calling takes an edge. James and John leave their father, Zebedee, in the boat with their hired men and go off "in his company" (NAB). Like them, we are not just summoned to follow Jesus, but to become this new way of being family, of being in households, of relating to one another in society and transforming all institutions to reveal a new order, a new harmony and communion born of the Spirit and word of God. In a very real sense we don't leave behind people or our jobs or our place in the world; instead, we leave how, why, with whom, and in whom we live and dwell. This will be progressive, turning everything about our lives, relationships, and ways of living upside down. We will rub shoulders with total strangers, who because they are also in the company of Jesus will be as close as blood relatives but closer in baptism and the cross.

This specific image of fishing is foundational in spirituality and ministry and in ways of speaking about discipleship. References to the prophetic roots of being called to catch people have been cited in many books, including *Say to This Mountain: Mark's Story of Discipleship* (by Ched Myers et al.).

> In the Hebrew Bible, the metaphor of "people like fish" appears in prophetic censures of apostate Israel and of the rich and powerful:
>
> > "I am now sending for many fishermen, says God, and they shall catch [the people of Israel] . . ." (Jeremiah 16:16)
> >
> > "The time is surely coming upon you when they shall take you away with fishhooks . . ." (Amos 4:2)
> >
> > "Thus says God: I am against you, Pharaoh king of Egypt. . . . I will put hooks into your jaws, and make the fish of your channels stick to your scales . . ." (Ezekiel 29:3f)
>
> Jesus is, in other words, summoning working folk to join him in overturning the structures of power and privilege in the world! (p. 10)

These allusions are a far cry from the often romantic notions of leaving all behind and following Jesus in religious life or priesthood. The call is much more radical than any call to a specific lifestyle or vocation. Jesus is calling anyone who hears his word to break with accepted structures and ways of living. The words that are used in the translations are to "leave" (*Christian Community Bible* [CCB]) or to "abandon" (NAB) your way of making a living as it is understood in the world or by your family, although you are still bound to your family and to making a living in the world. It breaks or tears apart the existing social mores yet still uses them as the foundation for a new life in God.

"They come after him" is the literal translation of what we call "following after Jesus" (*opiso mou*). In *The Beginning of the Gospel: Introducing the Gospel According to Mark*, Eugene LaVerdiere explains the crucial difference between being a disciple and following Jesus.

> Note that the word "disciple" (*mathetes*) is not used in the story of their call (1:16-20). Nor would it be used later in the story of Levi's call (2:13-14). Jesus did not call disciples just to be disciples. He called them to follow him. There is a difference.
>
> Following Jesus is more fundamental than being a disciple. Following is a matter of being and living. Being a disciple is a matter of learning. The correlative for disciple is teacher (*didaskalos*) or scribe (*grammateus*). The correlative for following (*akoloutheon*) is leading (*proagon*; see 10:32; and 16:7). For Jesus' followers, following meant three things: being with Jesus, patterning their lives on his life and taking up his mission. For that, they had a lot to learn. To be good followers of Jesus, they had to be his disciples. (1:64-65)

In a sense, following Jesus takes us as the person each of us is and makes us another kind of person altogether.

The Journey Begins

Now there are five of them, the first four, as images of each of us, following after Jesus. They come to Capernaum, and the scene is set for the first public experience of how Jesus' very presence sets in motion all kinds of power demanding a response. It is all about power.

> Shortly afterward they came to Capernaum, and on the sabbath he entered the synagogue and began to teach. The people were spellbound by his teaching because he taught with authority, and not like the scribes.
>
> There appeared in their synagogue a man with an unclean spirit that shrieked: "What do you want of us, Jesus of Nazareth? Have you come to destroy us? I know who you are—the holy One of God!" Jesus rebuked him sharply: "Be quiet! Come out of the man!" At that the unclean spirit convulsed the man violently and with a loud shriek came out of him. All who looked on were amazed. They began to ask one another: "What does this mean? A completely new teaching in a

spirit of authority! He gives orders to unclean spirits and they obey!" From that point on his reputation spread throughout the surrounding region of Galilee. (1:21-28)

This is one of Mark's many "sandwiches" in which a dramatic story appears in the middle of another account. Jesus' words and preaching entrance people (unlike the scribes) and they listen. His presence, words, and actions are described as "a completely new teaching in a spirit of authority!" The dramatic story is of a man with an unclean spirit who cries out in recognition of Jesus. Jesus immediately silences him, calling him back to himself. This encounter between Jesus, "the holy one of God," and the man possessed takes place on the sabbath, on the holy ground of the synagogue.

It is a story of displacing power. Jesus, who has moved into the synagogue to teach and preach, has displaced the scribes from their accustomed territory. It marks the beginning of Jesus' moving toward the temple in Jerusalem and toward his death and resurrection. From the very first, it is a clash of powers. Jesus begins immediately to manifest the power of God familiar to the people from the writings of the prophets. Mark's first chapter is so steeped in Isaiah, especially chapter 42, that the two can be read almost in tandem. Mark's description of what Jesus is doing corresponds closely to Isaiah's description of what God does for his people Israel and of what a servant does that brings pleasure to God.

> Thus says God, the LORD,
>   who created the heavens and stretched them out,
>   who spreads out the earth with its crops,
> Who gives breath to its people
>   and spirit to those who walk on it:
> I, the LORD, have called you for the victory of justice,
>   I have grasped you by the hand;
> I formed you, and set you
>   as a covenant of the people,
>   a light for the nations,
> To open the eyes of the blind,
>   To bring out prisoners from confinement,
>   and from the dungeon, those who live in darkness.
> I am the LORD, this is my name;
>   my glory I give to no other,
>   nor my praise to idols.
> See, the earlier things have come to pass,
>   new ones I now foretell;
> Before they spring into being,
>   I announce them to you. (Is 42:5-9 NAB)

In the mouth and person of Jesus something new has appeared on earth. It is ever ancient and old, but in Jesus' flesh it has power and authority, freshness, and an attractiveness that is lacking in the teaching of the scribes and the teachers of the law in institutional religion. In comparison, their words sound dead and hollow, empty of God's glory and lacking in any power except that invested in their status as scribes. The people recognize something in Jesus that is alluring and dangerous.

The story of the man possessed startles with its vehemence and violence, its unexpectedness. And while the people's reaction to Jesus' teaching seems to be positive, it is also one of astonishment and amazement. This describes, however, how Jesus was received and not necessarily approval of what he was saying. The leaders of the synagogue also showed a strong reaction to Jesus' presence, but it was one of resistance. Jesus' right to preach came not from them but from God. So the confrontation begins. The man with the unclean or evil spirit cries out against Jesus, recognizing him and his power. The verbs and adverbs in the account are all powerful—destroy, rebuked sharply, convulsed violently—as were Jesus' more powerful commands "Be quiet! Come out of him!"

This is more a story of Jesus' first clash with those who will resist him and his teaching and later seek to destroy him than a story of exorcism. The leaders sense that the Holy One of God will destroy their ways of doing and being religious in the synagogue and temple in collusion with state power. The story emphatically states that Jesus' power is not only stronger but of a nature different from their powers. They recognize him as Jesus of Nazareth, but even more as the Holy One of God. Jesus' demonstrations of power will force people to choose which power they will follow: the power of God in the good news of God's rule or the powers of those in opposition to God, those who are self-serving, destructive of others, or idolizing and worshiping what is not of God. In the words of Isaiah, Jesus' power is used to renew the covenant of the people and their God and to bring out prisoners who live in darkness, those possessed by evil or unclean spirits.

This is a very disturbing story. Using personal language, Jesus commands the spirit inside the man to "Be quiet!"—the same words he will later use to silence the winds and water of the storm that is threatening the boat the disciples are in (Mk 4:39). The spirit-possessed man knows who Jesus is, and he is intent on wanting to know if Jesus is going to destroy "us" (note that he speaks in the plural, on behalf of all those in the synagogue), those he associates and colludes with, those whom he serves. He knows Jesus not as someone to be followed or believed but as someone to be resisted and eventually destroyed. This is the voice of the evil or unclean spirit within him. And Jesus silences him with just a few words based on the authority of the Spirit of God within him.

We must remember and take to heart that the gospel is not only or even primarily about specific incidents two thousand years ago; rather, it is about us, right now. This is not primarily a miracle story to be interpreted as the account of someone needing exorcism of a demon/devil.

The terms "Satan" or "evil spirit" have a number of meanings throughout the text, with the first being "the hinderer," or one who blocks (or puts a stumbling block in the way of) or distorts, and so keeps someone from becoming a follower or a beloved child of God. This initial encounter sets forth whether or not each of us will respond to Jesus' teachings and actions, whether we will resist and become hostile to Jesus, or if we will choose to become a follower of Jesus. We know who Jesus is, but do we know Jesus? Do we know him as a follower? As the Holy One of God, the Christ, the Son of God?

Jesus' word convulses the man violently and he shrieks aloud, but the unclean spirit obeys and leaves him. The people wonder, "What does this mean?" What does it mean for our religious practices, our rules and ways of doing things? What effects will it have on people and authority, on "the scribes and the teachers of the law today" and on us? (We should note that the man is described as one *with* an unclean or evil spirit. Similarly, those we are *with*—in our religious beliefs, our work, our churches, our civic and political groups—do they lead us into a closer relationship with Jesus or do they distance us from it?) The unclean spirit knows who Jesus is. It is this presence of Jesus, the power of God made flesh, that will destroy all other powers, judging them and their effects on others and also judging those who use them.

From Synagogue to House

Immediately Jesus leaves the synagogue and, with James and John, enters the house of Simon and Andrew. Older translations use the word "immediately" a number of times in the next three lines.

> Simeon's mother-in-law lay ill with a fever, and the first thing they did [immediately] was to tell him about her. He went over to her [immediately] and grasped her by the hand and helped her up [raised her up], and [immediately] the fever left her. She immediately began to wait on them. (1:29-31—older translations in brackets)

When read to oneself, the text may appear awkward or repetitious, but when it is proclaimed aloud the repetition of the word immediately becomes a mantra, a demand, that situates listeners in that moment. A furious pace develops. When Jesus leaves the synagogue with his followers, they are quick to tell him of the illness of Simon's mother-in-law and her immediate need. The word fever wasn't often used to describe something like the flu or a bad cold, but an illness that was dangerous or even life-threatening. Jesus quickly goes to her and "grasps her by the hand and pulls her up." Some translations say "helped her up," and others "raised her up." These are the same words that will describe the resurrection of Jesus in the last chapter of Mark.

So the power of God goes forth; it moves out to those beyond the realm of institutional religious practice and worship into the house of the followers of Jesus. This is Jesus, in the words of the prophet Isaiah, who has "called you for the victory of justice" and "grasped you by the hand." This images the work of Jesus, raising us from the dead, saving us from evil, grasping us for the victory of justice, wrenching us away from the violence of evil and the shallowness of selfish ritual. There is no sickness, physical, psychological, or spiritual, that, once touched by Jesus, can stand against the power of God. And Simon's mother-in-law's response to Jesus is immediate: she rises from her bed and begins to wait on them.

I am often amazed that this last line offends many, especially women, who may cynically respond, "That's why she was healed, to be a servant to the men." But they have missed the meaning of the phrase "to wait on them," which is the term used for a deacon. She "ministers" to him, just as the "angels ministered to him during his time in the desert." Jesus has gone out to Simon's mother-in-law in her disease and grasped her by the hand for the victory of justice. In gratitude for his taking hold of her and giving her life to do his work, she responds wholeheartedly. Now the first four followers of Jesus become five in number.

That Simon has a mother-in-law means, of course, that he is married. Although his mother-in-law lives in his house, there is no mention of his wife or children, which is unusual, as is the fact that his mother-in-law lives in his house. When I was teaching this passage in a small community on the coast of India, a woman remarked, "Oh, his wife must have died, maybe in childbirth, and he took his mother-in-law into his house to care for her, or she lived with them since the marriage." To her it was obvious. I was surprised. I had never thought of that explanation, but it makes perfect sense.

People often speculate about how old Simon and Andrew, James and John were—since Jesus was about thirty years old. They think of all pictures they've seen of Peter, most of which portray Peter as an old man with a beard. In this Indian community, the men suggested that the apostles were maybe in their middle or upper twenties, except for John, who is described as young—perhaps he was around fifteen. The Indian men noted that fishing is hard work, especially net fishing. Simon and Andrew have their own boats, and James and John still work with their father and hired help, which means that they were at least making a living day to day, enough for their extended families of cousins, aunts and uncles, in-laws and children. After a moment of silence, one of the older Indian women said, "I never thought of Peter as actually married—but what if his wife died, or his child, and he took in his mother-in-law? He was a good man, righteous and caring, and Jesus would have known that. He would have observed that when he was watching them at work, feeding their families before they sold what was left over." Immediately, they made the story theirs. They were talking about their lives and with Jesus in the midst of them at that moment.

The gospel *is* about us and about our lives. All of us are called to be followers of Jesus with each other, carrying our families and our work with us, all of it to be touched by Jesus and transformed. By our baptism we are all grasped by the hand for the victory of justice and wrenched away from all that hinders us from following as beloved children and servants of God. What we have been given so generously, with God in Jesus always and immediately going out to us in our need, inviting us closer into the kingdom of God, we must in turn share with others—all others. This is how the word spreads.

As the day dies in the area of Galilee, other people come to the house, bringing their sick and all those "possessed by demons" or with "evil spirits" to be healed. "Before long the whole town was gathered outside the door." They press in on the house, trying to get near to Jesus. Most of us are ill in some way, sometimes physically, and often we are possessed by evil spirits. The list is long and may include addictions; patterns of destructive behavior; selfishness that affects all those around us; vices that we repeatedly practice; emotions such as anger, pride, despair, laziness, greed, envy, and hatred that control our actions; self-absorption that is empty of compassion; refusing to love or forgive; viciousness and violence. And we are told that Jesus would not allow those who were "possessed" to speak, "because they [the demons] knew him." This phrase may, and probably should, disturb us. Just knowing of Jesus does not give us the right or the authority to speak of him when others are around.

Simon's house, run by his mother-in-law, becomes a household of God, a church, a gathering of those in need of healing and forgiveness. Some older translations use the phrase "the whole world was pressing up against the door." This is the new gathering place, the new company of Jesus. It embraces those in need of healing and those healed and grasped for the victory of justice, helping the multitudes who come to Jesus.

Then the story moves right along. We find Jesus rising early, getting away from everyone and going off to a lonely place in the desert to be "absorbed in prayer." Jesus returns to the desert, to that place where God is most intimate with him. He is absorbed in prayer and absorbed in the Trinity, being who he truly is, fed and sustained by God so that he can give to all those who come to him. This will be the pattern of his days and nights with people and with God. It is the people, often his own followers, who pull him away from being absorbed singularly in prayer and the full presence of God. The next few lines tell of the meaning of the life of Jesus. When Simon finds Jesus (notice that Simon does not pray with him), he announces, "Everybody is looking for you!" Jesus then begins his journey with his followers coming after him: "Let us move on to the neighboring villages so that I may proclaim the good news there also. That is what I have come to do" (1:37-38). And, like an itinerant preacher, he goes to the synagogues throughout the whole of Galilee. He and his followers are always on the move.

The final story in the first chapter is the story of a leper who approaches Jesus from out of nowhere. The man is suddenly there with a request. He kneels down in open worship of Jesus and addresses him: "If you will to do so, you can cure me." The leper and Jesus are both breaking all the customs and laws regarding lepers, who are both isolated and feared. Jesus' response, which is staggering in its tenderness, goes against everything in his culture, society, and religion.

> Moved with pity, Jesus stretched out his hand, touched him, and said: "I do will it. Be cured." The leprosy left him then and there [immediately], and he was cured. Jesus gave him a stern warning and sent him on his way. "Not a word to anyone, now," he said. "Go off and present yourself to the priest and offer for your cure what Moses prescribed. That should be a proof for them." (1:41-44)

God's kingdom excludes no one! There is no one who is not invited to be touched, healed, forgiven, embraced, and brought into the family, the new household. Some older translations read "Jesus embraced him!" Jesus is moved by pity, the word used to describe Jesus as a servant who does not bruise what is already weak and does not allow what has become a smoldering wick to be extinguished. The word "pity" has many meanings. It is both the desire to vomit at the suffering you see and the anger that propels you literally into giving birth to something new in response to such suffering.

Jesus seems very aware that he is breaking the long-held beliefs of society and touching people's fears and that there will be increasing resistance to what he does by touching and healing and bringing hope by his words and pity. He seeks to bring the good news of the kingdom of God to people within the existing structures of religion. He does not want to antagonize them, although he is aware of their resistance and their hostility. He also seems aware that he is on a path leading to confrontation with the authorities.

Jesus tells the leper to obey the Law, to offer sacrifice in gratitude to God for his healing, but not to tell anyone about his healing. He is to keep to himself what God has done for him through the touch, will, and pity of Jesus. But the man does not obey; he goes off and makes the story known. It seems odd that the man simply "went off" after such an intimate meeting with Jesus. But the text then states that he started "proclaiming the whole matter freely," telling what Jesus had done for him. There is no indication that he returned to the company of Jesus or learned to follow him more closely or was taught by him even though he apparently had faith that Jesus could heal him. And his public announcement had consequences for Jesus. Mark states, "As a result of this, it was no longer possible for Jesus to enter a town openly. He stayed on in desert places; yet people kept coming to him from all sides" (1:45). According to the beliefs of the time, once Jesus touched the leper he himself became unclean and dangerous and was to be shunned. He became one of "them," the unclean, to be excluded from the community's life of commerce, religion, and worship, and he had to make his abode outside the dwelling place of people.

Again, the person healed is sternly warned to "be quiet." Because he disobeys, more fame, or notoriety, surrounds Jesus. The story begins to spread that Jesus is breaking the laws of the people, of the religious establishment, and, even more to the point, that Jesus is upsetting the way relationships and groups of people are controlled in society through fear and exclusion and by being labeled sinners or unclean. This could result from sickness or sin or a lapse in faithfulness to the covenant.

So Jesus moves to the fringes of society, away from the cities and synagogues to deserted places. Even so, people everywhere go out of their way, still seeking him. As his power and presence are loose in the world, other powers of the world are starting to resist and gather force to face him. Herein lies a stern warning for us. Do we take what we experience of Jesus personally and talk about it freely? Do we then return to Jesus and his company to aid others and to follow Jesus? Do we hold on to what we have been given in Jesus' pity for ourselves alone and not reform our lives to the good news of God? It is not enough to relate personally to Jesus and then live off of a moment of healing or connection. Instead, we must return again and again to Jesus' word and to the company of other followers and walk the way together. Like Jesus' disciples, we have a lot to learn about who this Jesus, the Holy One of God, truly is. And this is certainly more than any one of us might know individually.

By the end of the first chapter, Jesus is already excluded from the community and set apart as one who carries the burden of others' sin. He is seen as tainted by his association with sinners, a choice he has made of his own will because of his pity for human beings. Such pity is the mark of God and the mark of God's beloved son and servant. It is also the mark of the new community, the new household that lives in obedience to the Law and with pity for others, willingly putting themselves in jeopardy to set others free and to save others in desperate straits. Jesus and those who come after him are to befriend and embrace the lowest castes of society, the people on the fringe who have been forced outside by others. Touching those we fear the most, like Jesus, makes us most human and most obedient to God.

Today that "mark of pity" has the same enormous ramifications that it had in the time of Jesus. Pity may draw us into association with the sick, with those deemed dangerous to the community, those feared because of their behavior, those with HIV/AIDS and other diseases, those with mental illness or addictions to drugs or alcohol, and those who resort to sexual abuse and violence. Yet it is to "them" that Jesus immediately moves closer. The kingdom of God comes first to them. Jesus' victory of justice comes first to the victims of injustice and selfishness, especially to the victims of religious structures that add to people's burdens rather than serving them in imitation of God. By the end of the first chapter we are summoned to obey and imitate Christ and to have pity on those who suffer because of us. From this point on, the struggle between the powers of God and the powers of society and religious authorities will mount in force, and the followers of Jesus will be commanded to choose their way.

This opening chapter that looks at Mark 1 is longer than many other chapters in this study of Mark. Such in-depth attention will also focus on Mark 8, the story of another call, and on Mark 15 and 16. These are hinge chapters that are crucial to understanding what Jesus is trying to tell us about himself and what he summons us to as his followers. Images, verbs, phrases, teachings, and even stories of encountering Jesus will be repeated again and again and will overlap, reminding us of what has gone before. Learning to read or listen to Mark's account of Jesus' good news of God is like turning or spinning or even falling down from dizziness as we become aware of all that is entailed and learned. It is like an always moving spiral, leading us further down and further into our relationship with Jesus and with all the others who are connected to him. This is when we begin to be followers. This is where we turn our lives around. This is where we leave all else, our families, our livelihoods, our lifestyles, our ways of relating. This is also where we stay right where we are: with Jesus in the kingdom of God. Nothing is the same, although all is as it was before.

There is a Buddhist story—I call it "The Buddha Block"—that can call us again to what Jesus has begun in us.

Once upon a time there was a young child who learned early on that he had a marvelous talent. He could see all manner of things, creatures, people, faces in stones, rocks and boulders. He started small, working with pebbles that he chipped away at, uncovering tiny insects, snails, turtles and all kinds of animals. Then he moved to larger stones, seeing in them small dragons, horses, tigers, boars, foxes, birds, fish, and sometimes flowers and small figures of men and women. Next he was fascinated to start seeing children playing, fishermen, scholars, old men smoking their pipes, glorious birds, and faces of the great and lowly. As he grew older he grew better, both at seeing what was hidden in stone, rock face and mountain and at releasing them with his carving and sculpting.

And he grew famous. He was hired and paid royally to reproduce the faces, busts, and poses of the powerful, the rich, and the influential. He carved monuments and made sculptures of politicians, great men and women in villages and nations, and he became wealthy and renowned.

But, in all those years, he tendered a dream of his own. He was a devout Buddhist and wanted to find a stone, no matter its size, that contained a hidden Buddha. He wanted to release Buddha and carve it so that it would be lifelike. He wanted to reveal the compassion and mercy, the strength and wisdom of the Buddha so clearly that people who saw the statue would think and sense that they had actually met the Buddha! And so he spent all his spare time and also had others look for the stone that bound the Buddha. He referred to it as his Buddha block—that block of stone that held Buddha's form and face.

He searched everywhere in his homeland of Japan, studying all kinds of jade—green, white, and rare colors—but he found nothing. He heard of a quarry of granite in a place called New Hampshire and had tons of rock shipped over. He stared at it, walked around it and found nothing. He had marble quarried from Italy and still saw nothing. He spent years poring over stone, looking for the block that would release Buddha. And there was nothing. As he grew older he worried that if he didn't find the block of stone soon, he would no longer have the energy and strength needed to release Buddha's countenance and form to the world.

Finally, one day, he remembered the old priest who had lived in the monastery just down the road from where he lived and how, when he went to talk with him, he always seemed to have an answer. Even if he didn't leave with any specifics, somehow the priest's company, his presence, always gave him strength or confidence. The carver wondered if he was still there after all these years. He walked down to the monastery and noticed right away that it was now in a state of disrepair. Yet there in the temple, sitting quietly, was the old man. The carver was welcomed. Over tea he told the old priest of his dream and how for so long he had sought the right stone to release the Buddha. He also told of how close he was to despair that he would ever find it. Did the priest have any ideas on where to look, or what he could do next?

They sat in silence for a while and then the priest's face brightened. "Yes," he said, "I think I know exactly where you can find the stone you are looking for!" The sculptor was a little skeptical but interested. "Remember," the priest said, "there is an old garden at the very back of the monastery. It has old stones scattered about, some from the walls that once surrounded this place, but others discarded and unused by the builders over the years. Some are huge, ancient granite and others are small. Some blocks are already cut, some weathered. I'm sure you can find the stone you are looking for there."

The sculptor was delighted—of course! He rose to his feet, bowed to the old man and ran to the back of the monastery lands, easily finding the garden. It was exactly as the priest had described. The stones were different and magnificent. He would find one here, he was sure. He went around touching the stones, putting a finger to them, getting the taste of them, eyeing their shapes, sizes, and density, looking for cracks, looking for that one that would call out to him.

And then he noticed an old well, fashioned of great stones. It stood, rounded and high, reaching up to his chest. He went and fingered the stones, feeling something close. As he leaned over to see what they looked like on the other side, inside the well, he was startled to find himself looking at himself, in the fresh clear water a few feet down in the well. He looked for a moment, thinking about how he had gotten older and how he had changed, and then he was startled again by a hand on his shoulder. It was the old priest who had followed him down to the garden. The priest's words hit him like a hammer or stone as he gestured toward the carver's face in the water and applied more pressure to his shoulder. The sculptor saw the Buddha block. The Buddha block lay within himself! And he began to smile broadly.

The Buddhist monk who told me this story then turned to me, put his hand on my shoulder, and turned me to face my own reflection in the glass pane. He said, "Not Buddha block, but Jesus block! Yes? Good time to start releasing the Jesus within!" And he was smiling broadly. I immediately remembered Jesus' words: "Come follow me and I will make you a fisher of men and women."

Following Jesus is being remade in a new image, a new person, a beloved child of God and beloved servant, and it is also turning and returning the favor to anyone who might be there, waiting for a call or a gesture of invitation to come and join the company. Today, now, the kingdom of God is close at hand. Now is a good time to start releasing the Christ within us.

Let us pray, using the words of the psalms that Jesus and his followers knew by heart. We begin with the first one.

Psalm 1

Blessed is the one
who (follows not) does not go where the wicked gather,
or stands in the way of sinners,
or sits where the scoffers sit!

Instead he finds delight in the law of the Lord
And meditates day and night on his commandments.
She is like a tree planted near running water
Producing fruit in due season, its leaves never fade or wither.
Everything they do prospers.

But it is different with the wicked.
They are like chaff driven by the wind.
The wicked/the unclean will not stand when judgment comes,
Nor the sinners when the righteous assemble.
For the Lord watches over the way of the righteous but cuts off the way
of the wicked.

(a blending of translations from CCB and NAB)

CHAPTER 3

Mark My Words

Callings and Conflicts

Mark 2, 3, and 4

THE PATTERNS OF CHAPTERS 2, 3, AND 4 ARE SIMILAR. Each begins with a cure that is deliberately done in public, followed by a calling, and a teaching. There is a shift in chapter 4 to present a series of parables or teachings about the good news of God and the kingdom. This is followed by the story of Jesus silencing the sea, the skies, and the storm, as he and his disciples cross over to the other side. As Jesus preaches and teaches and then puts into action what his words proclaim, there are those who are fascinated by him and those who are resistant. His very presence demands a response because Jesus functions as a prophetic figure, calling everyone to repentance and forgiveness. His message demands that people choose to change or that they refuse to alter their lives after encountering him. Belief in Jesus can never be a private and personal affair alone because it has social, economic, and even political consequences.

But following Jesus isn't a one-time choice. There are moments of decision making that are pivotal. This is a process of conversion, a dawning awareness and a deepening of insight and wisdom that stem from an association with Jesus and with those with whom he chooses to dwell and whom he calls his own.

The new creation, the new order of the kingdom, grows as Jesus moves outward, with his disciples trailing along behind him. The first chapter fleshes out the nature of our calling, and we will learn, as followers and disciples and apostles what Jesus has in mind for those who come after him. Their lives are disrupted by Jesus' presence and call. Whether they are yet aware of it, they are breaking with the usual understandings of family ties, social and economical securities, cultural boundaries and national identities. They are, in effect, fundamentally reordering all their relationships. They will soon learn that Jesus has overturned each of their individual worlds, just as he is intent on overturning the world around them by ushering in the alternative life of the kingdom of God. They will need the company of others if they are going to sustain their conversion, others who are also called to follow, to come after Jesus. Jesus is now "catching" people, and they watch and observe how he does it so they learn to do it themselves in the future.

Jesus' first order is to issue a call to repentance. It will bring immediate, vocal, and almost universal persecution, both religious and political. But Jesus speaks with such authority that there are only two choices in response: obedience, faltering though it may be initially, or rejection. And there are many ways to reject him or to refuse to obey: ignoring him and his teachings; accepting personal healing, comfort, or whatever else is useful but continuing as before; being skeptical; provoking confrontation; cynical questioning; outright hostility; conspiring with others against him; rumor and deliberate misreading of his words and deeds; baiting him so that he will fall into a trap; and actively seeking to silence him.

His followers will experience different levels of conversion, a growing sense of urgency, and an awareness of what is involved in following Jesus and being known to associate with him. As the gospel continues, the disciples, and also ourselves, misunderstand more and more of what Jesus is asking and what being a follower of Jesus means in terms of practice, prayer, and worship in his community of the household of the kingdom of God. Immediately there will be moments of crisis between the authority and teaching of Jesus and that of the scribes, the teachers of the Law, the Pharisees, the leaders of the Roman Empire and those in Israel who live in collusion with them. For economic and political reasons, many will lay aside parts of the covenant of God to accommodate their situation with the Romans, whom they detest but need nonetheless. Even his family and relatives will find him hard to take and will seek to stop what he is doing. The gospel reveals that Jesus seems to be on a collision course with everyone!

Now begins the time when the disciples are called to "observe" Jesus, as he once observed them at their work. The verb covers many understandings: to see with your eyes; to see with your mind and so to perceive and know; to become acquainted with by experience; to look closely *at*—not to look away; to care for and pay heed to; to be seen, shown myself or appeared (from the website greekbible.com). And we walk with them, following Jesus and learning as we go.

But Jesus has the ability always to surprise us! That will be hard to get used to, though we will, like the disciples, try to do our best. This story from a Celtic collection of parables will help us remember what Jesus is about and what he would like from his followers.

Once upon a time there was a young man named Kevin. His father was a farmer, but Kevin wasn't much good at farming. He had trouble with the plow and left behind uneven rows, if you could even call them rows. He just couldn't get the hang of milking a cow and when shearing a sheep he nearly lost his own fingers or cut his clothes to ribbons. The farmer decided in his wisdom that his son had a different kind of wisdom and that his son would be better off as a priest. Dutifully Kevin obeyed. He was off to the city to the diocese to see the bishop.

Now the bishop was intent on finding out if Kevin was suitable for the priesthood and so asked him a number of questions. He began with the most basic: "Kevin, who created the heavens?" That was an easy one and Kevin replied: "The one who created the earth." And the bishop came back: "And who created the earth?" Kevin was quick (this was easy) with "The one who created all men and women, of course." The bishop kept pushing: "And who created men and women?" But this time, while Kevin's answer wasn't what the bishop expected, the answer came back surely, as though Kevin had done some thinking about the matter: "The one who created space for their souls in heaven!" The bishop tried once again: "And who created space for their souls in heaven?" Kevin smiled broadly: "Why the one who created heaven!" and they were both back at the place where they began. The bishop, who was frustrated and annoyed, told Kevin to look elsewhere for his calling. It obviously wasn't to the priesthood—he was, in fact, an idiot.

Now this didn't sit well with his father, as you might guess, who insulted Kevin, calling him a disgrace to the family name. Poor Kevin was dejected and didn't know what to do when he remembered that there was a wise old man, a hermit, who lived in a cave up the side of the mountain. He went to visit him and told him what had happened. The wise hermit told Kevin: "Ignore your father and the bishop, for that matter. It doesn't matter a whit what either of them thinks. What matters is the truth and the will of God. If you are to preach the gospel, have pity on the sick and the sinner and serve the people, then you'll do exactly what God wants you to do. But I do think I need to test you to see if you can obey the will of God."

So off the two of them went to a nearby lake. "Kevin, if you're going to be a fisherman and catch souls, we have to see if you're better at fishing than farming. Take my coracle—it has a fishing rod there and go out fishing. Then we'll see what God wants of you."

Obediently Kevin went out in the hermit's boat. He sat there with his line over the side for the rest of the day and all night. When morning came, he finally got a bite. He pulled the fish into the boat but as soon as he saw the poor fish thrashing about in the bottom of the boat, the hook caught in its flesh, poor Kevin couldn't bear it and gently, carefully removed the hook and threw the fish back into the water. Kevin sat there for a long while, until night came again, and then pulled the line into the boat. He was so filled with pity for the fish, that he knew this wasn't going to work—he would fail miserably as a fisherman. It was useless to try again. And he rowed back to the shore to meet the hermit.

As he pulled the coracle up on the shore, he turned to find the hermit standing there and smiling grandly, his eyes twinkling. Kevin heard him say: "Kevin, my boy, you passed the test swimmingly! You have all three qualities you need to be a priest, or better yet a public follower of Jesus. You sat and waited all day and night for a fish to take your bait—you have patience, enough to wait on folk for years to catch their minds, and hearts and souls, I suspect. And what is so important, you had pity on the poor fish—you'll certainly have pity on people and folk in need. And lastly, even though you knew you caused pain to the fish, you were humble enough to change and carefully set the fish free without letting your feelings of sadness or despair get in the way of saving the poor fish. You've got humility and the knowledge to keep changing yourself. You'll make a grand servant of the people."

Kevin was delighted. The hermit told him to get on with his life, to go back to his village and to the others in the surrounding countryside and to start preaching the gospel of God, helping any he could and being patient no matter how people reacted to him.

And so that is what Kevin did. He preached Jesus and he helped people in their needs, listening to them, sharing his bread, working and paying their bills, comforting them in their sorrows, standing by them in the hard times and letting a piece of him die with each of their deaths. As the years went by, Kevin was beloved, relied on by the people, heard of by total strangers whom he treated as dearest kin. So much for ecclesial power or the authority of ordination—Kevin was busy about the work of the kingdom of God, filling up all those empty spaces in heaven waiting to welcome men and women, after knowing a bit of that heaven here on earth.

Jesus is going to be about the work of testing his disciples, continuing to call them closer to him, deeper into his confidences and letting them observe how he preaches the good news. He wants them to see that he is the good news of God close at hand, in his flesh and blood and words and touch. Hopefully, they will learn by observing and by experiencing: They will know guilt by association with Jesus, learning to become as the beloved children and servants of God on earth. It will be a bumpy ride.

Forgiveness Offered and Given Over

After Jesus is baptized by John in the Jordan River in Galilee, he turns toward the desert to be known by God and to deepen his baptismal experience. Then he returns and walks along the lake in Galilee, calling men and women to come after him. He continues to travel the cities and synagogues of all of Galilee and then arrives in Capernaum where he begins to gather followers around him as he moves from the synagogues to private households. He continues alternating between deserted places for personal prayer and going out to the towns to preach and to heal by his words and touch. As he moves into rural areas people flock to him. When Jesus returns to Capernaum word spreads that he's back and people surge around the house where he stays. This will be his new home, his resting place, where his followers come together. This story is the model of how Jesus works.

> As the news spread that he was at home, so many people gathered that there was no longer room even outside the door. While Jesus was preaching the Word to them, some people brought a paralyzed man to him.
>
> The four men who carried him couldn't get near Jesus because of the crowd, so they opened the roof above the room where Jesus was and, through the hole, lowered the man on his mat. When Jesus saw the faith of these people, he said to the paralytic, "My son, your sins are forgiven."
>
> Now, some teachers of the Law who were sitting there wondered within themselves, "How can he speak like this insulting God? Who can forgive sins except God?"
>
> At once Jesus knew through his spirit what they were thinking and asked, "Why do you wonder? Is it easier to say to this paralyzed man, 'Your sins are forgiven,' or to say: 'Rise, take up your mat and walk?' But now you shall know that the Son of Man has authority on earth to forgive sins."
>
> And he said to the paralytic, "Stand up, take up your mat and go home." The man rose and, in the sight of all those people, he took up his mat and went out. All of them were astonished and praised God saying, "We have never seen anything like this!" (2:1a-12)

Jesus has been traveling throughout Galilee, preaching and teaching, and people keep coming to him to be healed and cured. His reputation as a miracle worker is dogging him, and it seems to handicap him when he wishes to preach about God's kingdom because the good news does not necessarily save one from suffering or death. Perhaps Jesus' stern warning to the leper is an attempt to keep people from associating his message primarily with escape from pain. We must remember why the gospel has been written: it is to help those who come to believe and are baptized face what can often follow—rejection, persecution, and suffering at the hands of those in authority and power who refuse to believe that Jesus' words are God's good news of the kingdom on earth.

In his book *The Gospel of Mark: A Reflective Commentary,* Denis McBride speaks of this connection between Jesus' power to heal and the stronger power to bring the good news of the kingdom of God into people's consciousness, and how a conflict may spring from their expectations of what Jesus will do for them.

It seems reasonable to suppose that if he [Jesus] believed his principal message of the kingdom was carried through preaching, people's stubborn focus on his miracle-working outside that context would make him angry. No amount of Jesus' healing is going to exempt people from experiencing pain or enduring suffering: to believe otherwise is dangerous foolishness, not least for Mark's readers. Mark will soon show how the Son of Man will illustrate that in his own experience when he endures unavoidable suffering for the sake of the kingdom. (p. 50)

This emphasis on healing reveals a lack of understanding of who Jesus is and what he is trying to do in the world. His intent seems to be to go beyond physical healing to radically alter people's lives so they will live more humanly and gracefully, following a new authority and power in the world. There will be many occasions when Jesus tells his own followers and those he heals not to speak. Often, they have missed the core and heart of who he is and what he is preaching. They want him to be something other than the beloved servant (who will also be the suffering servant) of God who obeys God alone.

As we return to the story, we see that there are people who are intent, even desperate, to get to him. They are faithful and true and also ingenious: they will not be deterred by a crowd or by doors! Houses at that time were often constructed with a back wall, two side portions that held up the roof, and a wide courtyard, an entryway that was more or less open space. Alternatively, the roof might be thatch supported by poles and mud walls, or, in better homes, loosely laid tiles without mortar, the way roofs are still constructed in many places of the world, such as rural India, Southeast Asia and other southern countries.

The people think that once they get to the roof, it will be easy enough to remove a section and replace it later. While they are doing this, however, there is likely a crowd down below. As they work at opening a space, mud, dust, straw, and pebbles fall down into the room below. Jesus is probably sitting up against the back wall, with teachers of the Law and scribes in somewhat honored places nearby, while the crowd packs in front and around the house. The teachers, scribes, and Pharisees are beginning to listen to what Jesus is teaching and beginning to ask questions. They may have listened to John but they were not necessarily converted by his words. They are not open to the one who comes after him teaching of the forgiveness of sins.

Jesus sees the faith and devotion of the friends of the paralyzed man and is moved by their persistence. Crowds can be a hindrance to Jesus' message, as they are here, as the people listen to his words and wait for something extraordinary to happen. But are they taking Jesus' words to heart?

Jesus sees their faith and is moved to speak to the man they lower into his presence. One translation has Jesus address the man as "My child" (*teknon*). This is a term of endearment and tender regard that has nothing to do with age. If you're literally a child, young in age, you are addressed as *paidion*, but even if you are an adult you can still be called *teknon*. Jesus says, "My child, your sins are forgiven." These words chill the hearts of the teachers listening, but this is the essence, the heart, of Jesus' message of the good news of God. We are forgiven in Jesus! Jesus does not say "I forgive your sins" but rather "Your sins are forgiven."

Immediately, some of the teachers are offended by Jesus' words. Jesus knows what they are thinking; he is aware already of how those in authority are reacting to him. Resistance to his message begins in earnest. Jesus' authority and teaching differ from those of the scribes and teachers of the Law, which were often ritualistic, involving a sacrifice in the temple or payment in exchange for forgiveness or acceptance back into the community. The power of Jesus lies in his word and in his presence. When he speaks like this, those in authority judge him to be blaspheming, as he appropriates to himself the power that belongs to God alone.

They start to harden their hearts against him, keeping quiet while making judgments and assumptions about him rather than looking at what he is doing or listening with an ear to obeying his words. Rather than accuse them, except to point out that he knows what they are thinking, he asks them a question: "Is it easier to say to this paralyzed man, 'Your sins are forgiven,' or to say: 'Rise, take up your mat and walk?'" Jesus then answers his own question, "But now you shall know that the Son of Man has authority (*exousian*) on earth to forgive sins." He turns from them to address the paralytic: "Stand up, take up your mat and go home."

This appears to be a way in which Jesus deals with conflict in Mark's gospel. He will begin speaking to a person or a group and then shift his focus, even in mid-sentence or thought, to direct the power of his words to others. Those he originally addressed must now watch and hear what he is doing and decide for themselves where they stand.

We are confronted with two options: is it easier to forgive sins or to give power to the legs of a man paralyzed and raise him to life, bringing him back into the community? Jesus seems to be intent on sharing his power to forgive. (Indeed, this may be easier to do than to raise up those paralyzed physically!) At that moment, he undermines and breaks the authority of the teachings of the scribes and teachers about forgiveness. We are forgiven in Jesus, the good news of God. As followers, we are given the power to forgive one another as God has forgiven us. Forgiveness, the heart and soul of Jesus' word of good news, is what brings life, raises people up from despair, and releases them from their prisons of brokenness, loneliness, and darkness. Jesus grasped Simon's mother-in-law to raise her up, but now his word alone has the power to bring life and movement.

Mark is questioning us. What lies in our hearts? Do we forgive, remembering that we have been forgiven and raised up in baptism? Do we believe in the word of God, the word of forgiveness with its power to bring life? If we're forgiven, like the paralytic, are we now going to great lengths to bring others into the presence of God, as did his friends? Do we, like the crowd, praise the goodness of God in Jesus, or do we, like those judging Jesus, judge others who seek to bring life to the outcast or publicly brand sinners and withhold forgiveness? The die is cast. From now on, everything that Jesus does and says will be scrutinized. He will be examined at every opportunity, and more and more people will find it difficult to take Jesus into their hearts and minds.

Jesus moves again, back to the lake. He is next seen walking along with a crowd when he catches sight of a tax collector sitting in his office. Remember that he also found his first four followers at their workplace. Jesus issues another individual call, this to Levi, son of Alpheus, whom we will know as Matthew. The calling is just two words that compose a demand and an invitation: "Follow me." And Levi, who practices a trade despised by the Jewish people, gets up and follows him! Taxes were collected from all on behalf of the Roman occupying authority and many tax collectors were notorious for collecting more than what was required to pay the Romans. They made their own fortunes, which afforded them lavish lifestyles on the backs of the poor, who had no recourse but to pay or suffer the consequences.

Although tax collectors were shunned by both the authorities and the people, we now find Jesus at Levi's house, and even eating with him. Levi has already invited others to hear Jesus preach. Mark reveals that a meal is often a usual place for hearing the gospel and such meals are often shared with others who are called to follow Jesus. Once more Jesus breaks a taboo by consorting with these people. His disciples are present, as are some teachers of the Law and members of the Pharisees. (Would they have remained in the courtyard or on the fringes, listening and watching?) Eugene LaVerdiere explains the monumental meaning of this meal.

> Joining at the same table was a powerful symbol of mutual respect and commitment among the participants. A meal could seal a new relationship. It could also bring about reconciliation. Those who shared in a meal welcomed one another in peace and extended their family unit even beyond the ordinary extended family. The meal transformed strangers and outsiders into friends. It also extended a community, incorporating new members. At table with Jesus, tax collectors and sinners joined those who heard the gospel and did the will of God. Later, Jesus would declare all such people to be his true relatives (Mk 3:20, 31-35). (*Beginning of the Gospel,* 1:84)

Jesus' actions and choices are upsetting the rules and rituals of society that determine who is inside and who is outside the domain of grace and what is needed to get back inside. The Pharisees in particular are shocked by Jesus' behavior. It helps to know why. The term "Pharisee" comes from the Hebrew word *perushim*, which means "the separated ones" or those who separated themselves from sinners and others who were deemed ritually unclean. They are horrified at what Jesus is doing, not because he is associating and eating with the common people, the *amme ha-arets*, but because he is spending time with those who are sinners, with evildoers, with those considered unclean and wicked. Denis McBride suggests how astounded and perplexed the Pharisees must have been as they watched Jesus at table with Levi and his friends.

> Many Pharisees were *soferim*, scholars or scribes not only of the Law, but also of the oral traditions, which detailed the requirements of the Sabbath, the dietary laws, the ritual laws of purity, and the regulations for tithing. Mark's phrase "the scribes of the Pharisees" refers to the scholars of the Pharisaic party. The Pharisees' dedication to being separate also expressed itself in *haveroth*, a table fellowship of friends. Both Jesus and the Pharisees believed that sharing a meal meant fellowship with God and with those who share the blessings of God. But whereas the Pharisees' table fellowship was limited to those whose lives were morally upright, Jesus' table fellowship was extended to all as a messianic symbol of God who cherishes all and graces all equally.
>
> The Pharisees object that Jesus eats with tax collectors and sinners. The term "sinners" refers to those who have flagrantly and persistently disobeyed the Law and have not repented. (*Gospel of Mark*, 54-55)

All of this leads up to the line that Jesus wants to proclaim aloud and in public. When the Pharisees question Jesus' disciples (not Jesus himself), Jesus overhears and answers them definitively. Why does he eat with sinners? "Healthy people don't need a doctor, but sick people do. I did not come to call the righteous but sinners" (Mk 2:17). In a nutshell this is God's good news.

Jesus' pastoral practice, so to speak, will differ from that of the Pharisees. As McBride says, "[Jesus's] practice is association, not separation; closeness not distance" (*Gospel of Mark*, 55-56). Jesus is very clear: God's forgiveness always comes first; it is a gift proffered long before there is any repentance. And eating with Jesus is a gift; it is not a reward for repenting but a way to be with him and follow him. In fact, sharing a meal is Jesus' primary way of preaching forgiveness, the gospel of God's kingdom here among us, and the call to continual conversion.

Jesus' words should stick in our ears and hearts. He has come not for the righteous but for sinners. The problem lies with those who will not admit that they are sinners, those who already think of themselves as righteous. When we forget that no one is righteous before God, we tend to judge others as not as worthy as ourselves to sit at table with Jesus. The way we view others reveals how we think of ourselves. If we refuse to eat with others or to forgive them, we reveal that *we* do not feel the need for forgiveness, that we are not like them. This sticking point is a locus of confrontation between Jesus and many of the leaders and teachers of the Pharisees. The Pharisees and teachers will continue to maintain that Jesus and his followers do not practice certain specifics of the Law in regard to fasting or picking grains of wheat on the sabbath or healing on the sabbath. They also maintain that Jesus is appropriating to himself what only God can do. But, again and again, Jesus refuses to let them use the Law to define God's love and mercy. He seeks to turn them to the power of forgiveness, mercy, reconciliation, inclusion of all, and to the idea that "the sabbath was made for man, not man for the sabbath. So the Son of Man is master even of the sabbath" (Mk 2:27).

Jesus will repeatedly return to stories of the tradition in the older testament to remind them of experiences of God other than their required rituals and set patterns of enforcing religious belief. Compassion for the hearts and lives of others is more important than adherence to the laws. Jesus also makes many allusions to what lies ahead, to the depth of resistance building in their hearts, which will result in their total rejection of him and, in the end, his death.

When the religious authorities question his followers about why they don't follow the rules of fasting, Jesus responds: "How can the wedding guests fast while the bridegroom is with them? As long as they have the bridegroom with them, they cannot fast. But the day will come when the bridegroom will be taken from them and on that day they will fast" (Mk 2:19-20). These words have an ominous undercurrent. This is the first mention in Mark of the shadow of the cross that will never be far from Jesus' consciousness and teaching. Mark seems intent on keeping that shadow of the cross in the background, as an undercurrent, reminding Jesus' disciples that they will share their master's call and what that can lead to. Following Jesus implies facing rejection and the pain of being marked as belonging to Jesus' company.

Giving Life and the Sabbath Law

Jesus goes back to the synagogue on the sabbath, the day devoted solely to the worship of God. The synagogue is turning into a battleground between Jesus and his followers and those who refuse to examine how their own practice of the Law might keep them from knowing the pity of God and compassion for others. A man with a paralyzed hand is present, and Jesus is being watched to see what he will do: Will he heal him? Will he break the sabbath law?

Jesus is not interested primarily in laws or even in healing. He is trying to get his opponents to look at what constitutes true worship of God and at how to keep holy the sabbath. But the conflict is engaged, and Jesus will heal the man with the paralyzed hand. Jesus tells him to move to the center so everyone can see him. He seems to be saying, Seeing someone in this condition, can you not be moved to pity? How can you quibble about laws and ignore that the sabbath is for praising God for creation, for life that is good? Do you not remember that this God of the living brought us out of Egypt into freedom and fullness of hope, making us his children and caring for us as a father? But the Pharisees are growing harder, or more resistant, realizing what his teaching might mean for their own lives.

Jesus makes his words—and their choice—very clear.

> Then he asked them, "What does the Law allow us to do on the sabbath? To do good or to do harm? To save life or to kill?" But they were silent.
> Then Jesus looked around at them with anger and deep sadness because they had closed their minds. And he said to the man, "Stretch out your hand." He stretched it out and his hand was healed. But as soon as the Pharisees left, they met with Herod's supporters, looking for a way to destroy Jesus. (2:4-6)

Although this is only the third chapter, a decision has already been made. Two groups who used to despise each other now conspire together to destroy Jesus. We should keep this firmly in mind as the gospel continues. Those who are baptized must be realistic about how others will react to them if they follow the way of Jesus. Jesus is described as angry and deeply saddened, grieved that these leaders have already closed their hearts to him. The paralyzed man lowered through the roof and the man with the paralyzed hand seem not nearly as paralyzed as those whose hearts are hardened. They seem unable to breathe or to rejoice or to be open to new possibilities.

So Jesus goes back to the lakeside, the waters of baptism. The crowds are growing and people from all over are seeking him out: "Judea, Jerusalem, Idumea, Transjordan and from the region of Tyre and Sidon, for they had heard of all that he was doing" (Mk 3:8). While rejection within his own society and religious community is growing, so is acceptance by those in need of his message and touch. Once again they crush against him, so he climbs into a boat to teach them. Once again those with unclean spirits recognize him. While they address him as "the Son of God," they seem to have little understanding of who he is or what he is teaching about God, that we are all called to be the beloved children of God. This is a challenge for us all of us. Do we recognize who Jesus is? Are we part of those who find themselves with unclean spirits or demons? Are we with those who are hard of heart, who reject his power? Are we part of those who seek no more than healing?

As many people seem to recognize Jesus, Jesus takes his disciples and withdraws in a boat. It seems almost as if he is withdrawing to an ark, a sanctuary of the new household of faith, which rides on the waters of baptism. The vocal crowds continue to demand what they can from Jesus, but all too soon they will be just as vocal in crying out for his crucifixion and death. As Jesus becomes known and popular, he is causing factions that abhor each other in politics, economics, and religion. Those who follow Herod and those who follow the Pharisees and the temple take counsel against Jesus. As we learn more about following Jesus, do we learn to obey him or do we question and refuse to follow more closely?

Midway through the third chapter of Mark, Jesus goes farther from the synagogue, moving into the hill country. He called "those he wanted," those who had decided to follow him, and they came to him. This third calling represents the naming of the twelve who became disciples and then later, after the death and resurrection of Jesus, became apostles. They were sent out to preach and "he gave them authority to drive out demons." This authority included announcing the forgiveness of God, eating at table with people, calling them to conversion and to following Jesus' way. The disciples were to persuade people to take the good news to heart and to grasp hold of it for the victory of justice and life in God. And so the Twelve were named, with the last name a sign of what is to come from within Jesus' own followers.

> These are the Twelve: Simon, to whom he gave the name Peter; James, son of Zebedee, and John his brother, to whom he gave the name Boanerges, which means "men of thunder"; Andrew, Philip, Bartholomew, Matthew, Thomas, James son of Alpheus, Thaddeus, Simon the Cananean and Judas Iscariot, the one who betrayed him. (3:16-19)

We know the names because we learn them as children. We often forget, though, that we could look in our community or our church today and list another twelve names of disciples, those who have been healed or called.

As the crowd grows, so does the number of Jesus' followers. It is likely that the Twelve are singled out because they became the leaders of the Markan church after the death and resurrection of Jesus. But it is being a follower of Jesus and a disciple in his company that is what is most important. Being called to be an apostle, one sent to found a community, does not necessarily mean being any closer to Jesus than other followers. It designates a role for someone who is to be at the service of others; it is not a position of authority from which to rule but a call to share his mission. In naming twelve, Jesus uses the image of a new family, seemingly a reference to the twelve tribes of Israel that were one in their covenant with Yahweh.

Although we know their names, we know very little about them as individuals, particularly Andrew, Philip, Bartholomew, James the son of Alpheus, Thaddeus, or Simon the Cananean (the Zealot). Peter, James, and

John, who come first, will figure in many of the stories to come. Although lists of the disciples usually begin with Simon Peter and end with Judas, there are often differences in naming the others. Matthias will later replace Judas, but he will never be mentioned again.

As the disciples gather around Jesus, they also signal a change as the focus moves from the tribes of Israel to the world beyond Jerusalem and Israel. Neither holiness nor awareness is a prerequisite for being chosen. Jesus is creating a new family, whose number will be greater by far than that of any extended family or even all the tribes of Israel. At the time Mark's gospel is written in the mid-sixties, Mark's church in Jerusalem is already formed of people from all over the Roman Empire, and many of the original Twelve are already dead.

When the Twelve returned home, the crowds pursued them relentlessly. The story that tells of their return is often ignored because people don't want to hear it or face what it might mean for Jesus' community.

> The crowd began to gather again and they [Jesus and the Twelve] couldn't even have a meal. Knowing what was happening his relatives came to take charge of him: "He is out of his mind," they said. Meanwhile, the teachers of the Law who had come from Jerusalem said, "He is in the power of Beelzebul: the chief of the demons helps him to drive out demons." (3:20b-22)

This is another of Mark's "sandwiches." It begins with Jesus' relatives declaring that he is out of his mind. They come to restrain him, or take him home, to silence him and stop his traveling and teaching, which attract the crowds. Then the teachers of the Law, representing the institutional structure, intervene, concluding that he is not out of his mind but is possessed by a demon, in fact by the chief of demons. Beelzebul, the power of Satan himself, turns Jesus' every action into evil. Jesus responds first to the accusations about the source of his power and whom he serves and then teaches about what is called "the sin against the Holy Spirit." Only later will he turn to his family and relatives and what they might think.

Mark's world of two thousand years ago was drastically different from our world today. Mark, and many of his contemporaries, believed in demons. What exactly did this mean for them? What does it mean for us? In his book *Jesus in Solidarity with His People*, William Reiser explains:

> Mark believed in the existence of demons. Many people today do not, at least not in the form of fallen spirits who have invaded and infested the human world. Demons provided Mark with a category for accounting for some unfortunate conditions that we today would explain in biological, psychological, or even social terms. We do not attribute epilepsy (Mk 9:14ff) or unnamed childhood diseases (Mk 7:25ff) or severe behavioral disorders (Mk 5:1ff) to the presence of

unclean spirits. Whenever we spot irrational behavior our first impulse is to suspect mental disorder and to seek medical expertise or clinical assistance. Truly pathological behavior, we know, can turn deadly. For the protection of society, some individuals need to be securely hospitalized and heavily medicated.

Yet for all the advances in scientific knowledge we cannot insulate ourselves against the crushing assaults of human wickedness and depravity. No one who has followed the stories over the past ten or twenty years of panic-stricken refugees from places like Rwanda, Angola, or Sudan could have failed to reflect on the staggering enormity of human suffering and the stark, gruesome sinfulness that has been responsible for so much of it.

Africa, of course, hardly stands alone. (p. 43)

The list of atrocities and human perversion is long and universal and can extend to every nation and country, every religious group and every government. What is demonic in society has always been there. Mark's communities would have known it firsthand from the persecution, brutality, and human depravity in the arenas of Rome and wherever the Roman Empire held sway. It was and is found in human beings, in institutions, in governments, and, more horribly, among those who claim to be religious emissaries of God. Because of free will, humanity has a side that can be described as inhuman and so demonic. In the twentieth century alone the human race has been noted for managing to kill more people than in the history of the whole human race, and many of those killings were under the banner of religious belief and obedience to a god's will.

Reiser continues to explain what Mark is speaking about.

Mark would have depicted all the hostile forces arrayed against humanity as, collectively, the power of the demons. And he knew two things in this regard. First, Mark realized that this power was no fiction; it existed, as anyone with eyes and ears could readily attest. And second, he knew that this power had to be confronted and broken. All human suffering, even ordinary diseases and infirmities, bore witness to the awful destructive energy behind sin, which, like a vicious hurricane or tornado, will strike the innocent and the guilty with blind intent. Pick up the most insignificant, run-of-the-mill thread of human weakness and eventually one will be led to the source, to the center, from which all evil proceeds.

That Jesus once stood within that center and had destroyed sin at its root was something Mark, as a Christian, firmly believed. That no one after Jesus would ever again have to stand in that center would have struck Mark as untrue to experience. The descent into hell (not Mark's phrasing) belongs to the Christian religious experience. Others besides Jesus would have to descend there and face the enemy of our human nature, but they would never have to make that descent and face that demon alone. The cosmic battle to the death with evil did not take place in the wilderness around the Jordan River but at the cross, and the cross was destined to be as integral to the lives of his disciples as it was to the mission of Jesus himself. (*Jesus in Solidarity*, 43-44)

Mark's gospel is about this struggle of good and evil in Jesus' life and in the lives of his followers, then and now. We do incalculable harm to one another and to our universe. We are fully capable of the behavior often depicted in movies and even in horrible events in the news. This is the face of sin, evil, injustice, and violence.

Such evil is often spoken about by demonizing the behavior or the person who does it, which is what the scribes seek to do with Jesus. The word *ba'al zebul* literally means "lord of the house," *ba'al* being a lord or ruler; in Jewish reality, this was not God but a source of power used to do evil. As the scribes pursue Jesus, they turn vicious and make no sense in their arguments about who Jesus is or whom he obeys. So Jesus teaches them, using their own words against them.

Summoning them, he then began to speak to them by way of examples: "How can Satan expel Satan? If a kingdom is torn by civil strife, that kingdom cannot last. If a household is divided according to loyalties, that household will not survive. Similarly, if Satan has suffered mutiny in his ranks and is torn by dissension, he cannot endure; he is finished. No one can enter a strong man's house and despoil his property unless he has first put him under restraint. Only then can he plunder his house. (3:23-27 NAB)

The scribes' and teachers' rash judgment of Jesus makes no sense. Jesus turns their analogy against them to show that Satan's rule and power are at an end. Jesus uses a brief parable, an example, to show that he is the strong man binding and restraining Satan or the forces of evil. He is not Satan's slave. He is Satan's opponent and Satan will lose the struggle. The word Satan means "hinderer," and Jesus is about freeing human beings from all that hinders them from being truly human as the beloved children of God. As Jesus is struggling against evil so will we, his followers, participate in that same struggle. It is a battle for forgiveness, truthfulness, justice, mercy, reconciliation, nonviolence, faithfulness, and obedience to God's will, even if it means death at the hands of those who reject resisting evil. Jesus' good news is that he will break the hold of evil in humans' hearts and lift the burden of human misery that is the consequence of sin, violence, hatred, and injustice. But these encounters are merely skirmishes. The final battleground will be the cross, and it will be fought in Jesus' body and soul, as it is in ours.

The scribes have accused him of having an unclean spirit and of being possessed by Satan himself; Jesus turns now to that initial accusation. His response is not easy to grasp, but it appears to be Jesus' own judgment on all who would denigrate his Word and his person as they refuse to change their own lives. He uses formal language.

"I give you my word, every sin will be forgiven mankind and all the blasphemies men utter, but whoever blasphemes against the Holy Spirit will never be forgiven. He carries the guilt of his sin without end." He spoke thus because they had said, "He is possessed by an unclean spirit." (3:28-30 NAB)

This angry denunciation of Jesus causes consternation and confusion. These are the words of a strong man who is mightier than John the Baptist, the words of the one who comes after him and baptizes with the Holy Spirit. The words going forth from the lips of Jesus the prophet of God speak the truth to those who would demean and belittle the truth of the word of God. He is confronting those who, because of their pride, power, or authority, have heartlessly and blindly decided to reject Jesus and the good news of God because it threatens them. They are also perversely denying the goodness of Jesus that is revealed in his words of forgiveness, pity, and compassion as he heals and brings unity and hope to the many who are desperately seeking God. Jesus is about freeing the oppressed and burdened from prisons and darkness and tending to those spent with exhaustion and suffering. Yet there are those who will denounce him as evil incarnate rather than look to themselves and their own sinfulness and collusion with evil. This is clearly a sin against the Holy Spirit. Not only do they reject Jesus and his message but they also decry Jesus as the evil one. Denis McBride describes their sin.

Jesus' act of liberating someone from bondage is called diabolic; kindness is called satanic; pastoral care is dismissed as the work of the devil. Language becomes meaningless in the service of such professional jealousy; words are used as vandals to lay waste what is manifestly good. To sustain the big lie, language itself is deformed. The ordinary people who go to Jesus can see what the scribes refuse to see: Jesus works through the power of the Spirit of God, a power for good that is stubbornly opposed to the destructive power of Satan. In choosing to ignore the transparent beneficence of Jesus' ministry, the scribes' ultimate irreverence is towards the Spirit of God. That is the sin against the Holy Spirit. (*Gospel of Mark*, 71-72)

But this chapter of Mark isn't over yet. There is one more layer of rejection, that of the group closest to Jesus. Jesus' family and relatives have heard of the choosing of the Twelve, this inner circle that is not based on

kinship and blood ties and does not include them. So, Jesus finally turns to
them.

> Then his mother and his brothers came. As they stood outside, they
> sent someone to call him. The crowd sitting around Jesus told him,
> "Your mother and your brothers are outside asking for you." He
> replied, "Who are my mother and my brothers?"
>
> And looking around at those who sat there he said, "Here are my
> mother and my brothers. Whoever does the will of God is brother
> and sister and mother to me." (3:31-35)

Jesus reinvents family and household based on the word of God, the will
of God, and faithfulness and obedience rather than on kinship or blood
ties. Intimacy in Jesus' family comes from responding to his call and following him and through baptism dwelling in the Trinity. Some translations
read that his family wanted to "seize him." The Greek word used, *kratēsai*,
is sometimes translated as "take charge of him." This is the same word
used in the accounts of Jesus' betrayal and arrest in the garden before his
trial. Closeness in family does not assure understanding who Jesus is, nor
does it necessarily influence a decision to follow him. True relatives are
defined not by marriage or blood connection but by faith and freedom.
Blood relatives can be followers of Jesus but like everyone else they have to
enter the household of Jesus, which means that everything would change at
its root and heart.

Jesus was born into a Jewish nation and religion that were governed by
men, often with inherited power. Jesus' new family, the church, would be
composed of men and women (brothers and sisters) whose authority is
based on the power of the Spirit received in baptism. The invitation to
become the new brothers and sisters and mother of Jesus was there for his
own family as well as for the whole of humanity. For many, this is one of
the hardest sayings of Jesus, but it is the way to opening the kingdom of
God to all the beloved children of God.

Parables and a Storm

Parables, a form of storytelling that does not come naturally to the Western mind, are a way Jesus often teaches. A parable is an experience of an
alternate reality, almost like a trapdoor into another world. Once there,
you can see what it's like and then decide to stay or to leave, to return permanently or to dismiss that other world and reject the teller. The story
assumes that the listener is open to another possibility, another way of seeing reality. Perhaps a person's past life and choices, sin or weaknesses have
prevented knowing the reality of God's truth.

Jesus is a master of telling stories. Mark recounts that Jesus sits in the boat, which has become a symbol for the church. The boat is an ark that saves and offers sanctuary to all. The crowd remains on the shore, listening. Jesus has already talked about new wine not being put into old wineskins and new patches not being sewn into old cloth. It seems clear that he is about something altogether new. This seems another allusion to Isaiah 42:

> See, the earlier things have come to pass,
>   new ones I now foretell;
>   Before they spring into being,
>   I announce them to you. (Is 42:9)

The parables are also callings that invite and also describe what has already happened and what is happening now, with their words building an experience of the kingdom of God. Listen, as Jesus commands us.

> "A farmer went out sowing. Some of what he sowed landed on the footpath, where the birds came along and ate it. Some of the seed landed on rocky ground where it had little soil; it sprouted immediately because the soil had no depth. Then, when the sun rose and scorched it, it began to wither for lack of roots. Again, some landed among thorns, which grew up and choked it off, and there was no yield of grain. Some seed, finally, landed on good soil and yielded grain that sprang up to produce at a rate of thirty- and sixty- and a hundredfold." Having spoken this parable, he added: "Let him who has ears to hear me, hear!" (4:3-9 NAB)

The parable is very familiar. Mark tells the story of Jesus preaching to his followers and Mark reminds his church that this isn't just a story: it is the truth of their own lives. One of the marvelous things about a parable is that parables have many layers and many different interpretations. A parable is also a jumping off place that allows each group that hears the parable to find insights from the Spirit in the word of God in the context of that particular community.

Jesus follows the parable with the bold statement that "to you the mystery of the reign of God has been confided" (4:11). It is a mystery that can be delved into repeatedly. It is a way of seeing, of understanding, and of living the kingdom of God, and it is surrounded by a larger reality. There is always more to say and more to appropriate each time it is heard. And it's been confided and entrusted to us by God. We've been taken into God's confidence, and we are offered a new relationship with the Father in Jesus, by the power of the Spirit of God.

Perhaps a good way to study this parable is to use the lens of the historical reality of Mark's time, when planting seeds and reaping the harvest were at the center of most people's lives. We know that the seed is Jesus' teaching, the good news, the word of God that is potent beyond belief. The parable begins with a farmer who goes out sowing, using a verb tense that encompasses past, present, and future all at once. (This could easily allude to the liturgical time-bound reality of sowing the seed of the gospel.) The image is of someone throwing the seed in great arcs, on both sides of his body, generous to a fault in scattering the seed everywhere! And the seeds land every which way—on footpaths, where the birds have a feast, and on rocky ground, where the seed sprouts immediately (that word again) but is quickly scorched and withers because there isn't enough soil to lay down roots. More seeds land in a thorny clump and are battling to get nourishment as they are crowded out by hardier plants with tough roots and spines to protect them. And none has a yield. These three types of soil have produced nothing from the seed. Finally some seed actually gets into properly prepared ground, and it starts to produce at amazing rates, a harvest beyond belief!

Listeners then and readers today understand that it is Jesus who has been throwing the seeds of the Word everywhere, indiscriminately. While some have left it for the birds, there were others who immediately grabbed at it and took what they could for themselves. The third group must contend with others who suck the life out of everything around them so the new shoots of the word don't stand a chance. These three groups were familiar to Mark's community. Large crowds heard Jesus preach, and many grabbed hold of his words. Many were touched by Jesus, literally or figuratively, and their way was eased and their bodies or minds were healed. Others found it threatening and trampled it underfoot. Many didn't have the foundation to sustain growth.

Although the prophets, especially Isaiah and John the Baptist, had gone before the Word to prepare the way, calling to repentance and conversion that would lead to forgiveness of sin, many did not repent or convert their ways and so could not absorb Jesus' teaching. In the events of the first three chapters this has already happened to many, from the leadership to members of Jesus' family. And we will find throughout the gospel that all too quickly those he called as followers and disciples will also fall into these groups. They will betray him, ignore and reject certain parts of his teaching, start looking elsewhere, or take only what they want. Some closest to him will deny him, curse him, run from him, and declare that they don't even know him. All of the Twelve, and especially those who will be in the inner circle, will suffer the fate of the seed in the first three groups. It will not be until after the resurrection that they finally understand the relationship offered them in Jesus with God the Father by the Spirit's power. Then the harvest will begin. It will be enormous, wildly impossible, starting at thirtyfold and growing in some places with a harvest of a hundredfold!

There was a saying in the early church that the blood of martyrs is the seed of Christians. The members of Mark's church experienced both blood and martyrdom as well as denial and betrayal by those who gave up the seed. But there were also many who returned to the field, the kingdom, the sanctuary of the church to take the seed once again within them to "take it to heart and yield at thirty- and sixty- and a hundred-fold" (Mk 4:20). Even Peter, who is listed first among the apostles, had to return after his betrayal and, once again, repent, be forgiven and again let the seed take root in his heart.

Other parables told by Jesus are as short but they can all be read in a new way to give glimpses into the kingdom. But each is also an invitation, a call to take a risk, to follow Jesus. What can happen is as staggeringly new as what Jesus means by talking about a hundredfold yield in a field. The parables are images of what Jesus is doing and what we as his followers should be doing. "Let him who has ears to hear me, hear!"

> "When the light comes, is it to be put under a tub or a bed? Surely it is put on a lampstand. Whatever is hidden will be disclosed, and whatever is kept secret will be brought to light. Listen then, if you have ears!"
>
> And he also said to them, "Pay attention to what you hear. In the measure you give, so shall you receive and still more will be given to you. For to the one who produces something, more will be given, and from him who does not produce anything, even what he has will be taken away from him."
>
> Jesus also said, "In the kingdom of God it is like this. A man scatters seed upon the soil. Whether he is asleep or awake, be it day or night, the seed sprouts and grows, he knows not how. The soil produces of itself; first the blade, then the ear, then the full grain in the ear. And when it is ripe for harvesting they take the sickle for the cutting: the time for harvest has come."
>
> Jesus also said, "What is the kingdom of God like? To what shall we compare it? It is like a mustard seed which, when sown, is the smallest of all the seeds scattered upon the soil. But once sown, it grows up and becomes the largest of the plants in the garden and even grows branches so big that the birds of the air can take shelter in its shade." (4:21a-32)

Many of these parables come in the form of questions, and Jesus often hints at the answers, giving intimations of where to dig into the story for the image that connects with the kingdom and the good news. The parables are quite like Buddhist *koans*, which must be absorbed into the mind and the heart before they teach. Often there isn't so much an answer as an "Aha!" moment of insight that immediately changes everything. Some parables become so familiar, including those above, that we don't really hear them.

But who is it who lights the lamp and keeps it burning? What is the oil in the lamp? Where is our supply? If the lamp is on a stand, what is it being used for? How comfortable are we at living with mystery, what we do not understand but obey? What is being revealed now in the church that seemed to be concealed before, perhaps because it was not yet needed and so was hidden from sight?

Do we really hear the gospel, or do we just read it? Do we hear Jesus today? Where? In whose voice and words? What do we say that is good news? What measure has been given to us? Are we hoarding it or sowing it generously like the sower? What do we clutch, refusing to share? What rule do we follow in forgiving? Do our measures look anything like Jesus' measure?

What happens while we sleep? Does this refer to actual sleep or to ministry and preaching the gospel? How much should we take credit for? What does the Word do of itself? Are we sowing the seed or wielding the sickle, or are we also helping with the watering and nurturing and growing? Are we being harvested? Do we belong to a community that produces enough wheat to feed others? How do we know when the crop is ready for the harvest? Where are those who lay down their lives, falling under the sickle, so that others can eat?

Farmers usually consider mustard seeds weeds, a blight in their fields that sucks up all the moisture from the other crops. Mustard takes over everything and is impossible to root out once it's sprouted. The kingdom is like that, and it's being deliberately planted in the fields! Mustard can make our eyes water and our noses run. Are we allergic or responsive to any bit of Word on the wind? Once mustard grows, it's home for the birds, the ones that gobble up the seed that falls on the footpath. Who are the birds, those who are familiar with footpaths, highways, and streets and are always looking for a home that welcomes them to build nests in its shade? Do we make friends with birds or know where the mustard grows?

The last line we must take to heart: "To them he spoke only by way of parable while he kept explaining things privately to his disciples" (4:33b). Does each of us belong to a group that studies the Word on a weekly basis? Are we learning privately and still listening publicly with everyone else to the word of God thrown out to the world?

The Storm and the Sea

As the day ends Jesus decides to take his disciples to the far shore of the lake. They leave the crowds behind and get into the boat. The story is familiar.

> It happened that a bad squall blew up. The waves were breaking over the boat and it began to ship water badly. Jesus was in the stern through it all, sound asleep on a cushion. They finally woke him and

said to him, "Teacher, does it not matter to you that we are going down?" He awoke and rebuked the wind and said to the sea: "Quiet! Be still!" The wind fell off and everything grew calm. Then he said to them, "Why are you so terrified? Why are you lacking in faith?" A great awe came over them at this. They kept saying to one another, "Who can this be that the wind and the sea obey him?" (4:37-41 NAB)

Jesus has been sharing his wisdom with them, teaching them and drawing them into the mysteries of the kingdom of God. He is also trying to draw them into his relationship with God, to open their minds and hearts to the depths of his message for anyone who will listen and obey. He draws them close, initiating them in knowledge that the crowds do not necessarily comprehend. He is making them family, dwelling with them and eating with them. But are they understanding?

In the account above, they go to the other side of the lake. Jesus has been preaching to his own, to the Jewish nation and his own family, but now the day ends and another day will begin as they cross to the Gentile shores. He has been rejected by many of his people, and now he will take the word of the seed and the light elsewhere. Jesus is in the boat, but there are other boats also crossing. There are many followers who are not Jews, but are Gentile converts and many cross with Jesus into another world. Immediately there are problems. The crossing is dangerous and the disciples panic.

But not Jesus, who is asleep in the boat! As the disciples see the storm come up quickly, they awaken him. The verb used in the original Greek can be translated as they "raised him from sleep." Jesus rose in the stern of the boat to command the winds and waters. While the words used can mean to awaken from sleep, they are also connected with Jesus' resurrection. It is likely that Mark is also writing about the risen Jesus in the boat of the church in the mid-sixties facing the harsh storms of persecution and martyrdom that threaten the church. The disciples call out to him as "teacher" and they chastise him for not caring about them.

Using the same words with which he addressed the man with the unclean spirit, the leper and others who thought they recognized him, he silences them. He stills the elements and forces of the earth, the sea, and the sky with the words: "Quiet! Be still!" and everything above and below, in heaven and on earth obeys him immediately. The disciples are nearly as terrified and stunned by Jesus' words and his power as they were by the storm's destructive power.

Jesus chides them, asking why they were so terrified and lacking in faith. The phrase used to describe their fear is used only once in the rest of scripture, and this is in the Book of Jonah when the sailors decide to throw Jonah overboard into the sea during another great storm and the great whale swallows him. It means "they were fearing a great fear." Very early on for the church, Jonah became a symbol for Jesus' death and burial and resurrection. It seems that perhaps the disciples were beginning to feel a great fear, far more powerful and disturbing than a storm on a lake.

Eugene LaVerdiere has some remarkable things to say about this passage:

> Unlike Jonah, Jesus was not fleeing his mission but fulfilling it. Still, for the disciples, who did not yet know who Jesus really was, this was not apparent. As the story ends, we are left with their question: "Who then is this whom even the wind and sea obey?" (4:41). . .
>
> Their fear could have come from the prospect of Jesus' death and resurrection, an event in which they themselves would participate through baptism (10:38-39). If so, a likely origin for the story would be early baptismal catechesis familiar to Mark's readers. (*Beginning of the Gospel*, 1:128)

Finally they ask the question that must be asked again and again: "Who can this be?" It is the question we must ask ourselves again and again in the context of our community. If we ask it only as individuals, we risk shrinking Jesus down to what we want him to be for us individually. For when the sun comes with scorching heat or the ground underneath us is shallow or there are many around us choking off our faith's source, it is likely that, like the disciples, we will produce no yield, leaving Jesus behind us and betraying our call.

These early chapters introduce the followers of Jesus to the mysteries of the kingdom and Jesus' teachings and they also signal future rejection, the storms and violence in society, in religious groups, in our families, and in our countries, where the news of Jesus is not received as good news. This bitter and painful experience of Mark's church is true in every generation. The gospel is a catechetical text and a mystagogic text for those who struggle to be faithful after their baptisms. Jesus is trying to open the eyes of his followers to a world that is blessed and forgiven. First we see and then we must choose.

A story that actually happened reveals the nature of life in the kingdom of God.

It was 1600 and the Dutch spectacle-maker Hans Lippersky was working in his shop, bent over the table doing the detailed and tedious task of repairing a lens. The door was always open so that as people came into the shop he wouldn't have to get up from his work. Two children who entered were intrigued by the lens and mirrors and strange implements in the window. Curious, they played with everything, delighted with new toys that showed them things so differently.

By accident, chance—grace, they picked up two lenses and looked through both of them at the same time and observed a weathervane on the roof of the church some distance away, but it looked so close! It was magnified in their seeing and they were excited. Laughing, they pointed the lenses at other things. They got so loud that Lippersky went to see what all the commotion was about and he discovered for himself the meaning of depth of magnification. But it was the discovery of the children that set him to making telescopes.

This is what Jesus has done for us. We look through the lens of Jesus, God's telescope, at our world, our church and our lives today and see them magnified and up close. The lens of Jesus draws the distant God of the past near to us. The word of God in the gospels, especially when listened to with others, is a double set of lenses that reveals truth. It's time for us all to start wearing these glasses.

Jesus' words "Quiet! Be still!" can quell the rising fear within us. They can also serve as corrective lenses when people begin to spread their individual versions of what they think is the gospel. And they can quiet those who wildly cry out theological concepts or descriptions with no basis of practice or understanding, devoid of their connection to serving others. There is a refrain familiar to us all: "Be still, and know that I am God!" Here is an old way of praying this refrain. It was taught to children, but is apt for those of us who are perhaps very young at being the children of God, the brothers and sisters and mother of Jesus. We can pray this now with new and fresh hearts.

> Quiet! Be still and know that I am God!
> Quiet! Be still and know that I am!
> Quiet! Be still and know!
> Quiet! Be still!
> Quiet! Be!
> Quiet!

CHAPTER 4

Making a Mark

Excursions and Expulsions

Mark 5

T HE NEXT THREE CHAPTERS, Mark 5, 6, and 7, are packed with stories of people who meet Jesus. All this happens on the other side of the lake, the Gentile side. These are the territories that are home to many of those who came to him earlier: Idumea, Transjordan, and the region of Tyre and Sidon (3:7-8). As Jesus moves out of Israel, he will repeat much of what he did in the synagogue and households, but now his frame of reference becomes more political as he takes on issues of nationalism, racism, and hatred of other peoples. It becomes even more important to see beneath the surface of the stories to the subversive nature of Mark's gospel. We are entering dangerous territory—the role of the followers of Jesus in relation to the empire, the state, and the collaborating authorities. This includes the military, religion, the economic system, and the aristocracy—in a word, the interlocking powers of church and state.

Mark's gospel was written for those living in Palestine and for Jews in territory occupied by the Romans at the time of Jesus. Beginning with chapters 5-7, it could also have been written for the Palestinians under Israeli domination, for the people of Iraq and Afghanistan under American occupation, for East Timor under Indonesian rule, or for any number of countries in Africa where the majority of the populations are strangled and butchered, caught between warlords and tribes with ancient hatreds to avenge. The audience could also include whole countries in the Southern Hemisphere enslaved to the more wealthy nations in the North through debt payments, the destruction of the environment and the pillaging of natural resources, and what John Paul II termed "aggressive, brutal capitalism."

In Jesus' time, Rome ruled with brutal disregard and disdain for the peoples of the empire, colluding with local ruling groups to protect Roman interests in the economy, such as slavery and natural resources. As needed, the Romans made accommodations with religious authorities intent on retaining some measure of control, even at the expense of their own people. The Jews hated the occupying Roman forces, but they also hated other groups of outsiders—basically those called Gentiles, which included anyone who wasn't Jewish—and often the feelings were mutual. There was also rancor among the leaders of the Jewish religion: chief priests, teachers of the Law, scribes, Sadducees, and elders, who were often wealthy and who controlled the temple structure. The leadership also included the Pharisees and Herodians, who vied to control the provinces through the synagogue structures. A system of taxation was in place that reduced the populace to misery. Ordinary Jews saw no distinction between church and state—they were one. What existed was a temple-state that was thoroughly corrupt after decades of collusion with the Roman Empire and military forces.

When Jesus began his ministry in the synagogue, he was accosted by a man with an unclean spirit. Jesus drove out the spirit using a new kind of power and authority that was "not like the scribes and Pharisees, or the teachers of the Law" (1:22). Now Jesus is on the other side of the Lake of Galilee and he will drive out another evil, unclean spirit. This spirit, whose name is Legion, a point-blank reference to Roman occupation of the area, inhabits a man who lives in the tombs. In both cases, the unclean spirits inhabiting the men call out to Jesus, fearing that Jesus will destroy them. Unclean spirits are also found today, in religious circles and groups, in nationalistic impulses and the military, in economic systems, and in the institutions of empire.

This second account contains many images of impurity that are taboo in Judaism, such as pagan territories, tombs, and pigs. It is likely that the story is so highly detailed and descriptive because Mark wants to make his message very clear to believers, many of whom have been persecuted, tortured, imprisoned, and murdered by the empire's forces.

The audience of Mark's gospel has lived under Roman occupation since birth. Because the military was constantly present, this story represents a major exorcism of the effects of empire and militarism, the slavery and human degradation that affect everyone in the area. Jesus' visitation to the other side of the lake will profoundly change the people and also call attention to the continuing brutality of the military presence.

Chapters 5, 6, and 7 show how Jesus will systematically challenge the powers that destroy people and how those who exercise power will be provoked by Jesus' actions. Jesus is intent on creating something new—a new cloth and new wine that will give possibilities of hope, life and freedom to the enslaved, the poor, the hungry, and the outcast. All the downtrodden are offered a place of privilege and welcomed to the table of the word and bread and also into the inner circles of Jesus' new household. The process begins by breaking down the enmity between Jew and Gentile, man and woman, outcast and insider, holy and unclean. These categories will no longer determine who may follow Jesus in the kingdom of God that is close at hand.

Because many of the stories in these chapters are about individuals and their effect on those around them, they are also stories about us. When Jesus' presence becomes a power to be reckoned with in our lives, far-reaching consequences can be set in motion. This is aptly illustrated by a Muslim story from the collection of Nasruddin, a mullah, or teacher, who, though appearing to be quite stupid, is always seeking to get his followers to think and reevaluate their positions and actions.

Once upon a time, Nasruddin gathered his students around him. He had been driving them hard for weeks with tests of memory and endurance and surprise questions. They looked forlorn and bedraggled as they stood before him. He laughed at them and said, "I have a surprise for you all!" As they all groaned, wondering what possibly could be coming next, he continued: "We're going to the circus for the next few days and I want you to watch and observe everything that you see—the acts, the animals, the vendors and food, the games and oddities, the jousts and competitions. I want your reactions to everything—the taste of the food, smells, what people do. Don't miss anything!"

This took a minute to register and then the students were delighted: this meant time off! But Nasruddin knew what they were thinking. "This is another kind of tool, of observation and testing. Don't slack off. Pay attention! You can go by yourself or you can wander around in twos and threes. The only thing I ask is that you all gather on the last day and meet me at the archery contest. I'm going to be one of the contestants. In fact I'm going to win. We need the money to feed all of you and keep you as we travel."

His disciples looked at him in amazement. It never ceased to catch them off guard when they learned of something else the master did with great skill! One of them said to him, "Master, we didn't know you were an archer. When did you learn that skill?"

The master laughed. "Oh, I've been reading about it for awhile."

They looked at him strangely and someone asked, "How long have you been practicing?"

The master looked sternly at him and replied, "I'm starting today. We need the money. Be there at the end of the circus, all of you. I want you there to cheer me on and celebrate when I win the contest!" They looked at each other, thinking that he was crazy and would embarrass them all. But they would obey and be there.

The end of the days at the circus came all too quickly. Nasruddin's students all gathered with the rest of the crowd to watch as he participated in the contest. He was the very last to pick up his bow. Each contestant had three arrows and three chances to hit the bull's-eye. The one who got the closest with his three tries would win.

Nasruddin stepped up to the line. The distance to the target seemed enormously far, but Nasruddin seemed confident. He laid his bow and arrow beside him, adjusted his cap military style and straightened his jacket. He stood stiffly as though at attention. He then bent to pick up his bow and with a soldier's stance and strength placed the arrow in the bow, glanced at the target and fired. His disciples groaned but the crowd laughed. The arrow went far over the mark and sailed off into the trees.

Nasruddin had two more arrows. As he picked up his second arrow, his cap fell off. He had begun to sweat profusely now, so he took off his jacket. Those close to him saw his hands shaking. His face turned bright red as he listened to everyone making jokes about his lack of skill. He quickly placed the arrow in the bow and let it fly. The laughter grew louder as the arrow barely made it halfway to the mark. The disciples began to slip back into the crowd, no longer wanting to watch the fiasco as a group. Only one arrow remained and he hadn't gotten anywhere near the target.

Nasruddin picked up his last arrow. He stood right on the mark and looked over at his students, now scattered here and there. Standing at ease, he carefully placed his last arrow in the bow and tensed the gut string. He eyed the target in the distance and then turned away for a moment to look at his disciples. He pulled back until everyone thought the bow would snap and sent the arrow whistling through the air. WHACK! The arrow hit the heart of the target, exactly on the mark. As the crowd stood silent, his students yelled and screamed, laughing as they slapped each other on the back. He had done it!

He collected the money and then collected his students, taking them off under the trees and picking up the other two arrows as he went. The students were all talking at once. One of them called out, "Master, Master, how did you do that? What happened? Those first two shots went wild. How did you hit it dead-on when you missed the mark so badly the first two times?"

The master eyed them all and shook his head. "That first time, that wasn't me."

"What?" they all were thinking. Someone spoke: "Who was it then?"

Nasruddin spoke. "What did I look like the first time?"

"A soldier," they all chimed in.

"Exactly! That was a soldier standing in a face-off with the enemy and in his fear he overshot the target. That wasn't me."

Another student asked, "What about the second arrow?"

Nasruddin cocked his head and answered, "That wasn't me either!"

"Oh," someone said, "who was it?"

"What did I look like?"

After a pause, someone said, "You were cowed and beaten. You were nervous. I saw you shaking, and sweating. You were worried, listening to everyone laughing at you and saying how stupid you were and thinking that everyone thought you were a joke."

"Exactly," Nasruddin said. "That man was insecure and humiliated and only cared what other people thought about him. He had no concentration, no confidence or faith and so he missed miserably, just like everyone thought he would. That wasn't me either!"

Someone immediately blurted out, "Oh, and the last one—he wasn't you either, I suppose?" All his followers laughed.

But Nasruddin looked at them steadily and said, "No, that was me!" They fell quiet, waiting for him to continue. "Don't you know me at all, after all this time with me? That was me! Haven't you learned that anything to do with the military and soldiering has to be about fear and insecurity and overpowering reactions and unnecessary strength? And don't you know that I do not care what anyone thinks of me, not you, or a crowd certainly? Don't you know who I am? I know exactly who I am and I've spent my whole life seeking never to miss the mark."

Nasruddin looked at them, said nothing more and walked away. His disciples trailed after him: it was time to go back to learning and tests.

The story illustrates so clearly what Jesus is trying to teach his disciples about living in the world of Gentiles and Jews, of men and women, of domination and oppression. The ideas and laws of other people have determined their identity. They must come to know this for themselves.

The Gerasene Demoniac

For those who live in the West, a great deal of Mark's gospel is difficult to understand. Most of us have no idea of life in occupied territory where the domination of the occupiers is violent, impersonal and destructive. Such a military environment destroys the bodies and souls of the human beings caught in it. When we study the gospel, if we individualize the stories, we sap them of the power that they have to overcome historical events. If we focus only on the characters in the stories, we forget that this is good news for the poor, for the masses of people struggling to live who represent more than two-thirds of the more than six billion people in the world today. After the death and resurrection of Jesus, Christianity was the fastest growing religious group in the world because it brought hope, a sense of worth, the knowledge of being loved by God, especially if you were poor or outcast, living without dignity. It is helpful to keep in mind the historical reality of Jesus and his followers during their lives and the first three hundred years or more after Jesus' death and resurrection.

Jesus lived in dangerous times. His country and, indeed, most of the known world, was under the jackboot of Roman imperialism. There is a tendency to romanticize the Roman empire, to speak of Roman law as if it were an instrument of protection for the poor and the weak rather than a cynical manipulation of power for the benefit of the rich. We forget that the long straight roads led to Rome to facilitate the transport of slaves and plunder to sate the appetite of its indolent inhabitants. We pass over the sexual exploitation of slaves, particularly of children, especially trained to pander to the whims of degraded men and women.

Gnaeus Julius Agricola (40-93 C.E.), Roman governor of Britain, on his way north to advance Roman rule to the Firth of Forth was confronted in the northeast by a local leader, Calgacus by name, who decided to make a stand. His speech to his men, before his inevitable defeat, is given to us by Tacitus, the son-in-law of Agricola but an honest historian. Here, in part, is the voice of the victim:

> Children and kin are by the law of nature each man's dearest possessions; they are swept away from us by conscription to be slaves in other lands; our wives, our sister(s), even when they escape a soldier's lust, are debauched by self-styled friends and guests. Our goods and chattels go for tribute; our lands and harvest in requisition of grain. . . . To plunder, butcher, steal, these things they misname empire; they create a desert and call it peace (Tacitus, *Agricola*, 30:3-31:2).

It is against this background of universal suffering and imperial aggression that we must read the strange story of the Gerasene Demoniac (O'Hanlon, *Mark My Words*, 69-70).

Recent study has revealed that the country of the Gerasenes, or the area referred to as the Decapolis, the ten cities on the eastern edge of the Roman Empire, was a place where many veteran soldiers had been given land to settle to aid in the stabilization of the empire's hold on the economy and natural resources and to produce food (see, e.g., Myers et al., *Say to This Mountain*, 58). The story of the Gerasene demoniac contains a number of military images, military vocabulary, and references to the effects of military occupation:

> They came to Gerasene territory on the other side of the lake. As he got out of the boat, he was immediately met by a man from the tombs who had an unclean spirit. The man had taken refuge among the tombs; he could no longer be restrained even with a chain. In fact, he had frequently been secured with handcuffs and chains, but had pulled the chains apart and smashed the fetters. No one had proved

strong enough to tame him. Uninterruptedly night and day, amid the tombs and on the hillsides, he screamed and gashed himself with stones. Catching sight of Jesus at a distance, he ran up and did him homage, shrieking in a loud voice, "Why meddle with me, Jesus, Son of God Most High? I implore you in God's name, do not torture me!" (Jesus had been saying to him, "Unclean spirit, come out of the man!") "What is your name?" Jesus asked him. "Legion is my name," he answered. "There are hundreds of us." He pleaded hard with Jesus not to drive them away from that neighborhood.

It happened that a large herd of swine was feeding there on the slope of the mountain. "Send us into the swine," they begged him. "Let us enter them." He gave the word, and with it the unclean spirits came out and entered the swine. The herd of about two thousand went rushing down the bluff into the lake, where they began to drown. The swineherds ran off and brought the news to field and village, and the people came to see what had happened. As they approached Jesus, they caught sight of the man who had been possessed by Legion sitting fully clothed and perfectly sane, and they were seized with fear. The spectators explained what had happened to the possessed man, and told them about the swine. Before long they were begging him to go away from their district. (5:1-17 NAB)

We will leave the ending of the story for later. The descriptions of the man possessed are almost too horrible to hear. Homeless, he lives in tombs among rotting bones and decaying flesh, a place that is feared and abhorred by people. Everything about the man is deteriorating: his mind, his flesh, his soul. He screams incoherently and mutilates himself, tearing at his skin until it bleeds. He's been bound with fetters and chains, tied up like an animal, and he has enormous strength born of despair and hate for himself and others. No one can control his destructive behavior.

It seems likely that Mark is using this man possessed by unclean spirits as an image of the occupying Roman forces. They are seen by the Jews as demonic, serving the unholy and unclean powers of evil. A vivid clue is given when, questioned by Jesus about his name, the demonic responds with the name "Legion," and adds, "There are hundreds of us." Readers have speculated that a legion comprised two thousand men (given the number of pigs), but that wasn't necessarily so. Many sources, including Joseph O'Hanlon's *Mark My Words* as well as documents in Scottish annals (the Firth of Forth in Scotland), say that a legion of the Roman army consisted of six thousand foot soldiers, one hundred twenty horsemen, and support units. When the Latin word *legio* entered the vocabulary of many conquered countries, it simply described a large number. Moreover, even at that time, the terms "swine" or "pigs" were often used to describe the despicable behavior of the occupying soldiers.

In the Greek, when the man with the unclean spirit confronts Jesus, the verb used is *hypantaō*, a strong word that means "to meet up against, to oppose or to engage in battle." This verb seems to refer to the fact that no one has the strength to bind or restrain the man. This brings us back to the declaration of Jesus that he is the strong man binding all evil (3:27 King James Version [KJV]), even Satan himself. The man gives homage to Jesus, indicating that he immediately recognizes Jesus' superior strength. He knows who Jesus is, like the man in the synagogue in the first chapter of Mark. By the time of Mark's writing, the Roman Empire certainly knew the power and the strength that reside in the presence of the risen Lord and his followers and that the empire could not stand against it. In the first story, Jesus is given the title "the Holy One of God," indicating for Jews worship and obedience of his awesome nature. In the account of the demoniac in Gentile territory, Jesus is addressed as "Son of the Most High God," a term often used to refer to Zeus (*hypsistos*), as well as a title used by Jews in the diaspora.

The evil spirits within the man beg, acknowledging the power of Jesus, not to be driven out of the territory. This seemingly is another use of military images: trying to "make terms for a settlement" and to avoid being sent out of the district, meaning the occupied territory of Palestine. The man represents an area that needs cleansing, healing, reordering, and re-creating.

Legion's desperate plea is to be sent into the pigs. For Jews, this was about as low as anyone could sink. The ritual codes of Leviticus and Deuteronomy forbid the eating of pigs. In the story of the prodigal son, Luke describes the son's desperate state by saying that he has been reduced to taking care of the master's pigs and is willing to eat their food. Any Jew would recoil viscerally from such a circumstance. Jesus dismisses Legion and as a band (similar perhaps to military recruits), they rush down the bluff (or charge into battle), falling over the cliffs and into the sea, where they drown. (Note that this latter phrase seems an echo of Pharaoh's army drowning in the Red Sea during the exodus.) The decision of Legion begins a stampede of self-destruction. Mark is exorcising the military presence and challenging the foreign invasion and occupation. This is also a description of Jesus as he liberates the oppressed, frees the captives, brings the people in darkness into the light, and even raises people from the dead.

Jesus has driven out the evil spirits that drove the man to such a frenzy of despair. The man is now "sitting fully clothed and perfectly sane." What is surprising and disturbing is the reaction of those who have gathered to watch. They "are seized with fear," and before long they are "begging him to go away from their district." We would expect the people to be grateful for what Jesus has done, but instead they are filled with dread and terror. But the message of Mark is that the empire and its military must be exorcised, restrained, and disarmed and that those who have suffered must be returned to being "fully clothed," not in battle gear or uniforms signaling death. And the people should be perfectly sane, in their right minds, rather than insanely killing, destroying themselves and others, and wreaking death all around them, turning creation into a land of tombs.

This message is echoed in words written over a decade ago by Philip Berrigan, a contemporary prophet:

> We were created to love God and one another. But when we accept the legalized role of killing, we switch allegiances. Our existence and soul shift as though in an earth tremor from the God of life to the "legions" of death. The military aborts the human vocation. . . .
>
> The Pentagon, Congress, weapon makers, the international market—for all parties involved, war is a bullish machine with a deafening bellow. Under its jurisdiction are more than a million soldiers to train, manage, and deploy; hundreds of bases to administer globally; extensive weapon research, procurement, and deployment to oversee; and $300 billion allocated annually for new weapons systems and "combat readiness." No lethal task is too formidable for its over two million military and civilian employees, nothing too daunting for its vast network of academic and technical researchers across the land.
>
> There are no chains, no restraints on this spirit which runs rampant in our culture and economy. In pursuit of its own prosperity, the spirit of the Pentagon has roamed the world, untouched by international law, constitutional restraints, the law of God, or any other potentially inhibiting voice of command. Such irreproachability is translated piously into one euphemism or another: "the national interest," "protection of world markets," "preservation of our way of life." Who will restrain the spirit of death? Who will bind the Strong Man (Mark 3:27)? Who will summon us from exile and madness? ("Exorcising the Demons," 16, 21)

While we might recoil from the words of Berrigan, we must force ourselves to listen as we study the text of Mark. It is essential to Jesus' teaching and to following him. We cannot simply ignore the parts of the gospel that we find problematic. We cannot refuse to see what is written in the text simply because it lays bare the reality of our world and our collusion with it. We must learn to listen to the word of God, in scripture and in the texts of the followers of Jesus. Mark's own community struggled with the overwhelming power of the Roman Empire and the calculated destruction of anyone who sought to bind that power. They knew and recognized how dangerous Jesus' words of freedom were, words that called people to live without violence and to use the Spirit of God given to us in baptism to bind any power that sought to destroy the bodies and souls of human beings.

Most of us are more experienced in seeking the meaning of texts for us as individuals rather than for the community. The community is essential, though, central to our belief and practice. In the Gospel of Mark, Jesus seems relentless in letting us observe who he is and what he is about, what his presence on earth means for creation and the children of God. Mark's own community indicated their interpretation of this text and the teachings of Jesus by refusing to serve in the military and refusing to baptize anyone in the military until they stopped killing or obeying the powers of evil and death. The entire gospel and this story in particular are why the early Christians refused to fight with the Jews against the Romans.

Philip Berrigan wrote further:

> The wars of our lifetime comprise a continuum of destruction and terror. War follows war without peace. No war is ever finished, as hatreds continue to fester. War kills the healing spirit, drives us mad, extinguishes our very humanity. . . .
>
> The loss of valuable animals attests to the waste of the military spirit, which places a harsh burden on us all. At least one estimate of the U.S. military's assets (no one knows for sure) hovers at about $1.3 trillion. But for all its prodigal extravagance and waste, the Pentagon is perennially and embarrassingly overfed. Unspent billions are fed annually into its coffers, with no accountability to the U.S. Treasury. Since 1946, the national investment in war and war preparations has amounted to approximately $12 trillion, and one can easily envision an unspent trillion or two tucked away in some secret fund to finance the next war. Under Pentagon management, the military costs U.S. citizens about $500 billion annually, a sum which includes financing, veterans' benefits, and the Department of Energy budget.
>
> An accurate estimate of military waste would also include the cost to U.S. residents of our national debtor status and near bankruptcy, the pollution of air and water, the deaths by cancer of unwitting citizens "downwind" from war games, the horrors of domestic violence, and the misery of violent streets. ("Exorcising the Demons," 16-21)

This quotation is from the same biblical reflection cited previously. One of the pages has a highlighted sentence that reads: "For nearly two millennia, we Christians have been co-opted into reconstituting Pharaoh's army" (p. 20). If we think about the severe ramifications that would result from treating this text seriously in our communities and our nation and how we operate around the world (the United States does operate as an empire today), we should not be surprised that those who witnessed the exorcising of Legion begged Jesus to leave their district! They are not eager to have the Roman authorities notice what is happening and so return with another legion. So the people refuse Jesus' power, his good news of the kingdom of God.

The same is not true of the man who was released from his bondage.

As they approached Jesus, they caught sight of the man who had been possessed by Legion sitting fully clothed and perfectly sane, and they were seized with fear. . . . As Jesus was getting into the boat, the man who had been possessed was pressing to accompany him. Jesus did not grant his request, but told him instead: "Go home to your family and make it clear to them how much the Lord in his mercy has done for you." At that the man went off and began to proclaim throughout the Ten Cities what Jesus had done for him. They were amazed at what they heard. (5:15-20)

The man who has been cured, like Peter's mother-in-law, wants to become a follower of Jesus. But this man is a Gentile. This account, written for Mark's churches thirty to forty years after the resurrection, calls attention to the fact that Jesus had crossed over to the other side of the lake, the Gentile side. The implication is that if the healed man was to become a follower, he would have to get into the boat and cross back to the Jewish side of the lake. But, as shown in the Acts of the Apostles, the church had decreed that Gentiles did not have to become Jewish in order to become followers of Jesus. Thus, in Mark's story, Jesus refuses to let the man go with him. Instead, he sends the man back to his own people, commissioning him to tell the story of what God in his great mercy has done for him. Eugene LaVerdiere explains this twist in the story.

> Jesus consequently told the man to return to his home (*eis ton oikon*) and to his people (*pro tous sous*). He was to announce (*apaggeilon*) to them all that the Lord (*ho kyrios*) in his mercy had done for him (Mk 5:19). He was to be the Lord's forerunner for the mission among the Gentiles, whose story will be told later in the third section of the Gospel (6:6b-8:21).
>
> John the baptizer, a Jew, had prepared the way for Jesus' mission among the Jews. The Gerasene, a Gentile, would prepare the way for his mission among the Gentiles. So it is that the former demoniac went off to proclaim (*keryssein*) what the Lord had done for him in the Decapolis, the Ten (Greek) Cities and their territories (5:20a).
>
> Earlier the people who had come to Jesus and seen the former demoniac were filled with fear (*ephobethesan*, 5:15) just as those in the boat with Jesus had been filled with fear when Jesus calmed the storm (4:41). However, all those in the Decapolis who heard the forerunner's proclamation were filled with wonder (*ethaumazon*, 5:20b). Everything was now ready for the Gentile mission. (*Beginning of the Gospel*, 1:132)

The separation and hatred between Jew and Gentile are explicit. While the separation between man and woman, rich and impoverished, young and old remains, the story of the healing of the daughter of Jairus and of the Jewish woman with a hemorrhage begins to hammer away at such distinctions within the community of believers. Jesus' company and the kingdom of God draw all in with equal welcome, healing, and acceptance. Women as well as men are publicly honored for their great faith. All will be comforted, healed, and raised to new life, but the poor will be taken care of first.

The Daughter of Jairus and the Hemorrhaging Woman

A man named Jairus seeks Jesus out on behalf of his twelve-year-old daughter. In Israel at that time she would be considered a young woman. The story of Jairus's daughter is interrupted by another story that describes an unnamed woman who has suffered for twelve years. While these might appear to be two separate events, they form one story: each encounter is to be seen in the light of the other. In fact, the interruption reveals an important message to Jesus' disciples, Jairus, and the crowd. Jesus has already established that he is stronger than any demonic power, and now we witness a demonstration of Jesus' power over sickness and even death. In addition, Jesus banishes the artificial and callous categories of being ritually clean or unclean, meaning untouchable at the time of Mark.

In the Greek text, Jairus's very name would be a clue to what is going to happen:. *onomati 'Iairos* means "he who will be awakened or he is enlightened." Jairus (*Iairos*) is a man of some stature and authority. As a synagogue president, he is its highest official in liturgy, ritual, and administration. We learn more about him in the sotry.

> One of the officials of the synagogue, a man named Jairus, came near. Seeing Jesus, he fell at his feet and made this earnest appeal: "My little daughter is critically ill. Please come and lay your hands on her so that she may get well and live." The two went off together and a large crowd followed, pushing against Jesus. (5:22-24)

Jairus may have a position of power in his community and religion, but he is first a father desperate for his daughter. He approaches Jesus with a faith born of that grief and helplessness that come from facing sickness that will likely end in death. He falls at Jesus' feet, a beggar in need. This is a public act of reverence that asserts his belief and hope in the power of Jesus over illness. He asks Jesus to visit his home to lay hands on his daughter. This offers a clue that Mark's story is catechetical teaching based on an actual occurrence. The words used are interesting because the Jews did not practice the laying on of hands in healing. The laying on of hands was a ritual developed in the Christian communities (see Jas 5:14 and Acts 9:12, 17-18; 28:8).

This story of Jesus and his followers also forms a story of healing for the church of Mark's time. The language used can be understood literally, meaning physical healing, but it can also mean being saved in Christ and given everlasting life.

As Jesus goes with Jairus, the crowd that followed Jesus from the lakeshore presses around him. The interruption occurs in the middle of the crowd. This is a critical juncture, because the girl is dying and every moment counts. The interruption is caused by a desperate woman. Sickness and death reduce everyone, men and women, rich and poor, young and old, to a common humanity. It is important to note that, like the young girl, this woman also is unnamed.

> There was a woman in the area who had been afflicted with a hemorrhage for a dozen years. She had received treatment at the hands of doctors of every sort and exhausted her savings in the process, yet she got no relief; on the contrary, she only grew worse. She had heard about Jesus and came up behind him in the crowd and put her hand to his cloak. "If I just touch his clothing," she thought, "I shall get well." Immediately her flow of blood dried up and the feeling that she was cured of her affliction ran through her whole body. Jesus was conscious at once that healing power had gone out from him. Wheeling about in the crowd, he began to ask, "Who touched my clothing?" His disciples said to him, "You can see how this crowd hems you in, yet you ask, 'Who touched me?'" Despite this, he kept looking around to see the woman who had done it. Fearful and beginning to tremble now as she realized what had happened, the woman came and fell in front of him and told him the whole truth. He said to her, "Daughter, it is your faith that has cured you. Go in peace and be free of this illness." (5:25-34)

The heart-wrenching description of the woman's condition is described in detail so that there is no mistaking how unclean she is. Religious laws were detailed and ruthless in their definition. Not only is she unclean, but her clothing, everything she touched, the furniture she sits on and, of course, anyone who accidentally touches her becomes unclean. She is supposed to be quarantined. Similar to the man in the tombs, she couldn't be more isolated or abandoned. And she has been abused by doctors who have taken all her money. Now totally impoverished, she has no where to turn.

At the time of Jesus, health care depended a great deal on economic status. Those who were rich could afford a house physician or a local doctor so that a sick person could be restored to his or her place. The poor did not have this advantage and would often depend on herbs or cures passed on in the oral tradition, or they would wait for a more or less competent itinerant healer to come through their village. This woman, who has been ill for a dozen years, has lost everything: money, her position in the community, companionship, comfort, dignity, a place to live. But she has heard about Jesus and feels that if she can just get near him, even touch his clothing, she will be made well. It is a tremendous risk on her part and also puts Jesus in jeopardy, as a touch from her would defile him. Apparently she has heard about Jesus and knows that he does not abide by the ritual purity laws or any law that contributes to the suffering and isolation of human beings. By breaking the same laws that he does, she also opposes the structures that have so debilitated her life, reducing her to someone to be scorned. She must sense what Jesus is doing because she has learned the hard way what these strictures and hard-hearted social codes have done to her. With a great deal at risk, she goes up behind Jesus and touches his cloak.

In the past we've seen that the words and presence of Jesus both have power. Now it seems that even Jesus' clothing has power. The sign that Jesus' presence had healed the man in the tombs was that the man appeared "fully clothed" (Mk 5:15). This immediately calls to mind the ritual of baptism. Anyone who has been baptized, saved in the waters and the word and Spirit, is clothed in garments symbolic of our being "clothed from on high." These stories also echo accounts in the Books of Kings of healings done by Elijah (1 Kgs 17:17-24) and Elisha (2 Kgs 4:18-37). Jesus' clothes are symbolic of Elijah and Elisha's mantle, the cloak of power that hides Jesus from eyes that do not want to see and from people who do not want their lives touched or altered by his presence.

Immediately (that word again!) the woman senses in her whole body (*egnō tō somati*) that she is whole again (*euthys*). The woman and Jesus both know that power has been transferred (*epignous en autō*), forming a relationship of mutuality through touch. Someone has understood him!

Touching is a decisive mark of Jesus' interactions with people, and the fact that Jesus has chosen to touch the unclean is explosive in a society that controls by the power to decide who is to be touched and who is untouchable. Joseph O'Hanlon has written a marvelous paragraph on the significance of Jesus' touch.

> Touching is an amazingly common feature of Mark's Gospel. Sometimes Jesus stretches out to touch people; on other occasions, he takes them by the hand. Here is a list well worth the trouble of looking up: 1:31; 1:41; 3:10; 5:27; 5:28; 5:30; 5:31; 6:5; 6:56; 7:32; 7:33; 8:22; 8:23; 9:27; 10:13; 10:16. What is amazing is that by touching the sick Jesus is taking on their status, that is, he becomes unclean. Or, rather, he abolishes the whole demeaning business of human uncleanness. He refuses to accept that human misery and the human processes of begetting and child-bearing, of being ill and dying, put one outside God's concern. . . . What Jesus is saying so eloquently in his hands

outstretched to touch and caress is that humanity's ailments do not incur divine anger; rather they incite divine pity. (*Mark My Words,* 78)

The woman's touching Jesus conveys respect and awareness of who he is. It also indicates that she has heard him preaching. This is faith! Jesus not only wants to see her; he wants others to know what faith is like, especially his disciples, who still don't understand at all what is happening. Jesus immediately recognizes the woman's touch of his cloak and asks, "Who touched my clothing?" The disciples show their lack of understanding by their response: "You can see how this crowd hems you in, yet you ask, 'Who touched me?'"

It is not surprising that the woman is now "fearful and beginning to tremble." This is a response that will appear again and again as people witness the power of God. She comes to stand before Jesus and falls on her knees before him—as did Jairus in his effort to get Jesus' attention—to pour out her heart and soul. Jesus appears to take pleasure in her presence, for he addresses her as "Daughter," saying that her faith has saved her. She is told, "Go in peace and be free of this illness." This is the only time in Mark's entire gospel that the blessing "Go in peace" is on Jesus' lips. It is Jesus' further gift of a promise for a life that is lived more gracefully and abundantly in faith. Oh, if only Jesus' followers would realize what he is doing and respond as she does!

And now back to the story of Jesus and Jairus that has been interrupted.

While Jesus was still speaking, some people arrived from the official's house to inform him, "Your daughter is dead. Why trouble the Master any further?" But Jesus ignored what they said and told the official, "Do not fear, just believe." And he allowed no one to follow him except Peter, James and John, the brother of James.

When they arrived at the house, Jesus saw a great commotion with people weeping and wailing loudly. Jesus entered and said to them, "Why all this commotion and weeping? The child is not dead but asleep."

They laughed at him. But Jesus sent them outside and went with the child's father and mother and his companions into the room where the child lay. Taking her by the hand, he said to her, "Talitha Kumi!" which means: "Little girl, get up!"

The girl got up at once and began to walk around. (She was twelve years old.) The parents were astonished, greatly astonished. Jesus strictly ordered them not to let anyone know about it, and told them to give her something to eat. (Mark 5:35-42)

Jesus has lingered with the woman who touched him and before he has sent her off with his blessing, dour messengers arrive with the news that sounds so final: "Your daughter is dead. Why trouble the Master any further?" They seem almost embarrassed by Jairus's public display of entreaty, and it is clear that they don't think this teacher has anything to say about the finality of death, which intrudes so rudely on everyone's life. But Jesus is not deterred by death or by any other human experience. His first concern is for Jairus, who is grieving and despairing—his child has died while Jesus was engaged with someone unclean. Jesus turns to Jairus and says: "Do not fear, just believe." Jesus has just finished talking with the woman and blessing her for her faith; now she serves as a model for Jairus. He is simply to believe as she did! So Jesus and Jairus, accompanied by Peter, James, and his brother John, the three disciples who are often singled out to witness and observe more closely, enter the house.

Mark appears to layer meanings in the account that follows. The phrase "to sleep" often means to die, but for Christians falling asleep also means to sleep in the resurrected Christ, awaiting the fullness of life. The story of waking the young girl from sleep is not only about her resuscitation; it is also about all those who are raised to life in baptism to live in the power of the Spirit. Jesus approaches the child with her mother and father and Peter, James, and John, indicating that this is also about the family of Jesus and who belongs to it. Before raising the child, Jesus speaks to those outside the house, those who do not believe and ridicule him. As Jesus moves inside, the house becomes the church, the home for the rituals of being born in water and the Spirit and being fed. He takes the girl by the hand and raises her up, as he has done with Peter's mother-in-law and the paralytic. As before, this appears to be a reference to his own resurrection (Mk 14:28 and 16:6).

The girl begins to walk around and family members are astonished. In Greek this same expression is used to describe Jesus' own family when he welcomes both Gentiles and Jews into his home. Jesus then orders them not to speak of this at all but to feed the girl. This may seem an odd request, but it follows the pattern established by Mark. Jesus silences those who do not believe, as he did with the possessed man in the synagogue. He does not silence the man at the tombs or the woman who has touched his cloak. Jesus has given the girl a share in his new life, making sure that she is fed properly, in both body and soul. He is building a new family, a community of believers.

Every detail in the stories is significant. It is important to spend time with scripture and to try to dig out the multiple meanings that can enrich our faith and practice beyond just personal interpretations. The insight of others is needed as we continue our conversion and growth in faith. Ched Myers and his colleagues point out some of these connections in *Say to This Mountain*:

> In the art of narrative, every detail is there for a reason, and Mark's "aside" that the girl was twelve years old is a good case in point. She

has lived affluently for twelve years, and is just on the edge of puberty. In contrast, the bleeding woman had suffered for twelve years, permanently infertile. This number symbolizes the twelve tribes of Israel (3:13), and represents the key to the social meaning of this doublet. Within the "family" of Israel, these "daughters" represent the privileged and the impoverished, respectively. Because of such inequity, the body politic of the synagogue is "on the verge of death."

The healing journey must, however, take a necessary detour that stops to listen to the pain of the crowd. Only when the outcast woman is restored to true "daughterhood" can the daughter of the synagogue be restored to true life. That is the faith the privileged must learn from the poor. This story thus shows a characteristic of the sovereignty of God that Jesus will later address: The "last will be first" and the "least will be the greatest" (see 10:31, 43). (p. 66)

It seems that Jesus' family begins with the largest group of people with the greatest needs or the deepest misery. Jesus shows his disregard for the practices of the religious establishment, which were often marked by insensitivity to those broken in body and spirit. The stories tell about forming a family and a community, a church where Jew and Gentile, man and woman, rich and poor, young and old are all one in Christ. Those who are healed are desperate. Jairus will do anything for his child. The woman with the hemorrhage is so desperate that she will break accepted laws. Will we do the same for family? And not just our blood kinship or birth families, but for the family into which we were baptized, the family with whom we share bread and wine? Driven by love, Jairus is willing to beg, to give up his reputation and risk derision. He will do anything for his daughter, and Jesus goes off with him. Would we do the same?

Jairus's daughter was in jeopardy as are so many children today. More than twenty-four thousand die needlessly each day of starvation and 25 percent of children in the United States are severely malnourished. The numbers are larger among blacks, Hispanics, and Native Americans—where up to 60 percent of children may live without the basic necessities of clean water, food, and medical care. It is the children who have suffered the most from the wars of the last fifty years. In Iraq alone, more than four million children have died in twelve years. In Sierra Leone, Liberia, Sudan, and Uganda hundreds of thousands of children as young as four or five are soldiers. Yet the United States hasn't signed the Children Soldiers' Treaty, and so sixteen-year-olds can sign up for the military. Neither has the United States signed the Landmine Treaty in order to restrict their use in "theatres" around the world. The largest problems worldwide are starvation and the lack of potable water. In addition, HIV/AIDS is a plague of epidemic proportions in Africa and, increasingly, in other parts of the world. Do we care? Will Jesus accompany us to help them? Jairus is instructed to grab hold of faith as the woman with the flow of blood reached out to touch Jesus' garment.

It is striking to note that both of the women in these stories, these daughters, are newborns after twelve years and bear the marks of the family of Jesus. They are clothed in the garment of resurrection and given right mind, body, and soul. They are sent out in peace to proclaim the goodness of God. They know that fear is useless, only faith is sound. While their own lives were unraveling, Jesus made a new cloth of them, tying the fringes and tassels together in prayer. Now they wear a seamless garment of life that is a cloak of justice and healing that goes out from its edges to those in need.

Jesus' family, found on the margins, ignores society's fear of contagion and difference and insists that no one is unacceptable. These are the people Jesus seeks out to touch. (Sadly, many of these people some of us won't touch.) Jesus gives new birth to them through compassion, inclusion, respect, and mercy. This family doesn't speak glibly of holiness, knowing that the whole truth of holiness does not lie in outward adherence to rules. These people remember the line from Isaiah, "I will hold your hand to make you firm" (Is 42:6) and practice what Jesus has taught them.

An old story from Hans Christian Andersen called "Leap Frog" or "The King's Little Daughter" illustrates how one perceives reality from the point of view of those beloved, or in need, even when it makes us appear to be foolish. Do we stand closest to the least in the world?

Once upon a time there was a king with a single daughter whom he loved dearly. No matter what was going on in his kingdom, he was always thinking about her life and her future. Now there were three different creatures always fighting in the kingdom, a frog, a cricket, and a flea. They argued continually about who was the most important and who was the most powerful. Finally, the king decided to have a contest to determine who could jump the highest and the winner would get to be his little daughter's friend forever. Circles and lines were drawn in the sand and crowds gathered to see what would happen. And, of course, the king and his daughter were present.

The flea jumped first and he went so high that he disappeared altogether and was never seen again. The king declared him out-of-bounds and disqualified him.

Next the cricket jumped, or rather he pranced around, rubbing his legs, and jumped—right into the face of the king! The king brushed him aside, swatted him, declared the cricket in contempt and disqualified.

Last of all was the frog—he looked around at the people, the advisors and the king and promptly jumped straight into the lap of the little girl. He was the winner! The king declared that there was no one higher in all the kingdom than his daughter and declared the frog the winner.

The flea was annoyed. Not fair! So he went off and lived with the animals, the cats and dogs. Perhaps you've met him? The cricket was not happy. He went away to live in the weeds and rushes and he is always telling his version of the story. Listen and you'll hear him.

And the king, ah, he is a bit like God, who considers the least in our world the highest. All are invited in; all are sons and daughters, welcomed, touched and grasped by the hand to dwell in peace, sharing food and astonishing the world. This is what family is for—and only this—to share the merciful and life-giving power of God with others.

Let us pray Psalm 131, which is short and so sweet.

> O Lord, my heart is not proud
> nor do I have arrogant eyes.
> I am not engrossed in ambitious matters,
> nor in things too great for me.
>
> I have quieted and stilled my soul
> like a weaned child on its mother's lap;
> like a contented child is my soul.
> Hope in the Lord, O Israel,
> now and forever.

CHAPTER 5

Jesus—Mark My Ways

Mark 6 and 7

CHAPTERS 6 AND 7 OF MARK present Jesus in a variety of roles: at home as the carpenter's son everyone thinks they know; Jesus the teacher who sends out disciples ahead of him as preachers and healers; Jesus the shepherd of those lost; Jesus the prophet; Jesus who walks on water; and Jesus who heals.

It starts off on a sour note. Jesus goes home to Nazareth, a backwater village where perhaps 120 to 150 people lived at the time of Jesus, according to the estimate of archeologists. The largest number would be part of Jesus' extended family. Members of one's family, often the harshest critics, are also often reluctant to see one of their own change, especially if they are jealous or feel threatened by the changed behavior. Mark uses this account to bring a cycle to completion: Jesus is being utterly rejected, from the highest authorities to his own kin.

Years ago I came across "Legends of Ahimsa," a short collection of stories by Daniel Rhodes. These stories of Ahimsa have become favorites of mine. Because I read the stories so long ago and have told them so many times, my version never quite matches the original. Although short, this story is not simple, but it provides an excellent introduction to the rejection of Jesus by those who think they know him.

> Once upon a time there was a master potter named Ahimsa who lived in the village of Karuna. He had many apprentices and disciples who learned the art of making pots from him. This involved long and often tedious study—learning about clays and molds, about furnaces, fuel, heat, firing times and glazes, about form and function, and this was only basic knowledge. The master was always throwing out unexpected questions about what he was teaching or what would happen after a firing or a session with the clay.
>
> One day the master returned from a trip to the city to sell his pots. He seemed unusually happy and the students guessed that it had been a

great success. All but one of his pots had sold and at high prices. The master carelessly tossed the one unsold piece under the work table.

The next morning when the students arrived to begin a new batch of pots, they were surprised to see the discarded pot, with sprigs of blossoms at its base, sitting in a niche above them. This was the place of honor reserved for pots that received special recognition. They knew that these pots were to be studied, contemplated and imitated.

The master potter spoke: "Look hard and long at this pot. Follow its lines and form with your eye. Catch the light on the glaze on the surface at different times during the day and evening. Try to penetrate its form and subtlety, its gracefulness and strength. Try to figure out why it was not sold, why no one wanted it. It is our new standard of excellence and promise."

The students knew it would be a long time before they understood that pot, or how their master's mind and soul and his fingers moved on the clay. (Adapted from *Potter's Companion*, ed. Larsen, 174-78)

Chapters 6 and 7 will introduce us again and again to the one not welcomed, the man misunderstood or viewed with contempt, the person the whole town thought they knew, though they knew little of him because they had not known him with any depth. These chapters will help respond to the question "Who can this be?" (4:41b). Note that this story of rejection by his family in the synagogue of Nazareth echoes the story of his family's earlier rejection in Capernaum when his "mother and brothers" stayed outside rather than entering to hear him teach (3:31-32).

Leaving that place, Jesus returned to his own country, and his disciples followed him. When the sabbath came, he began teaching in the synagogue, and most of those who heard him were astonished. They commented, "How did this come to him? What kind of wisdom has been given to him that he also performs such miracles? Who is he but the carpenter, the son of Mary and the brother of James and Joset and Judas and Simon? His sisters, too, are they not here among us?" So they took offense at him.

And Jesus said to them, "Prophets are despised only in their own country, among their relatives and in their own family." And he could work no miracles there, but only healed a few sick people by laying his hands on them. Jesus himself was astounded at their unbelief. (6:1-6a)

Jesus' family and neighbors can't believe that the one they have been waiting for could actually come from their own town. What Jesus actually said or what wisdom he sought to share with those he had grown up with has not been recorded. These familiar people would have heard the stories about him, including his teaching with parables. They cannot reconcile the Jesus they knew with this new Jesus. How he has changed!

They listen and are astonished and then they start talking to one another. Using modern language, their attitude might be "Who in the world does he think he is? Where does he get these ideas? Who's he trying to impress?" They know him by his trade and his work. He's a carpenter—in Greek *tekton*, a highly skilled and trained person who works in stone or metal or wood. Furthermore, they know his family and they list the names of his four brothers and his sisters, who are unnamed and uncounted, as was the custom.

Obviously, Jesus came from a family and had brothers and sisters. James, the brother of the Lord, figures in the Acts of the Apostles (12:17b; 15:13; 21:18) and elsewhere (see Gal 2:9, 12 and 1 Cor 15:7) and plays a strong role in the early Christian communities. (Note that an African church father, Tertullian [ca. 160-225], in asserting the full humanity of Jesus, considered the brothers of Jesus [and so also his sisters], true brothers; see Tertullian, *Against Marcion* 4.19.)

When those who have known him for a long time refer to him, they call him the son of Mary. Rarely, if ever, in Jewish society was a man referred to as the son of his mother, even if his mother was a widow. Such a reference was seen as an insult, a slur on his origins. They've known him for decades as an ordinary person. Cynically they dismiss him or reduce him to his work and his family.

The text adds that "they took offense at him." Jesus scandalized them; he became a stumbling block or a snare that would trip them. Joseph O'Hanlon points out:

> Amongst early Christians the word ["took offense at him"] was something of a technical term (see, for example Rom 9:32; 1 Cor 1:23; 1 Cor 8:13; 2 Cor 11:29; Gal 5:11; 1 Peter 2:8) for those, who on being confronted with the message of the gospel, found something in it (the lowly status of Jesus; his death by crucifixion; the resurrection or whatever) which prevented them from embracing Christian faith and discipleship. (*Mark My Words*, 88)

Their scorn causes Jesus to declare, "Prophets are despised only in their own country, among their relatives and in their own family." Jesus seems appalled at the people's resistance, their pettiness and their refusal to be open to him. He heals a few people by laying hands on them, but Jesus' power does not work for those who lack faith. The power of the Spirit is meant to be reciprocal and dialogical, but these people want no part of this new Jesus.

This brings a definitive split with his background; he becomes like a stranger to his own. Immediately Jesus summons the Twelve and sends them out two by two to share his wisdom and power and work. The following passages describe the lifestyle of Christian disciples. This is the "Way" in a nutshell, covering everything from clothing and money to where they are to lodge and what to do if they face rejection. Stated concisely, it describes how the new family of Jesus is born and brought forth among strangers.

> He called the Twelve to him and began to send them out two by two, giving them authority over evil spirits. And he ordered them to take nothing for the journey except a staff; no food, no bag, no money in their belts. They were to wear sandals and were not to take an extra tunic.
>
> And he added, "In whatever house you are welcomed, stay there until you leave the place. If any place doesn't receive you and the people refuse to listen to you, leave after shaking the dust off your feet. It will be a testimony against them."
>
> So they set out to proclaim that this was the time to repent. They drove out many demons and healed many sick people by anointing them. (6:7-13)

Before the disciples return to report to Jesus comes the "filling" of another of Mark's sandwiches: the account of the awful death of John the Baptizer. But Mark is relating not only what happened to John the Baptizer but also what happens to Jesus, to the Twelve, and to all those sent out two by two, missionaries and preachers who are bringing the good news to strangers near and far. There will be both welcome and rejection, and always there will be the threat of death because of their message of the truth of the good news of God. This will be witnessed by Jesus, by John the Baptizer, and by many in the early Christian communities.

Those who go out in the name of Jesus to wrest people from the grip of Satan and grasp them by the hand for the victory of justice (Is 42) must take no more than what they absolutely need. They must rely on the hospitality of others whose openness to the word and the kingdom of God will also open doors for them to lodging, food, shelter, and acceptance of faith. The disciples are to preach the need for repentance, to anoint the sick with oil and work cures, following in the path of John the Baptizer, who went before the face of the Lord.

It is likely that this also served as a short primer for those in Mark's community who went forth from their own churches to prepare the way for others. Barnabas and Paul, and Mark, Silas, Timothy, and many others traveled together in the first fifty or more years bringing the gospel to the far-flung corners of the Roman Empire. If they were not received graciously as was the case with Jesus, they were to get up and leave and not look back. The description of how they are to travel is probably not to be taken literally; the point is how little they need on their journey and how much they are to rely on the generosity of those they visit. Their family is out there somewhere, waiting to be found, touched, and drawn into the kingdom.

The Death of John

Herod has heard of Jesus and of all the rumors flying around that Jesus is John the Baptizer come back from the dead. Others say Jesus is Elijah or that "he is a prophet equal to any of the prophets." Everyone at the time knew that prophets were searing in their truth-telling, protective of the poor and the innocent and those without recourse to power. Prophets were known to rely only on God, for no one else cared for the plight of the poor. And prophets always demanded justice from the rich and the powerful, scorning any worship of God that continued while the gulf between the poor and the wealthy grew wider. All this talk of prophets frightens Herod, because he has had John murdered while in prison. What if he has not really gotten rid of this annoying and relentless voice of God that accuses him of murder, adultery, and all other manner of evil?

The account of the death of John is gruesome and senseless. It demonstrates the excesses and brutality of Herod and his court. It also warns Mark's readers of the connections to the beginning of the gospel. John is in a long tradition of prophets, like Isaiah, and their words most certainly contributed to their deaths. Preaching the good news of God that Jesus has just shared with his followers, and not the gospel of Rome or of any other ruler, is always going to be connected to persecution and martyrdom. The passion of John is a strong reminder, even a warning, of what happens to the prophets: like Isaiah and John the Baptizer, Jesus and his many followers will be "delivered up" in the same way (Mk 13:9-13). This takes place during the mid-sixties of the first century, and Mark's communities know firsthand this martyrdom and how it keeps interrupting their lives with ruthless violence and vicious hatred.

At the end of the telling of John's death we read that his disciples "came and took his body and buried it." Just after this intimation of Jesus' own death and burial, we read that Jesus' disciples returned from their missions and told him of all that had happened to them. This gathering of Jesus' disciples is a prelude to the story of the feeding of the five thousand, which introduces the symbol of bread and the theme of feeding, which will figure so strongly in the rest of the gospel.

> Then he said to them: "Go off by yourselves to a remote place and have some rest." For there were so many people coming and going that the apostles had not time even to eat. And they went away in the boat to a secluded area by themselves.
>
> But people saw them leaving and many could guess where they were going. So, from all the towns they hurried there on foot, arriving ahead of them. (Mk 6:31-33)

The disciples have had a taste of Jesus' work in their short apprenticeship. They have gone out on their own for the first time to extend the power of Jesus, asking others to choose life or to remain in the death-hold of the world. But people of the world who are in need and searching are coming from everywhere so that the disciples can't even share a meal. Thus they set off in a boat (the church) to a deserted place (perhaps the privileged place of intimacy and knowledge of God in our tradition). But the masses of people cut them off and get there before them. Jesus embarks from the boat, a place of refuge and sanctuary, and has pity on the vast crowd.

The description of Jesus is telling: "He had compassion on them for they were like sheep without a shepherd. And he began a long teaching session with them" (6:34). This story brings echoes as ancient as Moses. Moses stood alone with God looking into the promised land, knowing that he would not enter. And he asked Yahweh to appoint a leader to take his place before the people so that "they may not be like sheep without a shepherd" (Nm 27:17). And so Yahweh appointed Joshua, the man whose name is a variation of Jesus' own name—they are both to be saviors of their people.

Jesus turns from his disciples. They have a choice—they can stay in the boat, which is for them a place of refuge, or they can follow him into the crowd. It often happens that when any of us seeks to go off to a place of refuge, the needs of others will call us back. We must be moved and formed by pity and compassion. Our presence with those in need brings to them the justice of God, which breaks down the barriers of sin, evil, and injustice that cause inequality, suffering, and violence. As Jesus moves toward the people, he is acting out the words of Jeremiah the prophet: "I will appoint shepherds who will take care of them. No longer will they fear or be terrified. No one will be lost" (Jer 23:4). Our task as followers of Jesus, as the children of God with Jesus, is to give comfort and to teach the newness and hope that live in the word of God. This is Jesus' mission and it is also ours.

This first feeding story takes place on the Jewish side of the lake. A second feeding story, told in Mark 8, takes place on the Gentile side. Here is the familiar one from Mark 6.

And he began a long teaching session with them.

It was now getting late, so his disciples came to him and said, "This is a lonely place and it is now late. You should send the people away and let them go to the farms and villages around here to buy themselves something to eat."

Jesus replied, "You yourselves give them something to eat." They answered, "If we are to give them food, we must go and buy two hundred silver coins' worth of bread." But Jesus said, "You have some loaves: how many? Go and see." The disciples found out and said, "There are five loaves and two fish."

Then he told them to have the people sit down together in groups on the green grass. This they did in groups of hundreds and fifties.

And Jesus took the five loaves and the two fish and, raising his eyes to heaven, he pronounced a blessing, broke the loaves and handed them to his disciples to distribute to the people. He also divided the two fish among them.

They all ate and everyone had enough. The disciples gathered up what was left and filled twelve baskets with broken pieces of bread and fish. Five thousand men had eaten there. (6:34b-44)

Once again Mark shows his knowledge of his audience. These are people who would be familiar with the stories of the ancient prophets, such as that of Elisha in 2 Kings 4:42-44.

A man came from Baal-shalishad bringing bread and wheat to the man of God. These were from the first part of the harvest, twenty loaves of barley and wheat. Elisha told him, "Give the loaves to these men that they may eat."

His servant said to him, "How am I to divide these loaves among one hundred men?" Elisha insisted, "Give them to the men that they may eat, for Yahweh says: They shall eat and have some left over." So the man set it before them; and they ate and had some left, as Yahweh had said.

While we may not be familiar with this story of Elisha, Mark undoubtedly had it in mind when he recounted the feeding of the five thousand. Elisha's servant reacted just like Jesus' disciples—he understandably balked at trying to feed such a large group with such a small amount of food. What would happen when the food ran out? In this story, however, Jesus' followers seem to be sadly lacking in pity; now that dusk is approaching, they don't even show simple concern for the crowds that have been with Jesus for hours through the heat of the day. Even though they've gathered in "a lonely place," they suggest sending the people off to fend for themselves.

Jesus' words, "You yourselves give them something to eat," must have shocked the disciples; perhaps they reacted indignantly. One older translation has Jesus telling them even more pointedly, "Feed them yourselves." For months now, Jesus has been feeding the disciples with the word, with teachings and wisdom, preaching, experiences of healing and power and of his presence among them. They have received many spiritual gifts, and they have lots to give away. But they are confused. Before Jesus told them not to take money or food along on their journeys, and now Jesus is telling them to feed this huge crowd of five thousand. They rebel: "Are we to go and spend two hundred days' wages for bread to feed them?" (6:37b NAB). Their protests echo ancient cries of the exodus. When the Hebrews wandering in the desert grew dissatisfied with the God-given gift of manna, they cried to Moses: "Who will give us meat to eat?" (Nm 11:4). Feeling responsible for them, Moses lamented before God.

Moses heard the people crying, family by family at the entrance to their tent and Yahweh became very angry.

This displeased Moses. Then Moses said to Yahweh, "Why have you treated your servant so badly? Is it because you do not love me that you burdened me with this people? Did I conceive all these people and did I give them birth? And now you want me to carry them in my bosom as a nurse carries an infant, to the land you promised on oath to their fathers? Where would I get meat for all these people, when they cry to me saying: 'Give us meat that we may eat?' I cannot, myself alone, carry all these people; the burden is too heavy for me." (Nm 11:10-14)

And for an entire month God provided them with meat in the desert. "And Yahweh said to Moses, 'Is Yahweh's arm shortened? Now you shall see whether or not my word is true'" (Nm 11:23).

In Mark's account, the disciples seem to be thinking in terms of market economics! But Jesus thinks differently. He is interested in sharing the available resources. So he asks what food they themselves have, undoubtedly aware that they had enough for themselves. Pooling their resources, they produced five loaves, which would have been fairly substantial rounded loaves, and two fish. As fishermen, they would likely have kept some of the meatiest fish for themselves. Jesus tells them to organize the huge crowd into groups of hundreds and fifties, sits them down, and gets ready to distribute the food.

Similar feeding stories occur at least six times in the gospels as characteristic signatures of Jesus or marks of his ministry. Such stories seem to be preludes to the Eucharist. The crowds are told to sit down (in some translations recline) on green grass! Although this was a remote place, perhaps even a desert, this is how people would seat themselves at a banquet. The word used in Greek for a banquet was *symposium*. In time the Christian Eucharist was conducted in much the same way, even to the groupings of people in fifties and hundreds. It is thought that the largest Christian community of that time, that in Corinth, was made up of three groups of no more than fifty people each.

Another image used by Mark, that of the green grass, calls to mind the image of the good shepherd in Psalm 23: "The Lord is my shepherd, I shall not want. He makes me lie down in green pastures." And later, "You spread a table before me in the presence of my foes. You anoint my head with oil; my cup is overflowing."

The predominant image in the feeding of this large crowd, however, evokes more the image of the exodus people being led and cared for and always having enough. The feeding story in chapter 8 will include more of the characteristics of Eucharist. Here in chapter 6, Jesus acts as the host or the head of a family when he stands to pray, raising his eyes to heaven and saying a blessing before he breaks the bread for his disciples to distribute to the crowd. For Jewish families, this represented a daily ritual before meals. In fact, Mark uses the word *eulogein*, which means a simple blessing, and not *eucharistein*, which will be used in chapter 8.

Naturally the question arises of where the bread came from. It came from Jesus, of course, but it also came from those who shared what they had when they saw Jesus sharing with them. It was very simple fare but it was enough. The NAB translation says "they had their fill." I find the wording of the Christian Community Bible more apt: "everyone had enough." "Enough" describes both a spirituality and an approach to economics that is based on sharing the resources at hand. This story of the feeding looks at daily life, sharing food and resources, which was part of the economic realities of the Christian communities during the Roman Empire and should be so among us today.

Ched Myers points out the significance of this approach to economics.

While theologians love to see "eucharistic" significance in the wilderness feeding, the Elisha story suggests that the economic dimension is paramount. Twice the disciples try to solve the problem of hungry masses by referring it to "market economics" (6:36f). But Jesus insists that the problem cannot be "sent away" and proposes instead a kind of enacted parable of just distribution, an alternative of self-sufficiency through a practice of sharing available resources.

The same themes are reiterated in the second, briefer feeding story (Mark 8:1-9), which takes place this time in Gentile territory of the Decapolis (7:31). Jesus again is moved by the plight of the crowd: "If I should send them away hungry, they will lose faith on the way" (8:3).

The disciples' response (8:4) this time is despair: "How can anyone find bread for all these people in the wilderness?" Which is to say, how can the problem be solved outside of the economic system of the dominant social order? Again, repetition being the key to pedagogical success, Mark narrates the solution: Jesus organizes, the people share, and all are satisfied (8:5-9).

These stories reflect the concrete historical situation of the majority of Galilee's rural population. Hunger and poverty were ubiquitous among those disenfranchised by a feudal system of land ownership and an economic system in which the countryside was bled dry by urban and foreign trading interests. The same perspective pervaded Jesus' sermon of parables, in which he brought theology to earth by using real-life, economic metaphors taken from the daily agrarian world to describe the kingdom. There Jesus envisioned a harvest of unprecedented yield (4:8), which would shatter the cycle of poverty in which the indentured peasant—the "sower"—was trapped.

In the wilderness feedings, this hope takes flesh in the "miracle of enough" for the hungry masses through a model of cooperative consumption. Mark will later make it clear that the discipleship community struggles to embody this economic alternative in its own life (10:28-31). (*Sojourners Magazine* [May 1987]: 32)

Toward the end of the account, when everyone has had "enough," twelve baskets of leftovers are gathered up. Like many other images carried over from the Hebrew scriptures, this seems a clear reference to the twelve tribes of Israel. Similarly, the reference to Jesus' "long teaching" with them may be a reference to the five books of Moses. And a word is certainly needed about the end of the story. The last phrase in the account, "Those who had eaten the loaves numbered five thousand men," grates on the ears of many readers today, especially women. This, however, is a story of the Jewish world of the time, a time when only men were counted.

As Jesus takes his disciples back and forth across the lake, from the Jewish side to the Gentile side, another feeding story will appear, although with different numbers of people and provisions. These trips across the lake, always accompanied by storms, waves, and turmoil, also serve as bridges. Jesus is joining communities into one: one body, one loaf, one baptism, where differences do not divide but enrich abundantly. Many themes come together in chapter 8, which opens a doorway into the kingdom of God here on earth and provides an intimation of life lived together as resurrection life in the Trinity. Mark's task is formidable as he seeks to bring us along slowly but surely on this journey of teaching and conversion that will lead to wholeness, to a community that respects diversity and welcomes all, with special attention to those who are the "least."

Mark 6:45–8:21

After the feeding of the five thousand, the disciples embark in the boat for another trip across the lake. With this next story, Mark draws us into the "heart of darkness," where the disciples must face the hard choices involved in being followers of Jesus. They will have to abandon many of their previously held traditions as they learn that the kingdom of God belongs to all peoples, not just to the Jews, and especially to the least among us, those who do not belong even among their own people. The disciples themselves begin to resist Jesus, just as we are tempted to do. This next account also begins with the word "immediately," but this time there are some specific reasons for hurrying the disciples off into the boat.

Jesus removes the disciples from the crowd and sends them off in the boat. Perhaps the disciples are reluctant to go. Perhaps they're starting to get cold feet and don't want Jesus to be away from them. Perhaps they are also struggling with what he seems to be asking them to do. How could they feed such a large crowd by themselves? And so Jesus orders them to get into the boat and go. Various translations say "insisted" or "obliged";

it seems clear that he compelled them to go. Jesus then separates himself from them, dismisses the crowds, and goes off to the mountain to pray.

Again, Jesus goes off to pray. In chapter 1, when the crowds started to gather, Jesus slipped away from his disciples and was "absorbed in prayer" (1:35). When the disciples found him, he revealed something about who he was and what he had come to do: "Let's go to the nearby villages so that I may preach there too; for that is why I came" (1:38). This happens again in chapter 6, and it will also happen in chapter 14.

What happens next is very different from the disciples' last journey on the sea (4:35-41). That time Jesus was asleep in the boat with them when they panicked out of fear and woke him. This time they are not in any danger. They are simply rowing against the wind and having a hard time making progress. They are, indeed, having a hard time of it—of being followers of Jesus. Jesus does not come to rescue them this time but rather to reveal more of who he is. The other time, during the storm, they asked, "Who is he?" (4:41). The brief account of Jesus walking on the water is a revelation of what Mark's community believes about Jesus the Risen Lord, that he is Jesus the Christ, the Son of God (1:1). The story contains many references to Old Testament accounts of theophanies and epiphanies, manifestations or showing forth of God.

> When evening came, the boat was far out on the lake while he was alone on the land. Jesus saw his disciples straining at the oars, for the wind was against them, and before daybreak he came to them walking on the lake; and he was going to pass them by.
> When they saw him walking on the lake, they thought it was a ghost and cried out; for they all saw him and were terrified. But at once he called to them, "Courage! It's me; don't be afraid." Then Jesus got into the boat with them and the wind died down. They were completely astonished, for they had not really grasped the fact of the loaves; their minds were dull. (6:47-52)

The disciples must be feeling overwhelmed at what is happening, and it must seem very much like rowing against the wind and getting nowhere. When Jesus comes to them, they are far out on the lake. Seeing Jesus walk toward them on the water would have caused them to think of stories they knew from the Hebrew tradition, such as that of God parting the waters of the Reed Sea to save the exodus people from the pharaoh's army (Ex 14:16-31). Mark's community would be steeped in the psalms and stories of the prophets, and throughout the gospel Mark alludes to many of them. Here are two important examples.

> Your path led through the sea, your way through the great water, but your footprints were nowhere to be seen.
> You led your people as a flock by the hand of Moses and Aaron. (Ps 77:20-21)

Thus says Yahweh,
who opened a way through the sea
and a path in the mighty waters,
who brought down chariots and horses,
a whole army of them,
and there they lay, never to rise again,
snuffed out like a wick.
But do not dwell on the past,
or remember the things of old.
Look, I am doing a new thing:
now it springs forth.
Do you not see?
I am opening up a way in the wilderness
And rivers in the desert. (Is 43:16-19)

These are tellings of the mighty works of God, and by walking on the water Jesus is announcing what the disciples must come to believe of him, that he is God.

As soon as Mark tells of Jesus walking on the lake, he notes that Jesus "was going to pass them by." The revelation of Jesus' power is bound to the phrase "He meant to pass them by," which is also found in the Book of Job and in Yahweh's dealings with Moses.

He alone stretches out the skies
and treads on the waves of the seas. . . .
He passes by, but I do not see him;
he moves on, but I do not notice him. (Job 9:8, 11)

Moses said: "Then let me see your Glory." And He said, "I will make all my goodness pass before you and proclaim the name of Yahweh before you. For I am gracious to whom I want to be gracious and I am merciful to whom I want to be merciful." (Ex 33:18-19)

And Yahweh came down in a cloud and stood there with him, and Moses called on the name of Yahweh.

Then Yahweh passed in front of him and cried out, "Yahweh, Yahweh is a God full of pity and mercy, slow to anger and abounding in truth and loving-kindness." (Ex 34:5-6)

Jesus is going to pass by the disciples as the beloved Son of God, but they are not going to see him. They have not really understood what he has been saying to them nor who he indeed is. When they see him, they are terrified. They think they're seeing a ghost. Jesus calls out to them, "Get hold of yourselves (courage). It is I (I am). Do not be afraid," and then gets into the boat with them. The original Greek (in parentheses) is also translated as

"Take heart, it is I, do not be afraid." This is Mark's first use of the proclamation "I am" from the mouth of Jesus. It will come to pass again in chapter 14 when the high priest, furious with Jesus, asks him, "Are you the Messiah, the Son of the Blessed One?" and Jesus responds, "I am" (14:61-62). The words *ego eimi* are formulaic and rarely used by Mark. They are spoken here to encourage, to take heart. And then Jesus uses a phrase that the disciples will hear quite often, "Do not be afraid."

Mark is telling his own community, and us for that matter, that we have no reason to fear—our God is with us in Jesus the beloved Son. No matter what the world does, no matter how overwhelming things may seem, no matter if we do not understand, no matter that the powers of evil mass against us, we must remember *ego eimi*, that Jesus, the saving presence of God, is with us.

Despite Jesus' pronouncement, this manifestation of God's power and presence in Jesus escapes the disciples. At this point Mark describes the disciples in the same terms used to describe the people of Nazareth, his own kin, the Pharisees and scribes, the Herodians and all those who have resisted Jesus: "They were taken aback by these happenings, for they had not understood about the loaves. On the contrary, their minds were completely closed to the meaning of the events" (6:51a-52). The King James translation says clearly that "their heart was hardened." They have joined the resistance to Jesus.

When the boat lands, though, the people recognize Jesus. All those who are sick and in desperate need run to him, bringing along those who cannot walk, and they beg him "to let them touch just the tassel of his cloak. All who touched him got well" (6:56). Crowds of people now believe, but, sadly, the disciples don't seem to be included. This short account of the faith of those in need appears as a bridge between the disciples' lack of understanding and the hardening of their hearts and the growing hostility and opposition on the part of the Pharisees to what Jesus is teaching and doing (7:1-23). The disciples' lack of understanding will come to a head in chapter 8, when they begin to verbalize their resistance and rejection of Jesus.

A story from the Zen tradition tells about Buddha's desire to pass on his wisdom to his disciples.

> When Buddha began to sense that he would be leaving his disciples for good and that the day of his death was drawing near, he decided to meet with them one last time to pass on his wisdom, graces, and power. He called the four disciples who had been with him the longest and asked them to state what they had gleaned from all their years of study and practice.
>
> Tao-fu, the first to speak, stated: "According to the way I see it, we should neither cling to words and letters nor dispense with them altogether—remembering that all things are useful instruments of the Tao."

"Hmmm," said Buddha, "to you I give my skin."

Next up was the nun Tsung-chih. "According to the way I see it, it's like Ananda's viewing of the Buddha land of Aksobhy, seeing it once and never again."

"Hmmm," said Buddha, "to you I give my flesh."

Tao-yu then came forward to speak. "According to the way I see it, the four elements are all empty; the five *skandhas* are all unreal. As I see it, there is nothing, not a thing that can be grasped."

"Hmmm," said Buddha, "to you I give my bone."

Last of all Hui-k'o came forward, but he did not speak. He just stood there, not a word. But he did bow with deep reverence toward the master and looked straight into his face.

"Hmmm," said Buddha, "to you I give my marrow!"

And it was he, they say, who became the Second Patriarch.

The story is insightful because it reminds us of how difficult it is to become a disciple. We must seek to understand all of the insights of the Master, not just the ones we have come to terms with or find attractive. It is not necessary to know the tenets of Buddhism to understand what the Buddha is trying to do. This is just what Jesus is trying to do, to initiate his followers into his very flesh and blood, his heart and soul, his mind and practice. They are simply not getting it. Or, perhaps, they don't want the entire package. We aren't so different. What is it in Jesus' words and practice that we don't want to hear? What is it that we don't want to put into practice? Why do we try at times to back off from Jesus and go on about our business, staying where we are comfortable?

The Hard-Heartedness of the Pharisees

Chapter 7 begins with a long and detailed argument between Jesus and the Pharisees. While the Pharisees figure strongly in the earlier accounts in Mark's gospel, notably those dealing with resistance to Jesus' teachings, they are barely mentioned in the accounts of Jesus' arrest and crucifixion. It seems likely that the long discussion in verses 1 through 23, along with many other instances, may indeed be more revelatory of what is happening midway through the first century between the Jewish community and the new Christian communities. Mark uses these teachers of the Law to demarcate the differences emerging between the two groups. Readers might keep in mind that while the debates between Jesus and the Pharisees tell of what actually happened at the time of Jesus, they also tell of what happened after Jesus' death and resurrection when the Christian Jews became more clearly defined and separated from the Jewish community. The members of Mark's community, like other communities that formed the early church, sought to define themselves not as Jewish but as Followers of the Way. They struggled with how much of Judaism, especially of the Judaic laws, should be retained and practiced.

Two of the thorniest areas were those of ritual purity and cleanliness and the laws regarding food. In this encounter between Jesus and the Pharisees, Jesus acts as teacher, trying to explain what is important and why the laws existed in the first place. Rigid adherence to a law can ignore a crucial call for the conversion of heart and practice. Jesus was very clear: no law was to be used to exclude another person, and no law was to override compassion, forgiveness, and a welcoming inclusion into the community.

The break between Judaism and Christianity cannot be ignored because it has fostered so much hostility, war, and death throughout history. From the time that Emperor Constantine declared Christianity an official religion (313), the Jewish community has felt the brunt of un-Christian hatred. Even today it is a dagger in the heart of Jewish-Christians relations. As a group the Christians refused to fight with the Jewish community in the struggle against the Romans to protect and re-instate the temple in Jerusalem as the center of religious and national life. This became a source of hatred on both sides, and, sadly, the gospels reflect some of that rancor. Because Mark was written in the mid- to late-sixties, Jews and Christians are on the edge of that war. In *Mark My Words* Joseph O'Hanlon describes the background for the confrontation between Jesus and the Pharisees in the first part of Mark 7.

> How are these matters to be explained? If we recall that there was a break-up between Judaism and Christianity and if we further remember the defeat of Israel by the Romans in the war (66-74 C.E.), the explanation is not hard to find. The war saw the destruction of the temple and the powerful aristocratic clergy in Jerusalem became redundant. The Jewish religion, if it was going to survive, would do so through the work of adaptable teachers of the Law, not conservative, out-of-work priests. The Pharisees were the one group within Judaism with the skills to ensure its survival. And they succeeded. Judaism today is, for the most part, the child of the Pharisees. What the Gospels reflect is not so much the quarrels of Jesus and his contemporaries, but the years of growing estrangement and of final rupture. (p. 118)

Mark has two concerns in this text. The first issue is the integration of many Gentiles into the Christian community, which was originally all Jewish, including, of course, Jesus himself. And the second issue is the identity of Jesus: who is he?

Hostility permeates these twenty-three verses. The ritual washings are not about cleanliness or hygiene but about becoming holy. The first set of ritual washings has to do with preparation for the fellowship of the meal. Although many of the rules pertain primarily to the priests, they were often taught to the people as signs of holiness. This followed instructions in Exodus ("You will be for me a kingdom of priests and a holy nation" [Ex 19:6]) and Leviticus ("You shall be holy for me as I am holy, Yahweh, your God, and I have set you apart from the nations to be mine" [Lv 20:26]). Again, it is helpful to remember that this disagreement also took place between the Jews and the Christians in Rome at Mark's time. Mark's communities were dealing with Jewish factions that had developed their own priorities, as had different communities of Christians. Mark wants to emphasize exactly what Jesus is teaching—inward devotion is much holier than any outward appearance of obedience to rules. To make his point even more strongly, Jesus quotes Isaiah when responding to the Pharisees' questions about ritual handwashing.

> Jesus answered, "You, shallow people! How well Isaiah prophesied of you when he wrote: *This people honors me with their lips, but their heart is far from me. The worship they offer me is worthless, for what they teach are only human rules.* You even put aside the commandment of God to hold fast to human tradition." (Mk 7:6-8)

The tone is harsh. And we must keep in mind that Jesus is also speaking to us, challenging us to look at our practices and our worship. Do our traditions and rules reveal that our hearts are surrendered to God in obedience? Or do they show that we are dabbling with words rather than being converted to the good news of God? Are we transforming and serving others who have been excluded by liturgical or pastoral practices?

What Jesus is criticizing can plague every religion. There is always the temptation and tendency to settle for what is acceptable liturgically or to focus on one specific moral issue. Believers who do this are missing the connection to the rest of life and to other human beings. We always need others to call us to examine ourselves so we know whether our actions truly worship and give glory to God or whether we simply pursue our own agendas, stroke our own egos, or reinforce our own power bases. In a word, how pure are we in our practice? Are we adept at pious words and practices but shallow in compassion, inclusion, and justice and peace-making? Are we truly forgiving? Are we really giving our lives in sacrifice to God?

In the account that follows Jesus further defines himself as a teacher who re-interprets the Law as he explains clearly what is essential in the Law and what demands obedience. I keep a quotation from Dom Helder Camara tacked on the wall where I write: "Do not fear the truth, hard as it may appear. It is your best friend and closest sister." I heard him say this in 1969 in a dingy restaurant in Puebla, Mexico, when he was defining what is absolutely foundational in a world of inequality, racism, nationalism, injustice, and violence. In these next verses of chapter 7, Jesus lays out what is absolutely essential with regard to cleanliness or holiness. At the time, traditions around these issues clearly separated Jew and Gentile and men and women. Jesus speaks to the Pharisees, the disciples, and the crowd and also to Mark's community of the first century and to us in the twenty-first century. Today in our churches we need to hear his words with their demanding call to obedience as surely as did the people of the first century.

> Jesus then called the people to him again and said to them, "Listen to me, all of you, and try to understand. Nothing that enters one from outside can make that person unclean. It is what comes out from within that makes unclean. Let everyone who has ears listen." . . .
> Thus Jesus declared that all foods are clean. (7:14-16, 19b)

Mark has located the debate between Jesus and the Pharisees within the community with Jesus at mealtime. Some of the disciples are eating without having washed their "unclean hands" (Mk 7:2), and the Pharisees question Jesus about this. There is obviously dissension about such practices within the community, and Jesus is drawing the disciples' attention to some of the defining marks of his new family. Jesus is trying to pull people from the death grip of what destroys, what is violent, and what is dehumanizing, and to grasp them for justice and peace, for compassion and mercy, for belonging to God.

> What comes out of a person is what defiles, for evil designs come out of the heart: theft, murder, adultery, jealousy, greed, maliciousness, deceit, indecency, slander, pride and folly. All these evil things come from within and make a person unclean. (7:20-23)

Different translations render these evils somewhat differently: they can also include envy, arrogance, an obtuse spirit, perverseness, blasphemy, licentiousness, and acts of malice. The precise wording may vary, but what is essential remains. These evils usually have unjust, violent, and demeaning effects on other people. We must be very careful not to get caught in the same patterns of religious practice that Jesus condemns. Using the verses from Mark, Eugene LaVerdiere explains how this can happen in four easy stages:

7:8	"You disregard God's commandment but cling to human tradition";
7:9	"You have set aside the commandment of God in order to uphold your tradition . . .";
7:13	"You nullify the word of God in favor of your tradition."
7:13b	"And you do many such things." (*The Beginning of the Gospel,* 1:194).

Actions we take today—or actions we fail to take—on behalf of God's people can also defile us and make us unclean or impure. These include neglecting people's needs for medicine and health care, for housing or water or education; supporting the death penalty, pre-emptive strikes, nuclear proliferation, or low-intensity warfare; aggressively pursuing capitalism; excluding immigrants and refugees; or denying the rights of members of other religions, races, and nationalities.

The Syrophoenician Woman

Jesus moves on to the territory of Tyre and Sidon, Gentile country north of Israel. He feels a need to get away in order to gain perspective on how his own people, his nation, and the religious community are reacting. Why are they rejecting him? Why are they refusing to understand the heart of his teaching? Why do they not see who he is, the beloved son of God? Can he draw together the Jewish and Gentile disciples and converts so that they can eat from one loaf during one meal at one table?

In the last feeding story, women were conspicuously absent, although women such as those we have already encountered do figure prominently in Mark's gospel, Simon's mother-in-law, the woman who touches his cloak, and Jairus's daughter. It seems that at times Mark uses the presence of women as a literary device to warn readers that something significant is coming. The presence of women also speaks to a shift in how Jesus' disciples are to live in the new household of God. There were undoubtedly many people in Mark's own community who did not welcome either Gentiles or women at meals or the Eucharist. These issues surface many times in the Book of Acts and were central in the development of the early church. Sadly, some followers of Jesus have always been less accepting or welcoming of women and strangers of other nationalities or ethnic groups, those they feel might be "unclean" or unworthy of admission to the one loaf. Mark makes clear that the divine doctrine of Jesus must have priority over any traditions that betray the heart of God's good news in Jesus.

The woman in this feeding story is a Gentile, a Greek born in Syrophoenicia. The Gospel of Matthew refers to her as the Canaanite woman. She is probably wealthy, well educated, and a free citizen, part of the upper class afforded many privileges by the Romans in the midst of rural peasants who were poor and mainly Jewish. The story's emphasis is not primarily on the healing of the woman's young daughter, though that is the initial request; rather, it centers on the conversation between the woman and Jesus about bread and food and who gets to eat.

[H]e entered a house and did not want anyone to know he was there, but he could not remain hidden. A woman whose small daughter had an evil spirit heard of him and came and fell at his feet. Now this woman was a pagan, a Syrophoenician by birth, and she begged him to drive the demon out of her daughter.

Jesus told her, "Let the children be fed first, for it is not right to take the children's bread and throw it to the dogs." But she replied, "Sir, even the dogs under the table eat the crumbs from the children's bread." Then Jesus said to her, "You may go your way; because of such a reply the demon has gone out of your daughter." And when the woman went home, she found her child lying in bed and the demon gone. (7:24b-30)

This is a most remarkable, and formidable, woman, which was essential for the Gentile believers and the women of the early church! She approaches Jesus on her knees, but she is breaking laws left and right. She is an outsider, a Gentile pagan, who has entered the house of a Jewish man. Even though she would have had a higher status than he in her culture and society, she abases herself and does him homage. Then she begs on behalf of her small daughter. This scene would have been an affront to many Jews and even to Jewish Christians who resisted sharing the table of the Lord with either Gentiles or women. The woman begs on her knees, and while Jesus speaks to her, he doesn't answer her question. He speaks of something else altogether—who gets to eat first.

Jesus' response often puzzles and irritates people. He says to the woman, "It is not right to take the children's bread and throw it to the dogs." This seems to go beyond rudeness! Is Jesus, a Jewish man, attacking a Gentile woman who has intruded upon him and his solitude? Or is Mark using this scene to reveal how coarse or cruel some members of the early Christian community can be toward others in the church?

It helps to realize that the conversation is that of equals, although she is on the floor and he is sitting down and she is a pagan and he is a Jew. Jesus is speaking with her, which most Jewish men wouldn't be doing at all, and their exchange has the style of a debate, of fending and parrying back and forth.

Their dialogue reminds me of a brief account from the 1950s when a Catholic visiting Poland was shown around by a Communist Party official. When the visitor asks, "Are you a Catholic?" the official replies with a smile, "Believing, not practicing." As the official continues to show the woman around, she asks another question: "Are you a Communist?" To this, the official replies, smiling: "Practicing, but not believing." This somewhat light-hearted telling conceals a deadly seriousness.

The Syrophoenician woman is not easily deterred or put off. She gives an immediate reply, pointing out that "even the dogs under the table eat the crumbs from the children's bread." She is clever, insistent, and persistent and relates to Jesus as an equal. Jesus acknowledges this. Because of her words, because of her faith, she can go, and her daughter is already healed!

Her message is that all (even pagan Gentiles and women) are welcome at the table, and Jesus agrees with her.

It should be noted that the woman addresses Jesus as "Sir" or in other translations as "Lord." This form of address is used only here in Mark's gospel, and it is on the lips of a woman who is a well-educated Gentile, a member of the group considered to be in league with the Roman oppressors. For the early Christians the word "Lord" (*Kyrie* in Greek) became the title of the Risen Christ. Mark places this title of belief in the resurrection of Jesus, the Son of God, in the mouth of this woman, revealing the place that should be accorded Gentiles and women in the churches. God's good news in Jesus telling of the kingdom of God belongs to everyone and cannot be confined to one group alone. The household of Jesus is a universal family.

The Healing of the Deaf Mute

The last account in Mark 7 tells of the need for all to share the one bread, to be fed as one people by Jesus. The ears of the deaf must be opened and their tongues loosed so they can praise and glorify the good news announced by Jesus. Some people bring to Jesus a man who is deaf and has a speech impediment in the hope that Jesus can help him. Mark tells us that Jesus takes the man off by himself, an action that imparts more importance to what is happening. The touching of the man's ears and tongue seems to connect this account with ancient baptismal rituals, remnants of which still remain. This story repeats bits from the earlier stories but also things that are altogether new and that reveal more of what Jesus is trying to do.

> Again Jesus set out; from the country of Tyre he passed through Sidon and skirting the sea of Galilee he came to the territory of Decapolis. There a deaf man who also had difficulty in speaking ["speech impediment" in NAB] was brought to him. They asked Jesus to lay his hand upon him.
>
> Jesus took him apart from the crowd, put his fingers into the man's ears and touched his tongue with spittle. Then, looking up to heaven, he groaned and said to him, "Ephphatha," that is, "Be opened."
>
> And his ears were opened, his tongue was loosened, and he began to speak clearly. Jesus ordered them not to tell anyone, but the more he insisted on this, the more they proclaimed it. The people were completely astonished and said, "He has done all things well; he makes the deaf hear and the dumb speak." (7:31-37)

Some expressions call to mind the writings of the prophets. For example, the man has a "speech impediment" (in Greek, *mogilalos*), a word used only one other time in the Bible, by Isaiah. It occurs in a song on the prophet's return from exile that celebrates what God will do and is doing for the people.

> "Have courage, do not fear.
> See, your God comes, demanding justice.
> He is the God who rewards,
> the God who comes to save you."
>
> Then will the eyes of the blind be opened
> and the ears of the deaf unsealed.
> Then will the lame leap as a hart
> and the tongue of the dumb sing and shout. (Is 35:4b-6)

This man can represent all the people who have been deaf to the word of God or impeded from proclaiming the gospel, including the Gentiles. Now they can hear and now they can speak out. These people, like their Jewish counterparts, have witnessed the healings of Jesus, but they seem to have missed his deeper message. So Jesus commands them to be quiet, as he has done so often with his own people.

This is the language of baptism. It is very physical and involves an intimate relationship between Jesus and the man. Jesus often touches people when he is healing, but this time a new feeling of ritual seems to be present. Jesus puts his fingers in the man's ears and uses his spittle to touch the man's tongue. Then Jesus looks up to heaven and groans aloud. This is probably the most graphic account of healing in the gospels. One time, in preparing for a class on this text, a friend caught me utterly off guard by taking me aside and repeating the gestures of Jesus. It's something I will not forget! This intimate gesture to me was filled with power.

And as the brief account ends, the unnamed Gentile can now hear and proclaim the gospel. His friends praise Jesus to the high heavens, saying, "He has done all things well." Finally, the household of God is coming together.

We are halfway through the Gospel of Mark. Chapter 8, which is a turning point for Jesus and his disciples, and for us today, comes next. This first half of Mark should have shaped us for what is to come. Recently I've traveled extensively in Southeast Asia, lecturing in Singapore, Manila, India, Thailand, Myanmar, Malaysia, China, and Japan. A tree common to all of these places is bamboo, and I sense a distinct connection between the nature of bamboo and the first half of Mark's gospel. Bamboo is a very strange plant, but it is versatile and has many wonderful uses. It can be used as a screen or a wall or for defense. It is the primary food of pandas, and as it is endangered by development, pandas are threatened with extinction. Because it is considered to bring good luck, most homes contain a plant or two. It is used to make vases, drinking vessels and flooring because it resists moisture, heat, and changes in temperature. It sways gracefully in the wind and through rain and snow and yet is sturdy enough to hold up a roof. It provides stakes to support other trees in gardens and around temples. And it creates haunting sounds and beautiful music in flutes and other musical instruments.

But bamboo seeds take at least five years to germinate and break through the ground. The seeds need proper spacing and constant tending with water and fertilizer. For five years the seed grows an intricate and extensive root system, and then suddenly it sprouts. Once sprouted, it literally shoots up and can grow as much as nine feet in six weeks! This is how Jesus has been tending his disciples. The seeds have been planted, and he is allowing an elaborate root system to develop that will allow for enormous, almost seemingly miraculous growth. But we are still in the underground, hidden root-building stage.

Let us pray.

> This is the answer that Job gave to Yahweh:
> I know that you are all powerful;
> no plan of yours can be thwarted.
> I spoke of things I did not understand,
> too wonderful for me to know.
> My ears had heard of you,
> but now my eyes have seen you.
> Therefore I retract all I have said,
> and in dust and ashes I repent. (Jb 42:1-6)

CHAPTER 6

Marked Forever

Mark 8 and 9

THE ACCOUNTS IN THE EARLIER CHAPTERS of Mark have demonstrated the faith of the Gentiles. They seem to hunger for the good news of God's kingdom that Jesus is announcing as strongly as anyone in the Jewish community. In fact, some believers among them, such as the Syrophoenician woman and the man who lives in the tombs, put the disciples to shame. Jesus has first fed his own Jewish community, and now Jesus has turned to the Gentile community. Historically, the faith moved from Jewish communities outward toward various Gentile communities, and eventually the two merged. This is the story told in the Acts of the Apostles.

Another story about reaching out to others can help us understand what is happening in Mark. Here is a story a rabbi told me many years ago; he claimed that it was true and that people still talked about it.

In the 1930s Scranton, Pennsylvania, was a rough town. These were hard times; and although people worked hard, there was never much to spare. People struggled to keep their families fed and a leak-proof roof over their heads. The Jewish community had a marvelous rabbi named Chaim Guterman. He was a very understanding man who was loved by everyone. He was a good listener and was filled with compassion for everyone. He knew everyone's name and always asked about those he hadn't seen for a while.

Many people wanted to do something for him, but there was little they could do because they had so little—an egg here and there, firewood or coal for the furnace. They did what they could. The baker was a little better off, and in the name of the community (although many thought he really did it for his own sense of satisfaction) he left a basket of freshly baked rolls on the front stoop of the rabbi's house each morning. Everyone on the street could smell them. Each morning, as soon as the rabbi had finished his prayers, he would open his front door and take the rolls to his wife and family for their breakfast. This enjoyable ritual went on for years and years. And every afternoon the rabbi would stop by the baker's to tell him how good the rolls were, thank him, and bless his work and everyone in the bakery.

One morning the rabbi went out to get the rolls and saw nothing there! He frowned, wondering if the baker was all right. He thought he would stop by later and see how things were with the baker's family. Unfortunately the day was hectic and he forgot. The next morning, when he opened the door, he was again disappointed to find no basket on the stoop. He reminded himself that he must see the baker's wife to make sure everything was all right. Again he got caught up in other things, and three days passed before he could stop for a visit.

The baker was delighted to see him. As the rabbi asked after his health and the health of his wife, his children, and the grandmother, the baker wondered what the rabbi was thinking. Finally, he said, "Rabbi, we're all just fine. There's no need to keep asking. In fact, we were starting to wonder if you were all right."

"Oh," the rabbi answered, puzzled. "Why would you worry about me? I'm fine, as you can see."

"Well, yes," said the baker, "but you didn't come by these last three days to tell me you enjoyed the rolls. Oh, not that you have to every day. It's just that you do come every day and I guess I've gotten used to it."

"That's the real reason why I'm here," said the rabbi. "You see, there haven't been any rolls for the last three days."

"What? That's impossible. I've delivered them right to your door every morning as I always have."

The two of them looked at each other in silence, and then the baker blurted out, "Someone must be stealing your rolls. And it must be an outsider, because everyone in our neighborhood knows those rolls are for you and your family. We should lie in wait for them and catch them in the act of stealing!"

The rabbi said, "Yes, we must be careful and see who is taking the rolls. But we are not going to pounce on them and embarrass them. If they are taking the rolls, they must be very hungry to steal three days in a row. We'll meet early tomorrow and see who it is. We have to help them." The baker wasn't exactly pleased with the rabbi's intention but agreed.

Next morning early, he put the basket by the rabbi's front door, as he always did, and then sauntered down the street and ducked into an alley where the rabbi waited. Within minutes a shabbily dressed woman appeared. She looked around and then quickly ran up the steps of the stoop, grabbed the basket of rolls, and ran down the street in the opposite direction. The rabbi grabbed hold of the baker to keep him from running after her.

Now they knew. The rabbi was pretty sure that he knew everyone in the neighborhood, but he hadn't recognized the woman. Either she was new in town or she was coming from somewhere else because she needed the food. The next morning he got up early and watched through the curtains in his front room. When she came up the steps, he opened the door. She froze. The rabbi smiled at her and then offered her the basket with the hot fresh rolls. "Here," he said, "they're yours, but my wife and children would love to have you come in and eat with us." The woman turned around and ran away.

The rabbi was disappointed. Maybe he had been too forceful. While he was talking with his wife in the kitchen, the doorbell rang. He ran back and opened the door. There was the woman but this time with three little children in tow. They were dressed in layers of clothes and looked hungry. The rabbi and his wife welcomed them in, and they had breakfast together.

The woman, who wasn't Jewish, said she had been prowling the streets looking for food for her children and couldn't believe her good luck when she saw the basket of fresh rolls on the stoop. The rabbi welcomed her into the neighborhood, and he and his family and the congregation helped her to find a place to live and a job. But the first thing the rabbi did was to introduce the woman to the baker. As they stood in the shop, the baker heard the rabbi say, "Oh, you will soon see how gracious the baker is. As soon as you're settled, he will bring you a basket of rolls every morning, just as he does for my family."

The woman was astounded and so was the baker. As soon as he caught the rabbi alone, he tried to beg off, saying, "Rabbi, those hot rolls every morning are just for your family." But the rabbi was firm: "If you can't afford the extra basket for her family, then my family will go without. This new family needs them, and for us, they're just extra treats." The baker was ashamed and offered to bring the rolls to both houses every morning.

As the rabbi thought about this experience with the woman and her children, he realized that others were also hurting. When he preached on the sabbath, his message was that God, blest be his Name, wants us to share our bread with the poor among us. He added that he was sure everyone knew someone who was poorer and more in need. And the congregation began setting up food pantries and also a program so that on certain days of the week anyone in need could work at the bakery or the grocery store or the butcher's or the dry goods store or the other stores and be paid so that they could get food. While the price of the food at the pantry was a pittance of the real cost, the people would have the knowledge that they had worked for what they bought.

Gradually the town began to change. When people crossed the unspoken boundaries of neighborhoods, the Jewish ghetto grew less defined, and other ethnic neighborhoods began to overlap as people talked with one another. It took years, but lots of groups, including churches and synagogues, joined together to make sure that no one would be hungry. And for decades after, no one ever went hungry in Scranton.

Don't we wish that life were more like that today? It has been before and it can be again. In fact, the foundation of Christianity, and of Judaism, is to share the resources that God has given us. Jesus is crossing the cultural divides, those unwritten but enforced boundaries of economic class, gender, race, religion, and ethnic tie, and he is pushing his disciples to do the same. All must eat together at one table. There can be no divides in the kingdom of God among God's beloved children. What God has done for the Jewish people, God does for everyone. At the time of Jesus, this was dangerous and new, and the disciples were disturbed by what Jesus was doing. They didn't want to be rushed; they had to be careful. They were already in trouble with the Jewish authorities and many people were scandalized by what Jesus was doing. Jesus, though, was drawn by the needs of the people. They stirred him to pity, to anger, and to action.

The first story in chapter 8 of Mark is another story of Jesus feeding a large crowd. In some ways it is similar to the first feeding story in Mark 6:34-44.

Soon afterwards Jesus was in the midst of another large crowd that obviously had nothing to eat. So he called his disciples and said to them, "I feel sorry for these people because they have been with me for three days and now have nothing to eat. If I send them to their homes hungry, they will faint on the way; some of them have come a long way."

His disciples replied, "Where in a deserted place like this could we get enough bread to feed these people?" He asked them, "How many loaves have you?" And they answered, "Seven."

Then he ordered the crowd to sit down on the ground. Taking the seven loaves and giving thanks, he broke them and handed them to his disciples to distribute. And they distributed them among the people. They also had some small fish, so Jesus said a blessing and asked that these be shared as well.

The people ate and were satisfied. The broken pieces were collected, seven wicker baskets full of leftovers. Now there had been about four thousand people. Jesus sent them away and immediately got into the boat with his disciples and went to the region of Dalmanutha. (Mk 8:1-10)

While this account has fewer details than the earlier one, a telling detail is Jesus' expression of concern for the crowd. From the beginning, Jesus is moved to pity and concern that the people might collapse along the way if they have to go home hungry after spending three days with him. It is Jesus who initiates the action and the disciples who question what he is doing.

Their involvement is limited: they distribute the bread and later the fish and collect the leftovers, but that is all. It seems that this entire chapter is pointing to Jesus and providing a startling new answer to the question "Who is he?"

The people have been with Jesus for "three days," which can be seen as a reference to the three days of the Tridium, the liturgical celebration of the life, death, and resurrection of Jesus. The crowd can represent the Gentile church that has experienced and will continue to experience the presence of the risen Lord. Jesus becomes the Lord of all. All are welcomed to eat at his table. The early church is witness to that reality. No distinction is made in this account between Jew and Gentile or between men and women. By the end, we know only that four thousand were filled; we don't know who they were.

The numbers of available provisions are also different. Where there were five loaves (the five books of Moses?) in chapter 6, there are now seven, perhaps a reference to the seven deacons from Gentile communities in Acts 6:3, 5, and 31:8. At the time, seven was also considered a number that could encompass all numbers and all peoples. In this story, the fish were distributed later, separate from the sharing of the bread, and no number is given. The focus seems to be clearly on the bread. And significantly, in the first story Jesus blessed God (*berakah* is the word used; in the Jewish tradition, Jews bless people and not objects). In this account Jesus also blesses the fish.

The ritual of Eucharist is so familiar that we seldom think that the ritual is based on making sure that everyone is fed, that everyone has enough to live on, just as God feeds and nourishes our hearts and souls. Our religious worship is meant not only to be symbolic or liturgical but also to identify a lifestyle characterized by an awareness and sharing of all food, water, and other resources so that everyone is satisfied. Every time we eat and break bread with one another in the Eucharist we are also supposed to remember those who are hungry.

Hunger and malnutrition kill more than five million children each year, and when we add in children who die from related diseases and a lack of water, the number increases to twenty-five million. In a 2004 statement, "The State of Food Insecurity in the World," the United Nations' Food and Agriculture Organization estimated that there were 852 million hungry people in the world in 2000-2002, up by 18 million from the mid-1990s and still growing. The FAO suggested a twofold approach to fighting hunger. The first step is to help the poor increase their ability to produce food or earn income to buy food while giving immediate aid to the most needy families and individuals. The second step calls for large-scale national and international programs to promote agricultural and rural development. To routinely share the Eucharist with others and not actively work to reduce hunger is hypocritical and insulting to the Lord, who is the bread of life.

The story is told of Bishop Samuel Ruiz of Chiapas, Mexico. As the leader of his diocese for years, he was pleased with the changes that had been implemented. The churches were filled to overflowing for masses, with many people coming for the sacraments and devotions. On Sunday afternoons after the masses in the cathedral were over, he would have his driver take him out to visit his flock. They would drive through the fields, countryside, and estates. One Sunday afternoon he was horrified to see one of his parishioners, someone he knew well, beating senseless an indigenous worker who was tied to a tree. Bishop Ruiz had the driver stop the car and he got out. The man, who didn't seem to be ashamed of what he was doing, told the bishop that the man was lazy and insubordinate and he was being beaten because he would not work an extra eight hours that day to finish the harvest. Although it was Sunday, the harvest was more important than worship.

Bishop Ruiz said that that was the day he woke up and realized that more than 60 percent of his diocese was composed of indigenous peoples living like slaves on large plantations and estates. He added that he had been like a fish in the water with his eyes wide open yet seeing nothing. Chapter 8 of Mark asks us, and the disciples of Jesus, if we have awakened? Do we see and understand anything at all? The disciples showed their continuing lack of understanding by their questions.

When the people have been fed, Jesus dismisses them and moves to get in the boat with his disciples. Once again the Pharisees come forward to argue with him. Mark's account says that they were looking for some heavenly sign from him. Jesus' response is revelatory: "With a sigh from the depths of his spirit he said, 'Why does this age seek a sign? I assure you, no such sign will be given it!' Then he left them, got into the boat again, and went off to the other shore" (8:12-13 NAB). Jesus is angry and speaks to them forcefully, using the language of a prophet in the tradition of Moses. The Pharisees would understand his reference—only those who do not believe ask for signs.

> Would that today you heard his voice!
> Do not be stubborn, as at Meribah,
> In the desert, on that day at Massah,
> When your ancestors challenged me,
> And they put me to the test.
>
> For forty years they wearied me and I said,
> "They are a people of inconstant heart;
> They have not known my ways."
> So I declared an oath in my anger,
> "Never shall they enter my rest." (Ps 95:7b-11)

Like Moses, the lawgiver and the liberator of his people, Jesus has been feeding the people in the desert, yet they do not see what God is doing.

Although this is a new generation, they are not unlike their ancestors in the desert who constantly murmured against Moses and asked for signs. Their hearts are hardened. Just before, Mark described the disciples as having hardened hearts (Mk 6:52). The hearts of Mark's own communities in the sixties were also hardening, and Mark was writing for them. Or are our hearts hardening and is Mark addressing us? Signs were not given then and signs are not given now. Signs are for unbelievers, for those whose hearts have gone cold. Jesus' own heart is moved to pity by these crowds of people who are hungry, thirsty, and suffering, and he feeds them with bread and fish while he also feeds them with hope, comfort, acceptance, inclusion, welcome, and dignity. Is this what our churches and communities are known for? Is this what is evoked by our liturgies? Or, even after being fed over and over again with a surfeit of riches in spirituality, prayer, worship, preaching, and music, is "this generation" just like the one that made Jesus so angry?

Throughout scripture, "this generation" is never used in a positive sense. In the Book of Deuteronomy it refers to the generation that fled from Egypt into the desert as "a deceitful and crooked generation" (Dt 32:5). This expression is associated with people who want proof, who test God, and who complain incessantly. Moses cried out to God about the generation he has been entrusted with: "Why do you find fault with me? Why do you put Yahweh to the test?" (Ex 17:2). This describes a people without faith. Unfortunately, this is also an apt description of the disciples in this next scene. They have seen and witnessed Jesus' teaching and healing, and all they can think about is whether or not they are going to go hungry.

The One Loaf

After the second feeding and the continuing dispute with the Pharisees, Jesus and the disciples climb back into the boat and cross to the other side. The following text (8:14-21) clearly shows the disciples' total lack of understanding of who Jesus is. At this point, Jesus sounds totally exasperated with them. His language carries echoes of Moses and the problems he faced as the Israelites grew dissatisfied in the desert (Dt 29:2-4).

> The disciples had forgotten to bring more bread and had only one loaf with them in the boat. Then Jesus warned them, "Keep your eyes open and beware of the yeast of the Pharisees and the yeast of Herod." And they said to one another, "He saw that we have no bread."
>
> Aware of this, Jesus asked them, "Why are you talking about the loaves you are short of? Do you not see or understand? Are your minds closed? Have you eyes that don't see and ears that don't hear? And do you not remember when I broke the five loaves among five

thousand? How many baskets full of leftovers did you collect?" They answered, "Twelve." "And having seven loaves for the four thousand, how many wicker baskets of leftovers did you collect?" They answered, "Seven." Then Jesus said to them, "Do you still not understand?" (8:14-21)

By speaking about leaven, Jesus is trying to warn them to be on their guard. Immediately the disciples conclude that the one loaf of bread they have isn't sufficient. Leaven (yeast), a bacteria that causes fermentation, is what causes the dough to rise. But leaven also refers to something hidden in something else and as used in scripture it usually had negative connotations, often referring to the evil tendencies and inclinations of the human heart (see, for example, 1 Cor 5:8). Leaven also means something that has a corrosive or destructive influence over a long period of time. It can be the malice, evil, or violence of those who keep others from knowing or following the truth. Leaven can also have a positive connotation. Jesus describes the coming of the kingdom of heaven like the action of leaven—slowly, it deeply penetrates the world and gradually transforms it.

But Jesus isn't talking about bread. Instead, he's warning them against slipping into the attitudes and practices of the Pharisees, "traditions" that have become more important than God's divine will for people. The leaven of the Pharisees includes all those things that Jesus talked about in Mark 7, those things men and women do in their hearts that divide and splinter the human community. He also warns them of the leaven of Herod—his immorality, his murder of the prophet John, his arrogance and brutality, which instilled fear into the people. This reference to leaven also refers back to some short parables of Mark 2, of not putting a new patch of cloth onto an old garment or placing new wine into old wineskins. What Jesus is doing is a new thing and should not be mixed with the old.

Jesus asks the disciples seven short questions. They can answer only two, the two questions about how many baskets were left over from the two feedings. They are hardening their hearts against Jesus. Early in the gospel the Pharisees quickly hardened their hearts against Jesus, sensing his power. Then in Jesus' hometown, hardness of heart prevented those who had grown up with him from hearing his words. Now resistance grows among the disciples. Jesus' first question to them is why they are worrying about having only one loaf of bread. Earlier when they went out to preach the good news, he told them to take nothing in their purses. They were to rely on the graciousness and hospitality and openness of others who were hungry for the gospel. Even though they have one loaf, they think they have none (8:16).

They do not understand that Jesus is with them in the boat and that he is the one loaf and that is all they need. If they do not see this, they can very easily end up like the Pharisees or others who refuse to see or listen or obey Jesus. And they don't understand the importance of the leftovers, the fragments of the food that was shared. There was enough to satisfy everyone's hunger, but there was even more! Jesus, the one loaf, is the bread that feeds and nourishes us, and there is more than enough for everyone. And we become what we eat. We become the good news of God sent out to feed others, to set others free, and to welcome them into the embrace of God's wholeness and forgiveness. We have everything we need. And Jesus' last question to the disciples is "Do you still not understand?"

The brief account that follows seems to connect to one of Jesus' questions to the disciples, "Have you eyes that don't see and ears that don't hear?" This time Jesus heals a blind man, as earlier he healed a deaf man with a speech impediment. This occurs in Bethsaida, reportedly Peter's hometown, and it appears as a clear message that Jesus is attempting to heal the blindness of Peter and the other disciples. In a sense the story is a further warning to the disciples to be on their guard, to keep their eyes open (8:15).

How well do we see? When someone asks us, we usually answer in terms of how good our vision is. It's 20/20 or 20/100 or we're nearsighted or farsighted or color-blind. This isn't the kind of sight to which Jesus referred. A story I often tell during Lent illustrates how blind we all are. This is a story of something that actually happened in a famous college of medicine in Glasgow, Scotland, that is known for its innovative surgeries and therapies for people with serious vision problems.

There is a doctor, a skilled surgeon on the faculty, who gives only one lecture a semester, and everyone goes to it. He is revered and respected for new techniques in surgery, and he is loved by his patients. Many of the students know of his reputation; and they want to be like him, a professional who is both physician and friend.

His lecture is in a packed auditorium, with the students sitting in the tiers of rows going up to the ceiling. Everyone who attends the lectures is sworn to secrecy, and no one ever tells what goes on. He has nearly a hundred doctoral or research students each semester, and they set up the experiment.

He begins by telling them that if they want to be good surgeons they must learn two things above all else. First, they must learn detail, to observe, to see what others miss. This is essential in a field of minute organs such as eyes, filled with tiny blood vessels and nerves. Their eyes must become microscopes and magnifying glasses.

The second thing they must learn, and this is harder, he warned, is to have tough stomachs that are not connected to their eyes. They will often be seeing ooze, bloody messes, and all sorts of things that are going to make them nauseous. "Well," he told them, "get over it, and get over it fast. You can't be in an operating room, bent over someone's eye, and decide you have to throw up because of what you smell or see. If you can't control your stomach muscles, well think about another area of medicine." This always elicits laughter because this is already some-thing they've learned. Then he tells them it is time to do an experiment to see if they have the guts to be doctors.

He steps aside to reveal rows and rows of small petri dishes with all sorts of things in them: ooze of every color and texture. He tells them that his assistants have been concocting all sorts of brew for the dishes for days. The students nod wearily. He tells them that anything and everything is in those dishes. Every student in the auditorium is to watch and do exactly as he does. If they choose not to, they can leave.

He arbitrarily picks up one of the dishes, swirls the mixture around with two or three of his fingers, and then lifts his hand to his mouth and sucks on his finger. There are groans, and already some students are looking a bit woozy.

"On your feet. Everyone file down, take your dish, and do exactly what I just did. You have to get past whatever your stomach tells you or you will not make it as a surgeon." They dutifully do as they're told. It's grim. Students are racing for the door and vomiting; some are wiping their mouths, others are valiantly laughing, and finally they are all done. They take their seats again, and he looks at them. "Well, I commend you. Every single one of you managed to do it. You've got possibilities!" "But," he continued, "every single one of you failed miserably."

They are shocked. What could he mean? He waits until it's quiet and says, "Let me show you." He picks up the dish again and stirs the mix-ture. With his fingers, he points out that he stirred it with two fingers, his index finger and ring finger, and then he sucked on his middle finger, which hadn't gone into the disgusting mixture. The students are appalled. He says to them solemnly, "What did I tell you was the first thing you had to learn? It was to see, to observe and to pick up every detail. You didn't and so you have all put yourselves through a horror, needlessly." This was a lesson they would not forget, and they joined the ranks of those who swore never to reveal what happened in that room that morning.

How well do we see who Jesus is and what Jesus is doing? Are we in need of having our eyes opened, like the blind man at Bethsaida?

When they came to Bethsaida, Jesus was asked to touch a blind man who was brought to him. He took the blind man by the hand and led him outside the village. When he had put spittle on his eyes and laid his hands upon him, he asked, "Can you see anything?" The man, who was beginning to see, replied, "I see people! They look like trees, but they move around." Then Jesus laid his hands on his eyes again and the man could see perfectly. His sight was restored and he could see everything clearly.

Then Jesus sent him home saying, "Do not return to the village." (8:22-26)

This story has many of the characteristics of the story of the deaf man with a speech impediment. Both men are taken away from the crowd, and the connection between them and Jesus is intimate, sensate, and intense. Jesus takes this blind man by the hand, as you would a child. This gesture implies that he can trust Jesus and that he will be cared for. Jesus again uses spittle, this time on the man's eyes, and then holds his hands over them. Healing did not instantly occur. As with the healing of the deaf man, when Jesus groaned, seeming to wrench the man free of his affliction, it takes effort. Jesus touches the man's eyes a second time before his sight is fully restored. After the first touch, the blind man says, "I see people! They look like trees, but they move around." This seems a strange thing to say, unless he could see once before. He knows what people and trees are supposed to look like. The second time the man can see perfectly; with his restored sight, the world is seen clearly.

It will take more than two times for Jesus to make his disciples see clearly what his words mean and who he is. Jesus has taken his own disciples off by themselves over and over again so that they can hear and know what others do not. Twice they have seen him feed the crowds, and twice they have failed to grasp what they are seeing.

As the account ends, Jesus admonishes the man not to return to his village. The warning means that he is not to go back to the old ways that hinder and block what Jesus is doing in the world. He is not to go back to the people he came from, people who rejected Jesus. The man is not to go back to the old traditions. And Jesus is also speaking to the disciples, and to us: if the man returns, he would find himself blind once more.

The disciples, sadly, "have eyes but no sight; ears but no hearing." The disciples will require more time to see, to understand and to soften their hearts to Jesus and to teaching. From this point, the disciples lose more and more of their vision and grow myopic. Their sight and understanding of Jesus have become blurred and indistinct because of their fears and lost hopes. It won't really be until after the resurrection that they will see everything clearly. It's interesting to note that the blind man saw people who looked like trees and that, strangely enough, it will be a tree that allows the disciples to see clearly. With the end of this story of the blind man, the next segment of the gospel begins. It in turn will close with another story of healing a blind man, this time a person named as Bartimaeus (10:46-52).

Who Do You Say That I Am?

For many scripture scholars and theologians, Jesus' question to the disciples, "Who do you say that I am?" is the halfway point in the Gospel of Mark. This is also the question put to us. As we grow in conversion and obedience to the word of God in Jesus, we must seek to answer it with more depth and more understanding. In the past, scholars have often referred to Mark's gospel as an account of the passion, with a few introductory questions and texts. It is better described as a primer on conversion, a summons to discipleship. True discipleship calls us to sink further and further in the waters of our baptisms, which are mysterious, fearful, and wondrously filled with grace.

At this midway point—there are only sixteen chapters in Mark—there is an immediacy that is relentless as it builds in intensity and demands our response. Along with the disciples, we must wrestle with words and the presence of God in Jesus, seeking to know the truth of who this man really is. In the words of Simone Weil in *Waiting for God*, "It is hard to sift through our lives to the actual truth of the person of Jesus." The last eight chapters of Mark bring another call—the call to the cross of Jesus and the call to deny one's self to follow in the footsteps of Jesus.

> Jesus set out with his disciples for the villages around Caesarea Philippi; and on the way he asked them, "Who do people say I am?" And they told him, "Some say you are John the Baptist; others say you are Elijah or one of the prophets."
>
> Then Jesus asked them, "but you, who do you say I am?" Peter answered, "You are the Messiah." And he ordered them not to tell anyone about him. (8:27-30)

As Jesus sets out with his disciples, "on the way" refers not only to a geographical path between points and between Jewish and Gentile regions and cities but also to a way of life, a way of obedience and service, a way of surrender. It is the way of Jesus that leads to the Father. It is the way of the cross. It is the way of prophets who speak truthfully, knowing that this may result in persecution or even death. This is also the way of Christian initiation demonstrating the way the Spirit works in a person's life and in the life of the church. One belongs to the way along with other followers of Jesus. Early on in Christian history, the first Christians were called the Followers of the Way (see Acts 9:2; 18:25; and 19:23).

At this point in his ministry, Jesus is interested in finding out from his disciples who they, and others who have been listening to him preach, believe him to be. The first question put to the disciples, "Who do people say that I am?" is easier to answer. The response is varied but consistent. People think Jesus is John the Baptist or Elijah or one of the other prophets, one who defends the honor of God and defines the nature of true worship of God and cares for the poor and works for the coming of peace with justice. A prophet listens only to the word of God and is often persecuted for that faithfulness.

Jesus then redirects the question to them (and to us): "Who do you say that I am?" Jesus wants them to take responsibility for what they are thinking and feeling and to speak aloud their belief or lack of it. Peter, who is the first to answer, speaks on behalf of all of them. "You are the Messiah." It seems surprising that Jesus warns them "not to tell anyone about him." This warning has been given a number of times, usually to people who are grateful for their healing but who do not understand who Jesus is and what he is teaching. They take one piece of what they have experienced or want Jesus to be and ignore what is most crucial to his person and presence. "You are the Messiah" sounds like the right answer. The term "Messiah" speaks clearly of the presence of God with the people in justice and peace.

However, at the time of Jesus there were conflicting ideas about the Messiah and what it would mean not only for the Jews but also for Romans and unbelievers. Religious hope was interlaced with more vehement political, economic, and nationalistic hopes of overthrowing the Romans and regaining the temple and Israel's place as a nation to be reckoned with in regard to wealth, prestige, power, and domination. And Peter and the disciples are not exempt from these secular hopes. They also have hopes and expectations of power, of leadership, and of securing a place at the top with Jesus, even though they have been taken aside and taught much more than the others.

This is a second call to conversion. It is the call to the cross and to following the Son of Man. It begins with a proclamation of what is going to befall Jesus, the Son of Man. Yahweh often addressed the prophets as "sons of man." (See, for example, the Book of Ezekiel where the term is used this way as many as ninety times.) In the newer testament, the Son of Man is a title that Jesus uses almost solely to speak about himself. It seems to represent Jesus' own understanding of who he believes himself to be, both as the beloved son and servant of God and as a prophet who will suffer much because of his faithfulness to God his Father. The Son of Man also appears in the Book of Daniel as a figure of judgment.

> I continued watching the nocturnal vision:
> One like a son of man came on the clouds of heaven. He faced the One of Great Age and was brought into his presence.
> Dominion, honor and kingship were given him, and all the peoples and nations of every language served him. His dominion is eternal and shall never pass away; his kingdom will never be destroyed. (Dn 7:13-14)

This figure in Daniel and in popular belief was someone who suffered much as one of the people. He was the poor Jew with no power but who was somehow involved in the judgment of the nation and the coming of the messianic kingdom of peace and justice.

Jesus uses this knowledge of Daniel in telling the disciples something of who he is, and the disciples must listen closely. We must also listen closely.

> Jesus then began to teach them that the Son of Man had to suffer many things and be rejected by the elders, the chief priests and the teachers of the Law. He would be killed, and after three days rise again. Jesus said all this quite openly, so that Peter took him aside and began to protest strongly. But Jesus, turning around and looking at his disciples, rebuked Peter saying, "Get behind me, Satan! You are thinking not as God does, but as people do." (Mk 8:31-33)

Jesus lays it out in front of them. This is what Jesus believes will happen to him. He has read and reflected on the prophets, especially Isaiah (see chapters 50-53). Jesus sees himself as the beloved son and servant of God, and that means, in the tradition of the prophets, that he will also suffer because of his obedience to God's word and will. He speaks of this openly.

Peter reacts strongly. He cannot accept Jesus' words. He does not want to face rejection and suffering, and he doesn't want Jesus to be speaking like that in front of the others. So Peter takes Jesus apart from the other disciples and protests. Some translations use the word "rebuke." It is a strong word, the same word that Jesus has used to quiet unclean spirits (Mk 1:25; 9:25) and to quiet the storm (Mk 4:39). And Jesus rebukes Peter.

Peter and the other disciples have made a decision to follow Jesus, but suffering and death are not part of their expectations or plans. Jesus turns around (a hint of the need for conversion), looks at all the disciples but speaks to Peter, rebuking him in the harshest of language: "Get out of my sight, you Satan! You are not judging by God's standards but by man's!" The message to Peter and to all of them is clear and blunt: "You're wrong. You're in my way. You have become a stumbling block to what I am and what I have come to do. Get behind me. Start following me and don't move out ahead of me with your ideas and ways." Jesus describes Peter as "Satan," which means "hinderer," because Peter is hindering Jesus' mission and message. He is preventing others from coming to know who Jesus really is. Jesus is revealed as the Son of Man who has come to judge all the nations with regard to what they have done for the poor for the sake of justice out of obedience to God. In Jesus' suffering he receives the power and the authority to judge justly all of humankind.

What Peter is doing is understandable. He is trying to dissuade Jesus from a path that will result in Jesus' humiliation, horrible suffering, and death. But Peter is also trying to turn Jesus aside from the way, the way of the loving son and servant that is the way of forgiveness and mercy, the way that heals and makes whole and includes everyone—man and woman, Jew and Gentile, the "unclean" and the righteous alike. All are being called home to be the beloved children of God.

Nonetheless, Peter's illusions must be faced directly and named for what they are: Satan. Subtly and pervasively, Peter is succumbing to fear, to wanting to be accepted, to wanting things to remain as they are, to siding with those who are hardening their hearts and wills against Jesus. In rejecting Jesus' description of what lies ahead, Peter is also rejecting Jesus' very being and that the cross is part of the way. Jesus must be very clear in describing what is going to be required of those who come after him.

> Then Jesus called the people and his disciples and said, "If you want to follow me, deny yourself, take up your cross and follow me. For if you choose to save your life, you will lose it; and if you lose your life for my sake and for the sake of the Gospel, you will save it.
> What good is it to gain the whole world but destroy yourself? There is nothing you can give to recover your life. I tell you: If anyone is ashamed of me and of my words among this adulterous and sinful people, the Son of Man will also be ashamed of him when he comes in the Glory of his Father with the holy angels." (8:34-38)

We need to keep in mind that Mark is writing this in the mid-sixties of the first century, long after the death and resurrection of Jesus, and that he is writing it for people who have been baptized and who, as a result, also face a similar fate of rejection and persecution. Some held fast after their baptisms, but others, like Peter, rejected Jesus and the reality of suffering and the cross as part of the way. Peter and others, and we ourselves, have at one time or another abandoned our commitments and the vows of our baptisms, which means abandonment of Jesus' teachings and person.

As a result of Jesus' first invitation to follow him, Peter, Andrew, James, and John and all the others abandoned their old ways of life, their work, and their understanding of the holy. This second call demands that they abandon their ideas of who God is and of how God brings the kingdom and good news of forgiveness into the world. They are to place themselves in the hands of God and not do things the way the world does them. Instead, they will follow this mysterious God that Jesus is seeking to reveal. And at the core of the way of Jesus is the cross, suffering, and death in obedience to God's word. We followers must be faithful in the face of what others will do to us because of our belonging to God and God alone. This second call to conversion, the call that includes the cross, makes responding to the initial call look easy.

What if everything we have done in our religious living and personal relationship with God has been for the wrong reasons? What if we do what we're supposed to do because we think we're going to be rewarded for it? What if we continue to be believers or go to church because of what it does for us? What if we use our religious practices to avoid facing conflict, confrontation, or the necessity of acting on the word of God? What if most of what we do in our religion is an attempt to save us from suffering, rejection, persecution, and death?

Jesus' words to his disciples and to the crowd—all those who are considering following him—are a clarion call to battle, a call to face opposition. They must be realistic about what being a Christian involves: rejection, suffering, death, and resurrection. We must begin by denying ourselves so that we will not deny Jesus. We must give up our desire and hope that God will intervene and save us or make our lives easier. If we seek to have a good life without being bound to others, we are denying Jesus. Instead we are to seek to do the will of God, to serve others, to grasp people by the hand and help them to resist injustice and whatever harms them. We must oppose all evil, which dehumanizes people.

Many theologians believe that Peter's protest in Mark 8:32 represents Peter's first open denial of Jesus and that Peter will continue to rail against Jesus' teachings and grow more resistant to Jesus' message about the coming of the kingdom. Peter's resistance will come to a head in the courtyard of the high priest when Peter curses and denies Jesus three times. Peter's faith will not be restored until after the death and resurrection of Jesus.

Jesus' words to the disciples and the crowd to "take up your cross and follow me" would have instilled horror in everyone who heard them. The Romans were hated as much for their brutality as they were for being an insensitive and sacrilegious occupying force, and crucifixion was the usual method of silencing anyone who moved against Rome. Thousands of executions took place. Crucifixion was imposed on those who had no power, those whom the Romans despised. Those crucified suffered a horrible death, a death of utter humiliation. Those who heard Jesus would have recoiled at his words.

And so Mark is telling his community of believers, those already baptized, that they may have to face this same reality. To believe is to open oneself to the possibility of martyrdom. A believer must be absolutely steadfast to follow the crucified and risen Lord, the Son of Man.

Jesus' words and witness to what God wants for all people lead to his rejection and death, but also to his resurrection. We should remember that Mark is writing years later with the gift of hindsight. The only hint the disciples had of what lay ahead was the prophetic words of Jesus about the rejection and persecution that might visit his followers. The difficulties faced by Jesus and his disciples are the same difficulties that face Jesus' followers today.

> Jesus did not get into trouble with the powers of his day simply by challenging his individual hearers. He challenged the very systems of his society—the cornerstones. Just as the values of Madison Avenue, Wall Street, and the Pentagon conflict with the gospel, so too with Jesus and the institutions of his time: he took on the power structures of his own day, religious and civil alike.
>
> Confrontation was not popular in first-century Palestine. It is not popular anywhere in the twenty-first. To bring gospel values to bear on labor practices, governmental decisions, and even religious traditions and policies is no more popular for a follower of Jesus than it was for him. He was told that they had their laws. Those who dare to bring his values to today's world are told the same thing.

Yes, discipleship does have its cost—anyone who has dared to bring the gospel to bear on his or her own life knows that. Discipleship has its cost—whether we feel it may be a good litmus test for discerning if we are truly following on his path, or pursuing a false trail. (Jeanne de Celles, "A New Heaven and a New Earth," quoted online on "Daily Dig," http://www.bruderhof.org)

We are now halfway through the gospel. This is the time for us to think hard about our path. Can we face the cross? Will we walk the way with Jesus? Will we lay aside our ways and fall in behind Jesus? These questions follow from the question Jesus poses to all his followers: "Who do you say that I am?" Who do we think God is in Jesus? What is demanded of us? Whom are we following? Are we following anyone other than ourselves and looking for what we can get out of the practice of religion? Is our faith just empty words or is it put into practice? Is our faith revelatory of the good news for the poor? Do we judge the world with the Son of Man by standing with those crying out for justice or do we stand in opposition to Jesus? These are not easy questions. It is time to turn our hearts and lives and our ideas of who we think Jesus is inside out. If we answer the call to conversion truthfully, we may be disgraced; if we rebuke Jesus, we may not make it into the kingdom of God. Like Peter, we may be the stone that blocks the path to Jesus for others.

Eugene LaVerdiere puts it clearly.

For Christians, refusing to lose one's life for Jesus' sake is the same as being ashamed of him. . . . Like the entire discourse (8:34-38), the saying is addressed to the Markan communities and anyone for whom the cross was a stumbling block or foolishness (see 1 Cor 1:23). Jesus spoke of those who are ashamed of him and his words as belonging to "this faithless and sinful generation." . . . There are those who belong to this generation, and there are those who do not belong.

While "this generation" stands in contrast with the final coming of the Son of Man, it does not refer to the present era, but rather to the people living in it. Nor does it refer to everyone in the present era, but only those who are ashamed of Christ and his words. (*The Beginning of the Gospel*, 2:37)

Do we belong to this generation or do we belong to the Son of Man, seeking to be faithful to our baptisms and to our new relationship to God and one another? The first line of the next chapter hints at what awaits us if we are faithful and true: "Truly I tell you, there are some here who will not die before they see the kingdom of God coming with power" (9:1). And chapter 9 continues with the story of the transfiguration of Jesus. The story begins with the words "Six days later." So it is on the seventh day that Peter, James, and John experience the glory of God shining through Jesus.

The disciples need to see him in his glory immediately. After all, Jesus has just announced to them what he faces and what all his followers and friends must face in the future—the cross.

The seventh day is Sunday and so this glimpse of glory is also a resurrection story. Mark draws often upon the post-Easter faith of his community and inserts it into the text as preparation for those facing baptism or reentry into the community. It is also written for those who want to enter more deeply into the mystery of who Jesus is, which will not be fully revealed until after his death and resurrection. Paradoxically, it is only in the cross that we can recognize Jesus for who he truly is, the beloved and loving son and servant of God. Believers will understand the allusions to Moses and Elijah in the text (Ex 24:16-17 and 1 Kgs 19). Like many in Mark's church, we read this account through the eyes of belief, whether we have failed or stayed faithful.

> Six days later, Jesus took with him Peter and James and John, and led them up a high mountain. There his appearance was changed before their eyes. Even his clothes shone, becoming as white as no bleach of this world could make them. Elijah and Moses appeared to them; the two were talking with Jesus.
>
> Then Peter spoke and said to Jesus, "Master, it is good that we are here; let us make three tents, one for you, one for Moses and one for Elijah." For he did not know what to say; they were overcome with awe. But a cloud formed, covering them in a shadow, and from the cloud came this word, "This is my Son, the Beloved; listen to him." And suddenly, as they looked around, they no longer saw anyone except Jesus with them. (9:2-8)

The story is one of awe and terror, of seeing and being blind, of listening and not hearing. Jesus has taken Peter, James, and John off to pray. And what happens to Jesus when he prays is a complete metamorphosis: his very person is altered and it shines through his clothing. Suddenly, Moses and Elijah appear in conversation with him. Both these towering leaders of the old covenant—Moses the liberator and the lawgiver, and Elijah the greatest of the prophets—died in peculiar ways. It is said that God alone knows where Moses died and that God loved him so much he was buried by God. Elijah is said not to have died but to have disappeared in a fiery chariot. It was believed that Elijah would appear again to signal the coming of the Messiah. Are they talking with Jesus about his death? We get the impression that the three disciples are too dazzled to understand what is being revealed to them.

Peter speaks and stumbles over his words. He is talking to overcome his fear. Then the voice of God the Father interrupts his planning. It is a voice that commands obedience from the disciples and confirms the authority of Jesus' words, mission, and person. The voice of God speaks from a cloud, a passing reference to the presence of Yahweh as a cloud by day and fire by night during the exodus (Ex 13:21). But this is a revelation of the Trinity. The words proclaimed from the cloud are echoes of Jesus' baptism, but here they seem to be aimed at the disciples. Less than a week before, they had been asked, "Who do you say that I am?" Now they are told who Jesus is: "This is my beloved Son. Listen to him."

The word "transfiguration" can be broken into two parts: "trans," a preposition that indicates a bridge across or through, and "figure," meaning the human body. Suddenly, for just a moment, the disciples can see through Jesus' body into the glory of God. Jesus' body is a bridge between God and us, though the disciples cannot begin to fathom what this means. The cross will be a bridge for us to God. The cross is the mark of the Christian. It marks pain and promise. It marks agony and acceptance, horror and hope, and it marks loneliness and complete and utter love.

The Gospel of Mark is written for believers, and we must never stop listening to Jesus as we are drawn into deeper intimacy and drawn closer to the cross and resurrection. Peter and the other disciples have a long way to go before they turn to pick up their cross and follow Jesus. For now, they shudder at its introduction into their lives and push it away.

When the disciples look around, they see only Jesus. Jesus is alone with them. For believers, this experience is filled with hope. There is only Jesus. Jesus is always with us and we are never alone. As they come down the mountain they are charged once again not to speak of what they have just witnessed. Again, it seems they still have no inkling of what it means. Only when "the Son of Man be risen from the dead" will anyone know that the crucified and risen Jesus is the Son of God, Son of Man, calling us to come after him.

The disciples discuss among themselves what the phrase "rising from the dead" might mean. Jesus is teaching them again, telling them that, yes, as it was foretold, Elijah would come before the Son of Man, and that Elijah has come, in the person of John the Baptist. He teaches them that the Son of Man must suffer greatly and be treated with contempt. He is trying to prepare them for his death, that everyone must die, even the Messiah. They don't want to hear of it. They can't imagine the Messiah dying before he brings the glory of God any more than they can imagine who Jesus actually is. It takes the experience of baptism and the transfiguring of our lives to plant the seed of resurrection in us. Jesus is intent on balancing their ideas of glory and power with the reality of the world and his coming death.

Why did Jesus take Peter, James, and John up the mountain with him to pray? These three have entered Jairus's house and have witnessed Jesus grasping the little girl by the hand and raising her up. They will be with him in the garden when he is handed over to be killed. Why did Jesus choose them? Why does Jesus choose any of us? A story about another teacher may help us better understand.

Once upon a time there was a master who had many disciples, and, of course, there was an inner group that was privy to his personal talks, explanations, and even shared prayer with him. One of the disciples who had left everything to follow him sought to gain entrance into that group.

One day a friend of his came to visit, and they walked together and talked. The disciple talked only of the master—his goodness, wisdom, understanding, and how privileged he was to be allowed to be one of his disciples. His friend listened closely and watched his friend's face. He was glowing and alive with his enthusiasm and love for his teacher. When questioned, the disciple said that he would do anything for his master, follow him anywhere, that he trusted him completely and was secure in being one of his followers. The friend left, wondering whether he too should leave everything and become a follower.

Later that same evening the master sent word for the disciple to come and walk with him awhile. The disciple was overjoyed. He was being singled out to walk with the master. What a blessing, what a gift. The master mentioned within moments that he had overheard the disciple speaking about him to his friend. Immediately the disciple said, "Master, I meant every word that I said. It is all true. I would go anywhere and do anything for you. I am so grateful that you have chosen me to be one of your disciples, and I'm so honored that you would take this time to walk with me. I am so overwhelmed by your goodness I don't know what to say."

The master waited until he had finished and then asked him quietly, "Do you know why I chose you to be one of my disciples?"

"Uh, no," replied the disciple. "I never thought that much about it."

"Well," said the master, "I chose you because you needed it more than a lot of others."

The disciple was devastated. The master did not say anything else and they continued to walk together, alone in the oncoming night.

The Healing of a Boy with a Demon and the Marks of Discipleship

Chapter 9 follows a pattern familiar to Mark. It begins with an experience of Jesus, such as the baptism or, as here, the transfiguration. The experience is followed by the revelation, "You are my Son" or "This is my Son. Listen to him." And then comes a confrontation, a struggle with a demon or Satan or an unclean spirit.

The account of the first confrontation in Mark 9 serves to highlight the disciples' growing confusion and their inability to accept what Jesus is saying or to recognize their need for prayer and conversion. It highlights Jesus' growing frustration with everyone around him, including his own disciples, who belong to "this faithless generation." The battle is over a child who is first described as "possessed by a dumb spirit" and later as having symptoms of epilepsy or an illness that causes severe convulsions.

The conversation is between Jesus and the boy's father, who is part of the crowd listening to discussions between the other disciples and some Jewish teachers of the Law. The man explains his son's illness and reports that Jesus' disciples were unable to help. It seems that Jesus cries out his frustration that so many have seen and yet don't believe: "You faithless people. How long must I be with you? How long must I put up with you? Bring him to me." The approaching passion is there in Jesus' words. Jesus then questions the father. "'How long has this been happening to him?' He replied, 'From childhood. And it has often thrown him into fire and into the water to destroy him. If you can do anything, have pity on us and help us.'" Jesus' response is very forceful.

> Jesus said to him, "Why do you say: 'If you can?' All things are possible for one who believes." Immediately the father of the boy cried out, "I do believe, but help the little faith I have."
>
> Jesus saw that the crowd was increasing rapidly, so he ordered the evil spirit, "Dumb and deaf spirit, I command you: Leave the boy and never enter him again." The evil spirit shook and convulsed the boy and with a terrible shriek came out. The boy lay like a corpse and people said, "He is dead." But Jesus took him by the hand and lifted him and the boy stood up.
>
> After Jesus had gone indoors, his disciples asked him privately, "Why couldn't we drive out the spirit?" And he answered, "Only prayer can drive out this kind, nothing else." (9:23-29)

Of immediate concern to Jesus is the father's faith, which is a necessary prelude to the child's release. The man's desperate cry of distress is enough. He is half-believing and half out of his mind with worry for his child. When Jesus commands the unclean spirit to drive it out, he is "binding the strong man" (Mk 3:27) one more time. The crowd thinks the child is dead, but when Jesus takes him by the hand, he stands up in the community of believers by the power of Jesus' word, touch, and presence.

Jesus' call to the father of the boy to reach deeper for faith is also a call to the disciples to bolster their faith. When they question Jesus about why they were not able to heal the boy, for the first time in Mark's gospel Jesus speaks of the need for prayer. The boy's father prays a heart-wrenching prayer on behalf of his child: "I do believe (*pisteuō*), but help my unbelief (*apistia*). This is also the situation of the disciples. They need to be crying out to Jesus as well! Mark is also reminding his own community that prayer is a necessary component of their share in Jesus' mission and of preparation for baptism. This story lays out two prerequisites for following Jesus: faith and prayer. Since following Jesus means participation in his ministry, the disciples must strive to work against human misery and to relieve distress with compassion born of prayer and attentiveness to Jesus' words.

Once again Jesus tries to make his disciples understand what they face as they draw near to Jerusalem and to his own death. As they travel together through Galilee once again, he repeats what he began telling them at Caesarea Philippi.

> . . . he was teaching the disciples. And he told them, "The Son of Man will be delivered into human hands. They will kill him, but three days after he has been killed, he will rise." The disciples, however, did not understand these words and they were afraid to ask him what he meant. (9:31-32)

Mark reports that the disciples are still not ready to listen. Their faith is weak and prayer is lacking. They are locked into their previous hopes and plans to be a part of Jesus' following with Jesus as the Messiah. They don't understand and they are even afraid to question Jesus. They don't want to hear the answer. This is the beginning of a breach between Jesus and his own disciples, who will betray him out of fear. They are walking the way with Jesus, but they are not paying attention to what the way means for believers.

> They came to Capernaum and, once inside the house, Jesus asked them, "What were you discussing on the way?" But they did not answer because they had been arguing about who was the greatest.
> Then he sat down, called the Twelve and said to them, "If someone wants to be first, let him be last of all and servant of all." Then he took a little child, placed it in their midst, and putting his arms around it he said to them, "Whoever welcomes a child such as this in my name, welcomes me; and whoever welcomes me, welcomes not me but the One who sent me." (9:33-37)

Jesus has been teaching the disciples to resist the dominant social order and not to view power and authority as the scribes and Pharisees do. Instead they are to see power embodying their own lives as they serve those most in need and show solidarity with those excluded and in pain. But the disciples are intent only on their own futures and how Jesus' power will benefit them.

In the passage above, Jesus reveals another mark of being a follower: a follower must be the last, a servant of all, who has no special privileges or status or security. The follower must be like a child. Jesus sits down, putting himself lower than the disciples. According to ancient traditions, he also placed himself as a teacher in the justice or mercy seat. As the child is held and encompassed by Jesus, so can the disciples, as beloved children of God, enter into unbelievable intimacy with the Master.

At the time of Jesus children lived a precarious existence because of disease, poverty, hunger, and violence. A child was not viewed as useful to society and had no power even to protect itself. Children obeyed those who were bigger, older, or were more powerful. They were, in fact, little more than slaves who lived at the beck and call of anyone who needed something. They were the last, the least, the most excluded, and without protection.

The situation of children was similar to that of others in the society: those who were old, handicapped, sick, illiterate, cast out as unclean. This group included peasants, farmers, shepherds, widows, slaves, the unemployed, aliens, immigrants, prisoners, homeless. They could all be arrested and tortured. In today's society, some of these people disappear or become political prisoners; others are cast out as sexually unacceptable. HIV/AIDS patients, people involved in human rights cases, those raped and brutalized by war, those belonging to the wrong religion, social class, race, or country could also be part of this sad group. And Jesus will be in their midst as he is arrested, tortured, mocked, humiliated, and crucified like a common political criminal or terrorist.

Power in Jesus' community is to be practiced without violence. Jesus embraces all, including the lowly, and power is exercised most effectively in service to these. Jesus easily put his arms around lepers, Samaritans, those despised in the community, those considered sinners beyond redemption. His words could have been: "Wrap your arms around them for they are me and they are my Father, the one who sent me. God is lowly, meek, peaceful, good, lenient, docile, rich in sympathy, compassion, mercy, forgiveness; he is not what you think. This is the God who has sent me, his servant-child, into the world to save it. If you follow me, you will know this God and you will also know him in suffering, in obedience and glory as I know him. This is again and again the call to the cross, the mark of the Christian.

Other Teachings

This story is followed by a series of short teachings that will continue in Mark 10. These teachings on how to deal with outsiders (those who aren't followers of Jesus or those who are not known to the disciples) are filled with hyperbole about avoiding sin and are followed by the familiar exhortation to be salt and to be at peace with one another. It seems almost as if Mark is gathering together as many teachings of Jesus as he can remember. Only one chapter (Mark 11) remains before Jesus enters Jerusalem. Then the remaining six chapters will take up the account of the last week of Jesus' life.

These teachings in Mark 10 and 11 reveal a broad definition of a follower of Jesus. Being a follower is determined by what a person does and why he or she does it. The disciples seem intent on controlling what others do and in sharing in Jesus' power. John's complaint about others healing in Jesus' name echoes Joshua's complaint to Moses that the Spirit has come upon those who supposedly weren't chosen (Nm 11:26f.). Jesus' response is blunt and clear—there is no inside track and there is no way to control the Spirit of God.

> John said to him, "Master, we saw someone who drove out demons by calling upon your name, and we tried to forbid him because he does not belong to our group." Jesus answered, "Do not forbid him, for no one who works a miracle in my name can soon after speak evil of me. For whoever is not against us is for us.
> "If anyone gives you a drink of water because you belong to Christ and bear his name, truly, I say to you, he will not go without reward." (9:38-41)

Ah, if only we Christians had used these many centuries to learn to be generous in acknowledging the good that others do and not so concerned when they "do not follow us." It seems that Jesus is saying that people can follow him without necessarily belonging to the community of his followers. A welcoming spirit, attentiveness, and generosity to another's needs and mighty deeds come from the Spirit and can't always be controlled by the followers of Jesus. It appears that God is bigger than church. We are not to belittle any other person's goodness, and we are to be careful not to make it harder for the poor to believe, to live, and to hope in God.

The short teachings that follow (9:42-49) emphasize the importance of not causing scandal to others. We are to be especially careful around those whose faith is weak that they not see us doing something wrong and thus imitate our behavior. Jesus is trying to make his disciples aware that they, and we, are always being observed. Jesus himself observed them carefully before issuing his call. We are to be attentive to what our hands, eyes, and feet are doing. The behaviors that follow from our ideas and feelings should not hinder others from entering the kingdom of God.

This portion of the Gospel of Mark should not be taken literally, or else the community would be without many eyes, limbs, hands, and feet. But it does stress how much our behavior and actions affect others and that we will be held accountable for our actions toward others. We must examine our consciences to see if we are being small or mean and if, indeed, we are refusing to see the Spirit at work in others whom we do not consider worthy.

The last saying in this chapter of Mark is a declaration and a warning: "Everyone will be salted with fire. Salt is excellent in its place; but if salt becomes tasteless, how can you season it? Keep salt in your hearts and you will be at peace with one another" (9:49-50 NAB). Originally, part of the baptismal ritual was to have the candidate's lips salted so the person would always hunger for the Word of the Lord. So if we have been salted with the

Word and the fire of the Spirit, what happens when we lose that salt? The Spirit of truth and justice, of integrity and wholeness given to us at baptism must be guarded and nourished. When it is nurtured, together with others, the household of God will be at peace.

It is helpful to know that all the sacrifices offered in the temple were first salted (Lv 2:13), and being salted with fire was a strong symbol of persecution and martyrdom, which Mark's own community was experiencing. The community had seen members torn apart by lions, burned, and tortured to death. Being "salted with fire" meant to be made strong in faithfulness and enabled to withstand long periods of physical pain. Mark's community needed be to reminded over and over again that such was Jesus' experience at the hands of others and that they too would know such suffering. But, in the end, they would always belong to God, handed over in sacrifice, and they would know the peace that abides in the household of Jesus.

Chapters 8 and 9 turn us toward the cross. I've titled this book *On Your Mark*, and this section on Mark 8 and 9 could well be titled "Get Set: Face the Cross." This is what lies ahead on Jesus' way. We are marked with the sign of the cross and given its power in baptism; and each time we sign ourselves, we recommit ourselves to our belief in the crucified and risen one, the Son of Man who will come in glory to judge all the nations of the world. Jesus invites us to walk with him ever more closely and to share not only in his mission and power to heal but also in his passion and pain. It is a long process that begins in the catechumenate, the preparation for baptism, and it will encompass our entire lives.

There is an old Celtic story that tells us what this process is like, how long it can take, and how confusing it can be. It also tells about how unaware we are of what is happening to us, as were the disciples and members of Mark's own communities. This short tale is called "The Stone of Truth."

Once upon a time, it is told, Patrick traveled through the village of Cong in Ireland. He was weary from his journey and rested, finding a boulder to lean on while he prayed and to rest his head on. It was this great rock that became known as the Stone of Truth. It was said that anyone who put their hands or feet upon the rock had to tell the truth; they could not lie. They didn't know what would happen to them if they did, but they didn't dare even try to not speak the truth.

One day a notorious thief, a man who claimed he didn't believe in God and had no time for those who did, passed through Cong. He had spent years robbing people, thinking only of himself. He was mean, violent, and selfish, and he tormented people. When night came, it was pitch dark with no moon, and he was running away after having robbed a neighboring village. He was running hard, carrying his bag of gold; and in the dark he tripped and fell over the boulder, the Stone of Truth. As the gold went flying in every direction, he gouged his forehead on a ridge that protruded from the stone. Getting up, he cursed and lamented his loss, deciding to go home to fix the gash on his forehead. Somehow the gash never seemed to heal, and it cut a long line straight across his forehead.

He could not believe the blow that fortune had dealt him. But he went on with his evil ways, robbing and threatening people whenever he could. Wouldn't you know it that another night as he ran with a bag of coins and silverware he fell over that dratted stone again! And he gouged his forehead again. This time the scar went from the top of his forehead straight down the bridge of his nose. From then on his life became miserable. Everyone who saw him laughed at him and pointed out his scar in the shape of the cross. The man who didn't believe in God and who had spent his life as a thief and tormenter of others was marked by God himself!

He hated being made fun of, and there seemed to be nothing he could do to get rid of the cross on his forehead. He hated the people who taunted him and he hated that Stone of Truth. He figured that he could at least get back at the stone. So he went and dug a huge hole and tried to roll the stone into it. It was much heavier than he expected and he couldn't budge it. Frustrated, he covered the stone with dirt and more stones to hide it from view, but each time he tried to cover it up the sheep would rub against it and expose the stone again.

One day he was so tired and frustrated that he sat down on the stone, began shedding tears, and cried out without even thinking, "O God, what can I do to get away from this stone, from this mark on my forehead, and from all these people mocking me? I'm miserable and alone and I hate living this way."

Just then a beggar, in far worse straits than he, walked by and saw him forlorn and miserable. The beggar saw someone in need of help. He sat down beside the man and offered him a piece of bread from his bag, saying, "Here, maybe I can help. You cried out to God in desperation and maybe I'm supposed to be the one that answers you on God's behalf."

But the man wanted nothing to do with a beggar, especially one preaching that he was from God. Because the beggar had nothing else to do, he simply sat there. The beggar sang a little and then he offered the man some bread, breaking off a crust. He pulled out a water skein and offered it along with the crust. Without thinking, the man took the bread and chewed on it in silence. The beggar smiled at him and said, "I don't know who you are but I do know this much. You prayed aloud to God. You shared and broke bread with a stranger, a beggar and a poor itinerant, and you're marked with the holy cross. You must be a true believer, a good Christian. And I thank you. You've made my way easier, letting me share with you. I know now that there are others like me, crying out in desperation to the God above." And the beggar embraced him and went on his way.

The man sat there and didn't know what to do. He sat there some more and then it hit him like a bolt of lightning or peal of thunder—or even a rock! He was being called to be a Christian. The mark was God trying to tell him that he wanted him to belong to him. It didn't matter what he'd done; what mattered was what he could do. That was it. From that day forward, he became a Christian.

Instead of stealing, he worked hard at any job he could find. He helped out when folks needed it, and he always shared what he was given. He prayed aloud for anyone he met along the way, calling down God's blessing on them, even including the sheep that had rubbed all the dirt off the stone. He blessed the stones and people like the beggar and Patrick of old, all who had a part in his coming to be a Christian. He cried a lot out of sheer gratitude.

The years went by. Eventually all the people who had known his past died and those who came along didn't know who he was. They saw the cross on his forehead and knew they could trust him, marked as he was by God. But he had to make sure that they knew the truth, so he gathered them all about and told them the story of how the Stone of Truth had marked him with the cross and how the beggar had broken bread with him when he cried out in his misery. They say he always ended his story with the same line, "That stone I stumbled over in the dark saved me, and that beggar gave me communion. What could I do but change?"

We, too, have all been marked along our way with the sign of the cross and we have had strangers break bread with us. And God has broken bread with us, as we will see in the next chapters of Mark. Though we may not often see the mark of our baptism and calling, we will always be marked with the sign of glory. The only prayer we need to close this chapter is the sign of the cross: In the name of the Father, the Son, and the Holy Spirit. Amen.

CHAPTER 7

Missing the Mark

Mark 10 and 11

CHAPTER 10 OF MARK is a small primer on what is essential to be a follower of Jesus. There is a confrontation on the question of marriage and divorce when Jesus teaches about faithfulness, which is followed by a teaching about children. Then there is an encounter with a rich young man who is more attached to his goods than to the person of Jesus. And then, for the third time, Jesus will warn his disciples of what is coming and will invite them to walk with him, to share more closely in his life, to share the hard times and the agony as well as the joy and the glory of being together in the presence of God. This is really the last chapter Mark devotes to Jesus' teaching and mission, for the remaining chapters focus on the last week of Jesus' life, his passion, death, and resurrection. So, in a way, chapter 10 pulls together the essentials of Jesus' teaching before Jesus turns his face toward Jerusalem.

A traditional story about discipleship may help reveal how the disciples felt and also how we might feel when we hear portions of Jesus' message that seem out of touch with our daily reality or that we just find hard to obey. This story is attributed to St. Francis of Assisi.

> Once upon a time there were two brothers who had heard of Francis and were captivated by his simplicity of life, his obedience to the word of God, his love of the poor and Lady Chastity. So they went together and begged Francis to accept them both.
>
> Francis looked at them and said, "Well, you both have to pass a test to see if you'd be a fit follower of mine. But you can take the test together." The two brothers were delighted. "Here's all you have to do. As you can see, I'm planting cabbages for the brothers' supper some day and I want you to do just as I do. Follow along behind me and plant as I do." The brothers looked at each other and smiled. They'd done a lot of planting during their days on the farm.
>
> Francis began, heading down the row in front of him. He took a cab-

bage out of the purse that he filled from the wheelbarrow and planted it, upside down with the roots sticking in the air! And then he did the same with the next one and the next one. Finally, he turned around and saw that neither of the brothers was moving to follow him. "Come on," he said, "with three of us working it won't take any time at all."

One of the brothers shrugged his shoulders, filled his purse with cabbages and fell in behind Francis. Francis left a lot of space so the brother could put his cabbages in, upside down with the roots in the air just like Francis did. And the second brother filled his purse with cabbages and followed behind his brother and Francis. But he was thinking to himself, "This is a test. Francis can't expect us to plant cabbages upside down. They won't have a chance at growing. I'll just go along and plant mine the right way, and turn Francis's and my stupid brother's right side up." And so he did.

Up and down the rows the three of them went. Francis was singing and planting cabbages upside down, and pretty soon the first brother started humming along, planting the cabbages upside down. Eventually the other brother hummed along as well, careful to set the cabbages right as he planted his. Finally they ran out of cabbages as the day was sliding toward its end. Francis and the two brothers sat together at the edge of the field, and then Francis walked up and down to see what the planted field looked like. Then he sat back down with the two brothers. They were anxious to hear what he had to say.

He looked at them both and said, "I can accept only one of you into my brotherhood. I'm sorry."

The brothers looked at each other, distraught. "Why? Why? Which one?" they chorused. Francis replied, "You, my friend, who obeyed me and planted exactly as I did. You can join me and the other brothers."

Then he looked sadly at the other brother and said, "I'm sorry, you just wouldn't last long among us. You don't know how to obey, and you do what you think should be done when you can't see the wisdom of what you are asked to do." The brothers wept. One went home with Francis and the other sat in the field, alone for the first time in his life.

This a wrenching story. More likely than not, we would also right the cabbages and miss the call to obedience. Just like the one brother, we often think we know better. We're just normal people, but Jesus is interested in normal folk who can *obey*. Jesus seeks people who hear his word and put it into practice, even if, and especially if, it seems not to jive with their usual way of doing things. The disciples are struggling to follow Jesus, and so are we. It isn't always easy, but the journey brings companionship and closeness to Jesus, and eventually the wisdom of Jesus will dawn upon us.

The previous chapter of Mark closed with a teaching about peace: "Have salt in yourselves and be at peace with one another" (9:50b). This chapter looks at obvious places and relationships where that peace was threatened in Mark's community; this also applies to Christian communities today.

Oddly enough, the teaching on marriage and divorce is related to being "salted with fire," which appears in the last two verses of Mark 9. The covenantal bond of marriage can represent Israel's covenantal bond with God. Ritually, that covenant was referred to as "a covenant of salt before the Lord" (Nm 18:19) and as an "inviolable" covenant binding on all the people and their sons and daughters. The people are exhorted not to "let the salt of the covenant of your God be lacking from your cereal offering" (Lv 2:13). Eugene LaVerdiere explains the meaning of this covenant of salt:

> Even in the New Testament, partaking of salt together was an expression of covenant. In Acts 1:4, we read that "while meeting with them, he enjoined them not to depart from Jerusalem, but to wait for 'the promise of the Father.'" The verb, translated as "meeting with," is *synalizo*, literally meaning "while having salt with." The simple verb *alizo* means to salt or give flavor. Jesus was restoring the flavor of the apostolic community, "salting" them that they might have flavor in themselves. (*The Beginning of the Gospel*, 2:63-64)

Jesus is intent on putting salt, on putting fire into his disciples' lives so they can serve as a prophetic alternative to the way other people live. Jesus' teaching on marriage and divorce is both a call to prophetic faithfulness and a pastoral response to a situation that was widespread in the Greco-Roman world and in Judaism and was also surfacing within the communities of the early churches, including Mark's.

The Pharisees approach Jesus and frame a question to test Jesus in relation to Moses. It is a question to which everyone already knows the answer: "Is it lawful for a husband to divorce his wife?" Everyone would know that the answer is yes. This is the teaching from the Book of Deuteronomy:

> If a man marries a woman, and then dislikes her because of some notable defect he discovers in her, he may write a certificate of divorce, give it to the woman, and send her out of his house.
>
> If afterwards she becomes the wife of another man and he also dislikes her and sends her out with a certificate of divorce; or, if this second man who took her to be his wife dies, the first husband who sent her away cannot take her back as wife, since she has been defiled. It is an abomination in the eyes of Yahweh for him to take her back. You shall not defile the land which Yahweh will give you for an inheritance. (Dt 24:1-4)

This section of Deuteronomy explains how a man could divorce his wife according to the Law. The phrase "because of some notable defect" was the

crux of the matter. Depending on the rabbinic school, that could be something very serious, such as adultery or promiscuous behavior (the school of
Shammai), or it could be something as trivial as burned food or finding
another woman more to his liking (school of Hillel). The man was then free
to remarry. The writ was supposed to protect the woman and allow her to
remarry, although the woman could not initiate a divorce. This was the situation within Judaism at the time of Jesus. In Roman society, both men and
women could divorce and remarry, and divorce was widespread in the
wealthy levels of society.

But Jesus is not easily trapped, and he answers their question with his
own question: "What law did Moses give you?" They are quick to answer:
"Moses allowed us to write a certificate of dismissal in order to divorce"
(Mk 10:3-4). Jesus then explains why Moses rewrote the law of original
faithfulness and why marriage is bound to God's faithfulness. And he condemns divorce for both men and women.

> Then Jesus said to them, "Moses wrote this law for you, because you
> are stubborn. But in the beginning of creation *God made them male
> and female*, and because of this, man *has to leave father and mother
> and be joined to his wife, and the two shall become one body.* So they
> are no longer two but one body. Therefore let no one separate what
> God has joined."
>
> When they were indoors at home, the disciples again asked him
> about this and he told them, "Whoever divorces his wife and marries
> another commits adultery against his wife, and the woman who
> divorces her husband and marries another also commits adultery."
> (9:5-12)

Jesus explains that the law was changed by Moses because of the stubborn-
ness, or "hardheartedness," of the people, especially the leaders. The term
"hardness of heart" is often used to describe those who resisted the word of
God in their lives or were slow to understand (6:52, 8:17). The Greek word
sklerokardia is the basis of the word scleroderma, which is an excruciating
disease that hardens the organs of the body, including the skin, until the person becomes entombed in one's own flesh. Jesus uses that word to describe
those who refuse to look at the word and the will of God and bend to the
needs of others in regard to the law. He does not attack the law; it is a fact,
as is the practice of divorce. But he reminds them that the original intent of
marriage was to become one, in covenant with God. In this way, he calls
everyone to rethink and reflect on the practice of divorce.

Then, and somewhat surprisingly, Jesus reveals the patriarchal nature of
the law, which serves only men and their wants. He condemns the law in
that regard, saying that the man sins against his wife when he divorces her
and marries another. That would have been quite a new idea for the Jewish community. A man who committed adultery with another man's wife

shamed that man; the woman was not the cause of shame. Then Jesus extends the teaching on divorce to include women, saying that a woman sins when she divorces her husband and marries another.

As previously noted, divorce was a reality both in Judaism and in the early Christian communities. Jesus' teaching emphasizes that divorce is a tragedy that goes against the hopes and design of God for human beings, male and female. While a tragedy, divorce was also a reality, as it is today. Jesus' teaching on divorce is, in fact, a prophetic call to faithfulness. He is calling his followers to a deeper commitment and truer covenant of faithfulness than others. This prophetic demand is balanced by the way Jesus treats everyone, especially those considered impure or unclean because of their failure to live up to the religious code. Failure in itself does not exclude a person from Jesus' following or from forgiveness or from inclusion in the community at the breaking of the bread. The call to conversion and repentance is issued again and again. As Jesus reminds people of the original power and meaning of marriage, he is calling them to faithfulness. This is the mark, the standard that Christians who follow Jesus must reach for, as they "deny themselves, pick up their cross and come after Jesus" (Mk 8:34).

Chapter 10 is thought to be part of a catechetical text that dealt with many concerns, including marriage and divorce, children, riches within the community, arrogance and selfishness, the reluctance to face suffering or to bear the cross, and blindness, or hardheartedness, to the teachings of Jesus. Jesus consistently calls his followers to faithfulness, to wholehearted obedience, and to sacrifice. They are to belong to God alone. This is the only way to bring peace among the members of the community.

In the next short teaching, Jesus turns to the children. At the time of Jesus, childhood was an extremely vulnerable age.

> In antiquity, childhood was a time of terror. Infant mortality rates sometimes reached 30 percent of live births. Sixty percent were dead by the age of sixteen. These figures reflect not only the ravages of unconquered diseases but also the outcomes of poor hygiene.
>
> Moreover, while Western cultures tend to place children first and risk everything to save the child above all, ancient Middle Eastern cultures would place the child last. The medieval Mediterranean theologian Thomas Aquinas taught that in a raging fire a husband was obliged to save his father first, then his mother, next his wife, and last of all his young child. When a famine came upon the land, children would be fed last, after the adults. Such priorities are still common in many non-Western cultures.
>
> Within the family and the community, the child had next to no status. A minor child was considered equal to a slave. Only after reaching maturity did a child become a free person with rights to inherit the family estate. (John J. Pilch, *The Cultural World of Jesus*, 139-40)

This reveals why parents would want Jesus to touch their children for protection, power, healing, and comfort. It also brings a certain perspective to the reaction of the disciples, who don't want them coming to bother Jesus. They rebuke the parents, just as they sought to stop someone else from casting out demons in Jesus' name. Instead of rejoicing over those who do come to Jesus, the disciples want to keep Jesus for themselves. Once again, Jesus' response to the children will surprise his followers.

> People were bringing their little children to him to have him touch them, but the disciples were scolding them for this. Jesus became indignant when he noticed it and said to them: "Let the children come to me and do not hinder them. It is to just such as these that the kingdom of God belongs. I assure you that whoever does not accept the reign of God like a little child shall not take part in it." Then he embraced them and blessed them, placing his hands on them. (10:13-16 NAB)

This is the only time that Mark uses the word "indignant" to describe Jesus' feelings, and his indignation is directed at his disciples. Earlier, Jesus had wrapped his arms around a small child in protective intimacy and security (9:36-37) to show his disciples who is truly great in his kingdom and to show them what being the least could mean for them. Now Jesus says that to learn to accept his teachings, one must become like a child; otherwise one will not understand and will not be included in the kingdom. The kingdom is here and now among us in Jesus and is open to all those who are like children in relation to God.

As Jesus includes children in his embrace and in his kingdom, he continues to draw into the inner circle of his new family those who were formerly excluded. He is drawing in those most in jeopardy or in need, those who are dependent in the way that children are totally dependent on adults for food, water, shelter, health care, or education, all that relates to their survival into adulthood. This is how Jesus is with God, and this is how we are to be with God.

In all these examples, Jesus uses hyperbole to convey the importance of what he is teaching. He is trying to grasp the attention of his disciples and others so they will hear what he is saying and see what he is doing with fresh eyes. Jesus' teaching is a call to change the way we act and how we feel. We are not to inadvertently harm the most vulnerable or to act in such a way that the least among us will be harmed by what we might do thoughtlessly or selfishly.

Jesus uses the children to teach his disciples, as he has used persons such as the Syrophoenician woman or the father of the boy with the deaf and dumb spirit, those whose faith has confronted the faithlessness of his followers. These are the ones who reveal how to have the kingdom of heaven now. Jesus touches them, blesses them, and embraces them. Closeness in the household of Jesus' family is not given to those who deserve it or are connected by blood ties, but to those who need it the most, have been denied it the most, and those whom no one else would think to touch.

Jesus touches the people no one else touches, especially in public. In Mark's stories up to this point, Jesus has touched people seven times. The first was the leper (1:41-42), a man who was considered repulsive, an untouchable. He touched or was touched by the woman who had been bleeding (5:25-34), another impure person who could defile and soil him. He also touched Jairus's daughter (5:41) and Peter's mother-in-law (1:31). Jesus touched other persons to heal them: the deaf man unable to speak (7:31-37) and the blind man (8:22-26). And now he touches the children (10:13b).

So we must ask, whom do we reach out to and touch? How do we touch them? Does our touch imply acceptance, inclusion, even welcome and the sharing of power? How do we feel when others see us touch these people? Jesus warned his disciples not to prevent the children from coming to him and not to prevent others from healing and bringing hope in his name. So we must also ask if we are preventing others from coming to Jesus or hearing the good news of God. Who do we think does not deserve to be in the presence of Jesus and draw close to his touch and healing hope?

Just as children must rely on the kindness, generosity, and devotion of others to grow up, so we are supposed to rely on the goodness of God and the goodness and devotion of others so that we can grow and mature in our faith and practice as followers of Jesus. The lowly of the earth can teach us to see ourselves in perspective.

The disciples do not seem to have understood and are more interested in arguing over "who is the greatest in the kingdom." Do they hear Jesus as he answers that question for them? The greatest are those who are faithful in marriage, children, and those who rely utterly on God and the generosity of others, the lowly of the world who are without power but who accept the word of God and take it to heart. Are we listening and watching as Jesus singles out models of "the greatest among us."

Before God, each of us, young and old, immature and mature, is the beloved child. We must learn to relate to God as children, to depend on God, to rely on his graciousness, and to be obedient to him. We are honored to be his servants and beloved, along with Jesus, but we must be mindful of the least, those without access to power who lie at the heart of God and have a position of honor and respect in the household of God, Jesus' new family.

Jesus is calling his followers to a relationship of trust and dependence on God that affords us the opportunity and the courage to depend on one another and be responsible for one another. A priest in Chicago once told a story that goes right to the heart of this teaching.

His mother, who had grown elderly and frail, lived in a two-story walk-up with the bedrooms and bath upstairs. He was staying at home

to care for her, and the ritual that began and ended each day was his carrying her downstairs and then upstairs—to spend the day downstairs
and then to prepare her for bed. Night wasn't the problem. He'd pick
her up, she'd wrap her arms around his neck and her legs around his
waist, and he would carry her up the stairs and put her to bed.

It was the morning that was frustrating and exhausting. He'd stand
at the top of the stairs on the landing with her in his arms, and she'd
have her arms around his neck and legs around his waist, and he'd start
down the steps. After maybe one or two steps she would reach for the
banister and clamp down on it like she was held by superglue. As he
would move down, unsuspecting, to the next step, he would be caught
off balance with one foot on each step. And an unchanging ritual
began. "Mother, let go. I can't move while you hold onto the banister."
And she would answer, "No, you're going to drop me." "Mother, have
I dropped you yet?" "No, but you could." "Mother, if you don't let go,
I am going to drop you!" and finally she would let go. After a couple
more steps, she'd clutch the banister again and the conversation would
repeat itself.

It took forever to get down the sixteen steps each morning. It became
a nightmare, something he dreaded facing every morning. How could he
get her down the stairs as she clutched and held on for dear life? Finally,
one morning, he just couldn't do it any longer. He sat at the top of the
stairs, nearly in tears. He was praying to be patient and then suddenly
thought, "Oh, my God, why am I getting so upset with my mother? This
is the way I act all the time with God. How could I be so stupid, so slow
to see what has been happening with God in my life?"

He sat on the steps for a long time, then got up and went back to pick
up his mother. His realization didn't stop her from clutching at the banister, but it did give him an insight into his own relationship with and
lack of trust in God and his need to be more compassionate with his
elderly and frightened mother.

When we first heard the story, some of us in the audience were laughing, but later I began thinking about banisters. There was one in my Nana's
house that was on a long curved stairway. It was made of gorgeous, highly
polished wood. The banister was decreed off-limits for children and no one
was allowed to slide down it. But we learned early on that sliding down it
was great fun. With a good start, we could fly all the way across the living
room; and if we timed it just right and got up enough speed, we could land
on the couch! That was confidence and trust, the kind of trust that Jesus
was trying to teach his disciples. This is the degree of trust that is necessary
to fall into the arms of God one day. Like sliding down the banister, we
have to practice it regularly with one another in covenants and relationships, by reaching out to those long shunned and untouched, and by letting
ourselves be carried and by carrying others up and down the stairs. Unless

we remember and become as children, there is a lot we will not be able to accept and absorb as beloved children of God with Jesus.

The Story of the Rich Man, or the "Undisciple" Story

Jesus has taught about family relationships, and now he turns to the issue that everyone has to attend to, that of economics, of wealth, security, possessions, and, for some, excess. The story is familiar and Jesus follows it with a teaching directed to his disciples and to all of us. This is a thorny issue for those of us who live in a society where money and security are tantamount. This teaching of Jesus clearly reveals another basic concept that stands in opposition to accepted practice or the "wisdom of the day." Listen to the story carefully because it describes the practice of a follower of Jesus who is bound in trust to the least of our brothers and sisters.

> Just as Jesus was setting out on his journey again, a man ran up, knelt before him and asked, "Good Master, what must I do to have eternal life?"
>
> Jesus answered, "Why do you call me good? No one is good but God alone. You know the commandments: Do not kill, do not commit adultery, do not steal, do not bear false witness, do not cheat, honor your father and mother." The man replied, "I have obeyed all these commandments since my childhood."
>
> Then Jesus looked steadily at him and loved him and he said, "For you, one thing is lacking. Go, sell what you have and give the money to the poor, and you will have riches in heaven. Then come and follow me." On hearing these words, his face fell and he went away sorrowful for he was a man of great wealth. (10:17-22)

The man who ran to Jesus in his eagerness asked the eternal question: "What must I do to have eternal life?" What he seeks appears in the Book of Daniel: "Many of those who sleep in the Region of the Dust will awake, some to everlasting life but others to eternal horror and shame (12:2).

Everlasting life is what the man wants from Jesus, or, rather, he wants to know what he must do in order to obtain this gift of God. The man is rich. He has a great deal of excess. He is attached to it and what it affords him: security, a place in the community, a reputation and a lifestyle. His riches, though, are a burden if he wants to follow Jesus. Within Jewish society and religious tradition, the man is impeccable. He has obeyed all the laws since his youth, which in itself is a feat not to be lightly brushed over. How many of us can say we have never killed, committed adultery, stolen anything, borne false witness, defrauded others, and always honored our parents? And this means not just our individual acts, but also the acts of groups to which we belong.

The first commandments come from the Decalogue (Ex 20:13-16); another commandment, from a list in Deuteronomy that concerns justice, equity, and charity (Dt 24:6-25:3), is added. It reads: "Do not exploit the lowly and the poor daily-wage earner, whether he be one of your brothers or a foreigner whom you find in your land in any of your cities" (24:14). While wealth had long been considered a blessing from God, the prophets, especially Amos, had attacked the wealthy as an insult to God when their wealth resulted from injustice or disobedience to the demand to share and to give alms.

There were really only two classes in Jewish society, the masses of people who worked the land and the few who were extremely wealthy. The rich young man had stature in his community, and he was earnest about learning what he must do. He wanted to know what he must do to inherit eternal life. He wanted a plan, a blueprint, to make sure that he was saved. Don't we all? But he has approached Jesus, and the way of Jesus is radically different from society's sense of what might constitute good.

Jesus begins by reacting to the young man's form of address. "Why do you call me good? No one is good but God alone." This may sound strange to us because we believe that Jesus is God, but Jesus, a Jew obedient to the word and will of God, saw himself in a privileged relationship; he was a beloved son who sought to love God with every fiber of his being. He will not allow the man to call him good. Goodness is relative and is dependent on the yardstick being used to evaluate it. Jesus' norm for goodness is the goodness of God. We must never think for a moment we are anywhere close to the goodness of God. So Jesus answers the man's question by stating what the man already knows. As a Jew he is required to obey the laws to inherit eternal life. And the young man immediately replies that he has been obedient to the Law since he was young.

We are then told, simply, that "Jesus looked steadily at him and loved him." Jesus didn't love him because he was good or because he had been obedient from childhood. Jesus certainly did not love him because he was rich. No, Jesus loved him as he loves every one of us. He looks at us and then tells us the truth about ourselves, about what we are lacking. Jesus then invites us to come along and follow him, to go off in his company and be a member of his household, to enter the kingdom of God like a child who is obedient and grateful to God.

Jesus then announces what is the stumbling block for the rich young man. He must give up his wealth. This is the one thing he does not want to do, but it is also the one thing that everyone who is called to follow Jesus must do. The disciples had to leave their fishing nets and boats and their families, and Matthew his counting tables and job. If this man can leave his possessions, he will "deny his very self" and begin the way with Jesus. He will have become a child, who, along with Jesus and the disciples, is dependent on God and ready to be part of the kingdom.

Jesus tells him to go and sell what he has and give it to the poor (heaven is with the poor) and then to follow. Although this is the blueprint he has asked for, he is unable to obey. He is unwilling to share his wealth with others, with those who need it most. He "will not lose his life to save it." He is caught in the profit of one who gains the whole world and yet forfeits his life (Mk 8:35-36).

Jesus has just invited the rich young man to join the inner circle of his family, but he does not take up the invitation. "On hearing these words, his face fell and he went away sorrowful." How many others invited by Jesus refused him because they were not willing to do the one thing that would connect them to the poor, the children, the outcast? How many times has that invitation been extended to us? How many times have we rejected it to go away in sadness?

We read that the rich young man went away sorrowful. What of Jesus? What was he thinking as he watched the young man turn away? What does Jesus think of us when we turn away because we will not accept renunciation as a mark of a follower of Jesus? What does Jesus think when we will not share even our excess with the poor?

Jesus uses the man's refusal to teach his disciples, and once again the disciples find Jesus' words shocking and unnerving.

Jesus looked around and said to his disciples, "How hard it is for those who have riches to enter the kingdom of God!" The disciples were shocked at these words, but Jesus insisted, "Children, how hard it is to enter the kingdom of God! It is easier for a camel to go through the eye of a needle than for one who is rich to enter the kingdom of God."

They were more astonished than ever and wondered, "Who, then, can be saved?" Jesus looked steadily at them and said, "For human beings it is impossible, but not for God; all things are possible with God."

Peter spoke up and said, "We have given up everything to follow you." Jesus answered, "Truly, there is no one who has left house or brothers and sisters, or mother or father, or children, or lands for my sake and for the Gospel, who will not receive his reward. I say to you: even in the midst of persecution he will receive a hundred times as many houses, brothers, sisters, mothers, children, and lands in the present time and in the world to come eternal life. Do pay attention: Many who now are first will be last, and the last, first." (10:23-31)

Jesus looks at his disciples, fixing his gaze on them in the same way he looked at the rich young man who just walked away from him. He loves them and he calls them "children" to acknowledge that they are his. They are in the embrace of his kingdom and in the care of his Father. Mark notes that the disciples are shocked at Jesus' teaching on wealth and that being a disciple makes demands on those who have excess wealth and possessions. According to the Law of Israel, which demanded justice toward the poor, and the prophets, who raged against those who disobeyed the Law, wealth is to be shared with the poor. The way the poor, the lowly, and the outcast were treated revealed whether or not the covenant was being honored and God was being truly worshiped. While the Law does not speak directly about giving to the poor, there is a tradition in Sirach that giving alms would atone for one's sin: "As water extinguishes the burning flames, alms-giving obtains pardon for sins" (Sir 3:30). Also, in the Book of Tobit, Tobit teaches his son what he must do in service to others to live uprightly.

> Give alms from what you have to those who act justly and do good. Do not be grudging when you give alms. Do not turn away your face from anyone who is poor so that God may not turn away his face from you. Give alms in proportion to the amount you have; if you have little, do not be afraid to give alms according to the little you have.
>
> In this way you are storing up treasure against the day of tribulation, because almsgiving frees us from death and keeps us from wandering in the darkness. For, in fact, almsgiving is, for the one who practices it, a previous treasure in the eyes of God. (Tb 4:7-11)

Jesus is extending that wisdom outward, making giving alms, or sharing what one has with the poor, a condition for having eternal life and entering now into God's kingdom as a disciple. Jesus repeats his warning to the disciples to emphasize its importance and then uses the image of the camel trying to go through the eye of a needle to nail home the difficulty (or impossibility!) of achieving the kingdom without concern for the poor.

This image distresses the disciples, who wonder, "Who, then, can be saved?" Peter speaks for them all, reminding Jesus that they have left everything to follow him. (It is good to remember, however, that they are pulling back from Jesus' call to renunciation and the cross.) Jesus seeks to give them heart, and hope. He assures them that anyone who wishes to follow him must give up house, family members, and lands; but in return they will gain a new household and community and a new family, and he reminds them once more that there will also be persecutions. Jesus confirms that his disciples will share in his passion and death but will also have eternal life in the age to come. The kingdom will return everything a hundredfold to God's children.

The last line of this account is very familiar: "Many who are now first will be last, and the last, first." Those who are first and foremost in this world will be last in eternal life, and the many who are without power and wealth in this world will be first in the kingdom. Once again, it is time to choose: Where do we stand—with the first in the world or with the last?

The Third Prediction of the Passion

Once again Jesus asks his disciples to walk with him. This time they are headed to Jerusalem and the cross, and this time the call to face suffering with him is more detailed and graphic. The disciples' response is not only negative, but they simply ignore Jesus' words altogether and proceed to seek his favor. James and John, the disciples, who, along with Peter, have been chosen to be with him when he raised Jairus's daughter from the dead and at the transfiguration, now seek places of power in Jesus' kingdom. Have they heard anything he has just said? Their callousness and their insensitivity, although born of fear, are also born of selfishness and sin. The Greek word for sin is translated literally as "missing the mark," and the disciples have missed it by a wide margin this time. As their hearts have hardened, they have misunderstood the marks of discipleship, and now they are refusing to hear Jesus' words. As the hardness spreads, they cannot see how it is opening a gap between them and Jesus. Once more Jesus invites them to stay close to him in his pain as well as in his mission of healing and feeding and drawing people together.

> They were on the road going up to Jerusalem, and Jesus was walking ahead. The Twelve were anxious and those who followed were afraid. Once more Jesus took the Twelve aside to tell them what was to happen to him, "You see we are going up to Jerusalem, and the Son of Man will be given over to the chief priests and the teachers of the Law. They will condemn him to death and hand him over to the foreigners who will make fun of him, spit on him, scourge him and finally kill him; but three days later he will rise." (10:32-34)

As Jesus is trying to explain the suffering of the cross to his disciples, so Mark is trying to explain to his believers that the cross, the passion and death of Jesus, is also part of what they will experience if they are faithful to God's word. This was the reality that would face Jesus in Jerusalem, and it was also the reality that many of the first-century Christians faced at the hands of the Roman Empire. One could not be baptized and ignore the integrity of the cross and the resurrection, pain and glory, the rejection of the world and the love of God the Father. Pain and glory were like both sides of the same hand.

The disciples, however, refuse even to speak to Jesus about what he has just said. In fact, James and John, two of the first disciples that Jesus called to his side, pick this moment to make their plea for power in Jesus' kingdom. They are trying to profit from the blood ties that come from being part of the extended family. They have learned nothing. What must Jesus have thought as he listened to their request?

James and John, the sons of Zebedee, came to Jesus and said to him, "Master, we want you to grant us what we are going to ask of you." And he said, "What do you want me to do for you?" They answered, "Grant us to sit one at your right and one at your left when you come in your glory."

But Jesus said to them, "You don't know what you are asking. Can you drink the cup that I drink or be baptized in the way that I am baptized?" They answered, "We can." And Jesus told them, "The cup that I drink you will drink, and you will be baptized in the way I am baptized. But to sit at my right or at my left is not mine to grant. It has been prepared for others."

On hearing this, the other ten were angry with James and John. (10:35-41)

The disciples are arguing about who is the greatest, but they are also laying bases for power. They are approaching Jesus as they would a ruler in their world, someone who can grant favors and privileged status and share power with them. They are still intent on his being the Messiah in their very limited understanding of that word. They want to make sure that he knows that they are family and that he "owes" it to them to put them in positions of authority and leadership in the new kingdom.

Once more Jesus tries to make them hear what he is saying and get them to see that what is coming is not the glory that they expect, but, instead, suffering and death. So Jesus asks them if they can drink of the cup that he is being offered and share in his baptism—"salted with fire"—and then be handed over to be crucified. When they promptly reply "We can," Jesus tells them that one day they will indeed share in his cup and baptism but that he does not have the power to grant them seats on his right and left. (The gospel later shows that these seats are given to the criminals crucified beside him.) The disciples have no idea what they are asking for; they seek honor, but what lies in the cup of which Jesus speaks is profound suffering, anguish, and pain. Jesus' power will come from the passion, and the disciples want the power without the passion that is its source.

The word "cup" used by Jesus has a rich background in the psalms. For example, Psalm 116:13, "I will lift up the cup of salvation and call on the name of the Lord," or Psalm 23, which speaks of a cup that overflows (23:5). For Jesus the cup refers to his baptism and his passion and suffering. For us it is the same. We are baptized into the death of Jesus, and we die with him so that we might also rise with him. Along with James and John, Jesus is asking all of us if we are willing to "lose our life" for the sake of the gospel. Jesus is asking if we will go with him to the cross.

The other ten disciples are indignant. James and John seem to have outmaneuvered them. The rest are as ambitious or eager for power. At the moment, the disciples are acting like a group of spoiled, petulant children. This is not appropriate behavior for the children of God and certainly not for the disciples of Jesus. So, once more, Jesus calls them together to teach them as clearly as he can the meaning of leadership in his community.

> Jesus . . . said, "As you know, the so-called rulers of the nations act as tyrants and their great ones oppress them. But it shall not be so among you; whoever would be great among you must be your servant, and whoever would be first among you shall make himself slave of all. Think of the Son of Man who has not come to be served but to serve and to give his life to redeem many." (Mk 10:42-45)

This is a complete reversal of what they know of authority under the Romans and among the Gentiles. Even within Israel, authority and power were heavy-handed and subject to the whims of favors, bribes, threats, and family ties. Jesus' description of the "rulers of the nations" is scathing; he has lived under Roman authority all his life. He is adamant in telling them that "it shall not be so among you." In Jesus' community, power is exercised and practiced by serving, as it is practiced by Jesus, the Son of Man. They must learn from him, carefully observe him, and imitate him now and even more so in the coming days when he enters Jerusalem.

In speaking of power, Jesus is very specific: "whoever would be great among you must be your servant, and whoever would be first among you shall make himself slave of all." A servant (the word is derived from the same word as "deacon") serves. Servants were free and were often hired to help out, being paid for their services in money or given a place to live and food. The emphasis, however, was on being free. Power in Jesus' household is at the bottom. But Jesus tells them that if they wish to be first they must be the *slaves* of all. A slave often did the same work as a servant and was also given housing and food, depending on the largesse of the owner. But no one ever chose to be a slave, who did not have freedom. Jesus is saying that to be first in his family a disciple must *choose* to be a slave, to belong to others and to serve the gospel as Jesus did, in obedience to God's will. In Jesus' kingdom, slaves will be more powerful than servants because they are bound more closely to the person of Jesus crucified. The community of Jesus, the body of Christ, the church as a whole is to be the slave for the many. This is the heart of Jesus' mission and his death, and it is rooted in one of the servant songs of Isaiah.

> For the anguish he suffered,
> He will see the light and obtain perfect knowledge.
> My just servant will justify the multitude;
> He will bear and take away their guilt.
>
> Therefore I will give him his portion among the great,
> And he will divide the spoils with the strong.

> For he surrendered himself to death
> And was even counted among the wicked,
> Bearing the sins of the multitude
> And interceding for sinners. (Is 53:11-12)

Joseph O'Hanlon writes of this call to Jesus' disciples and to the church to gain power and authority through service.

> The death of Jesus, the cross of Calvary, stands at the heart and defines the meaning of Christianity. It is the mystery which unlocks all mysteries. Christians will forever draw on the profound meaning of the cross and they will never exhaust its meaning. Mark places its meaning in the context of service. Thus he warns that service is the defining quality of Christianity. The Christian is called to that degree of service which can be seen on the cross of Jesus. There is no room for *lording it over them* in the Christian way. Authority is not a question of power, it is the duty of service. To be a Christian is to be last. To be a Christian in authority is to be even more last! (*Mark My Words*, 209-10)

Blind Bartimaeus

This chapter of Mark ends with another story of the healing of a blind man. In this account a blind beggar sees what the others do not see. While others have resisted, he obeys and follows Jesus up the road to Jerusalem. This last story before Jesus enters Jerusalem is also a model for baptism.

> They came to Jericho. As Jesus was leaving Jericho with his disciples and a large crowd, a blind beggar, Bartimaeus, the son of Timaeus, was sitting by the roadside. On hearing that it was Jesus of Nazareth passing by, he began to call out, "Son of David, Jesus, have mercy on me!" Many people scolded him and told him to be quiet, but he shouted all the louder, "Son of David, have mercy on me."
> Jesus stopped and said, "Call him." So they called the blind man, saying, "Take heart. Get up, he is calling you." He immediately threw aside his cloak, jumped up, and went to Jesus.
> Then Jesus asked him, "What do you want me to do for you?" The blind man said, "Master, let me see again!" And Jesus said to him, "Go your way, your faith has made you well." And immediately he could see, and he followed Jesus along the road. (10:46-52)

Jesus is leaving Jericho, which is a place full of violence and intrigue, with bandits and revolutionary groups within Judaism organizing resistance to Rome. Jesus, his disciples, and a crowd are all headed to Jerusalem, to the cross and glory. As they pass a blind beggar who has heard of Jesus and his teaching, he cries out in prayer and petition for Jesus to have pity on him. He addresses Jesus as the Son of David, the son of a king who reigns from a throne of mercy and represents the presence of justice with peace. He is rebuked by many, including the disciples, which was the reality of many who prepared for baptism. But he is persistent in his prayer.

Jesus hears him and stops; Jesus does not go to him, but he has the disciples call the man over to him. They use the same words that Jesus used to speak to his disciples when they were struggling to cross the lake: "Take heart. Get up, he is calling you." This is the church, after the death and resurrection of Jesus, calling people to baptism and to discipleship in words that urge them to have the courage to arise and follow Jesus. And the blind beggar throws aside his cloak, jumps up, and goes to Jesus. He lets go of all that he has, his shelter from the elements and the prying eyes of others, his clothing and his identity. In the baptismal language of the church, he lays aside his old life, his old person, and comes to Jesus, who will give him everything that he needs.

Jesus then addresses him, using the same words he used with James and John when they approached him: "What do you want me to do for you?" The man answers, "Master, I want to see." This is a request for baptism. He wants to know Jesus, to see life as Jesus sees it, with Jesus' wisdom and understanding, and that will be enough. In response, Jesus does not do anything to him, but simply speaks, commanding him, "Go your way; your faith has made you well."

These were the same words spoken to the hemorrhaging woman who reached out to touch him and the Syrophoenician woman. It was their faith that was their saving grace, and now they would go into their new life with peace, healing, and wholeness. Immediately (that word again), the man receives his sight and follows Jesus on the way. And the way is set toward Jerusalem, toward the passion and death of Jesus, and toward the release of the glory of the resurrection through Jesus' obedience. As the man's request for sight is a cry for baptism, so his following of Jesus' way now brings him into the community of believers, the church.

This story of the blind beggar forces us to ask if we actually see. Whom do we shunt or rebuke or quiet? Like the rich young man, do we need to imitate the blind man, dropping our cloaks and possessions along with the masks and defenses we use to help us to hide from the questioning of God? Even now, who is crying out for pity? Whose cries are we not hearing? Cries can come from a whimpering lone person on the street or cries can be as loud as those coming from Sudan or Niger.

A short story about Rabbi Menahem Mendl of Kotzk summarizes much of these last four chapters of Mark. It is from Elie Wiesel's book *Souls on Fire*.

A disciple tells [the Rebbe] his woes: "I come from Rizhin. There, everything is simple, everything is clear. I prayed and I knew I was praying; I studied and I knew I was studying. Here in Kotzk everything is mixed up, confused; I suffer from it, Rebbe. Terribly. I am lost. Please help me so I can pray and study as before. Please help me to stop suffering."

The Rebbe peers at his disciple in tears and asks: "And whoever told you that God is interested in your studies and your prayers? And what if He preferred your tears and your suffering?" (235)

Jerusalem

Chapter 11 of Mark is the opening reading for the Palm Sunday processions. Jesus sends two of his disciples ahead into Jerusalem to find a colt that is tethered at a gate and to bring it back to Jesus. They lay their cloaks on the donkey and Jesus rides it into the city.

> They went off and found the colt out in the street tied at the door. As they were untying it, some of the bystanders asked, "Why are you untying that colt?" They answered as Jesus had told them, and the people allowed them to continue.
>
> They brought the colt to Jesus, threw their cloaks on its back, and Jesus sat upon it. Many people also spread their cloaks on the road, while others spread leafy branches from the fields. Then the people who walked ahead and those who followed behind Jesus began to shout, "Hosannah! *Blessed is he who comes in the name of the Lord!* Blessed is the kingdom of our father David which comes! Hosannah in the highest!"
>
> So Jesus entered Jerusalem and went into the Temple. And after he had looked all around, as it was already late, he went out to Bethany with the Twelve. (11:4-11)

They have arrived in Jerusalem, the center of the world for the people of Israel, and, according to the writings of Isaiah, the center of a new world to come. We hear the following reading in Advent.

> In the last days, the mountain of Yahweh's house shall be set over the highest mountains and shall tower over the hills.
>
> All the nations will stream to it, saying, "Come, let us go to the mountain of the Lord, to the house of the God of Jacob, that he may teach us his ways and we may walk in his paths." (Is 2:2-3)

And it was believed that Jerusalem was where the judgment would take place: "On that day his feet will rest on the Mount of Olives, facing Jerusalem on the east and the Mount of Olives shall be split in two from east to west by a deep valley (Zec 14:4).

Zechariah also gives us the image of Jesus astride a colt.

> Rejoice greatly, daughter Zion!
> Shout for joy, daughter of Jerusalem!
> For your king is coming, just and victorious,
> humble and riding on a donkey,
> on a colt, the foal of a donkey.
> No more chariots in Ephraim,
> No more horses in Jerusalem,
> For he will do away with them.
> The warrior's bow shall be broken when he dictates peace to the
>   nations.
> He will reign from sea to sea,
> And from the River to the ends of the earth. (Zec 9:9-10)

As Jesus enters Jerusalem, subdued jubilation comes from the crowds of people, their memories and hopes for freedom born of years of brutal oppression. Jews viewed the reigns of David and Solomon as their golden age of glory, and they looked to a future that would repeat that reality. Although these images point to a coronation, shabby and poor as it may be, Jesus approaches the city humbly and peaceably, unlike a king coming to be crowned. Yet, by the time the week is finished, the same crowd will be crying for his execution. From the beginning, shadows of violence, of the cross and death, have clouded Mark's gospel. These shadows are all associated with Jerusalem, the city that kills the prophets.

This is the first time Jerusalem and the temple are mentioned in Mark, and many of the events of the next five days will take place in its shadow. On this, his first of three visits during these final days, Jesus does not remain in the city, but simply enters, visits the temple, looks around and leaves. The last days of Jesus will be spent in Bethany, a small village on the outskirts of the city, at the eastern foot of the Mount of Olives. He will spend his evenings there and go into the temple during the day.

The events in this chapter that deal with the Jews and the temple serve as a warning to Jesus' disciples, and the community of Mark, about what can happen to them. The day starts early, and it will be filled with confrontations, tests, and the incident in the temple. Jesus will use these experiences to teach his disciples about his way. And the day will end with more teaching about the temple as Jesus and his disciples sit on the Mount of Olives facing the temple (13:1-37).

The next account is another Marcan sandwich. The two pieces of bread both deal with a fig tree, and the filling of the sandwich is the account of the cleansing of the temple. Here is the first account of the fig tree.

The next day, when they were leaving Bethany, [Jesus] felt hungry. In the distance he noticed a fig tree covered with leaves, so he went to see if he could find anything on it. When he reached it, he found nothing but leaves, for it was not the season for figs. Then Jesus said to the fig tree, "May no one ever eat your fruit!" And his disciples heard these words. (11:12-14)

The story seems strange—Jesus is cursing a tree because it does not give fruit out of season. Surely Jesus should know that if the tree was leafing, it was not yet time for fruit. Fig trees leafed in March or April and usually had figs in June. But these three stories are bound together. Right before we read the first account of the fig tree, Mark has Jesus visit the temple, and then Mark announces that "it was already late" (11:11b). Time is running out—for the fig tree and for the temple (although the temple will not be physically destroyed until 70 C.E.).

This is the only time we read of Jesus being hungry. This hunger must go beyond ordinary food. Jesus is hungry for God's word and will to be realized in the coming of the kingdom of God. Jesus is also hungry for his own followers to understand what he is doing and to follow him whole-heartedly.

The image of the fig tree is significant because it was the belief among many Jews that when the Messiah did come, all of nature would respond abundantly, providing fruit and harvests in all seasons. But this fig tree is not producing fruit. Given that the story of the temple is wedged between the two references to the fig tree, the fig tree represents the temple. Mark is saying that the religion as practiced in the temple will no longer satisfy or feed anyone either. It is all leaves with no nourishing fruit. And Jesus curses the tree. Would the curse cause the tree to shrivel up, or would it make the fruit bitter or poisonous?

When they reach Jerusalem they enter the outer court of the temple, the court of the Gentiles. It had a number of uses, both religious and practical. It served as the area for the tables of the money changers and where temple fees could be paid in Tyrian coins, the closest coinage to the Hebrew shekel, especially the annual tax which served to make atonement for all adult males (Ex 30:13-16). It was also where salt, incense, wine, and oil could be bought as well as the unblemished animals that were used for sacrifices in the temple. The animals included oxen, sheep, goats, pigeons, and doves. There were also other markets intended for the convenience of pilgrims, under the jurisdiction of the Sanhedrin and the high priest. The courtyard would be filled with merchants, pilgrims, buyers and sellers, Jews and Gentiles alike.

The story of what Jesus does is forthright and startling. It is definitely a prophetic act on the part of Jesus. Jesus is not acting against the temple (he is only in the outer courtyard), but his actions will contribute to the hatred of those who are intent on getting rid of him because he is indirectly criticizing the entire structure of the temple and its required sacrifices. While Jesus' actions are not strong enough to attract the temple guards or the

Roman soldiers, they are duly noted by the scribes, the chief priests, and the elders of the temple leadership.

> When they reached Jerusalem, Jesus went to the Temple and began to drive away all the people he saw buying and selling there. He overturned the tables of the money-changers and the stools of those who sold pigeons. And he would not let anyone carry anything through the Temple area.
>
> Jesus then taught the people, "Does not God say in the Scriptures: *My house will be called a House of Prayer for all the nations?* But you have turned it into *a den of thieves*."
>
> The chief priests and the teachers of the Law heard of this, and they tried to find a way to destroy him. They were afraid of him because all the people were captivated by his teaching.
>
> When evening came, Jesus left the city. (11:15-19)

Chaos would have erupted in that area of the temple, with animals loose and birds flying off. There could have been a small riot as everyone scrambled to retrieve what they had lost. But the chaos occurred in an outer court of the temple. It seems that Jesus is interested in a symbolic action rather than in stopping preparations for worship in the temple. Jesus' actions call attention to the original purpose of the court of the Gentile: it was to be a place of prayer for all people. As financial transactions connected with the temple structure of sacrifice and worship increased, merchants profited from the buying and selling, and there was no space left for prayer, whether by Jew or Gentile.

Jesus then quotes Isaiah. It is God (Yahweh) who draws to himself foreigners who love the name of the Lord, and Jews who come from afar. The temple is there to bring them joy, and God will accept their sacrifices, "for my house shall be called a house of prayer for all peoples" (56:6-7). Instead the temple has become a "den of thieves." This pronouncement is a quote from the prophet Jeremiah. The seventh chapter of Jeremiah is sometimes called the "temple sermon" because Jeremiah castigates Jews who enter the temple and repeatedly cry out "This is the temple of the Lord" but have no intention of reforming their lives. They have abandoned doing justice and caring for the poor, the resident aliens, the orphans, and widows, and they follow strange gods when it suits them. This is a raging invective against worship that insults God and makes "God's house an abomination, a den of thieves" (Jer 7:11). Jesus' words about temple worship are very much in the tradition of the prophets of Israel.

Jesus is directing his protest against the authorities who are in charge of this charade and who profit from the marketplace they have made of the temple. He is angry that temple worship has deteriorated beyond repair, that it is insulting to God and demeaning to the people. It is self-serving, and its officiants are in collusion with those in power who collaborate with

Rome. It is an insult to the Jews and to the God of the Jews. It is obvious that the authorities are taking note of what Jesus is saying.

When evening comes, Jesus and his followers head out of the city and return to Bethany. And they follow the same pattern the next day and return to Jerusalem in the morning. This is when Peter sees the fig tree.

> Early next morning, as they walked along the road, the disciples saw the fig tree withered to its roots. Peter then said to him, "Master, look! The fig tree you cursed has withered."
>
> And Jesus replied, "Have faith in God. Truly, I say to you, if you say to this mountain: 'Get up and throw yourself into the sea,' and have no doubt in your heart but believe that what you say will happen, it will be done for you. Therefore, I tell you, whatever you ask in prayer, believe that you have received it, and it shall be done for you. And when you stand to pray, forgive whatever you may hold against anyone, so that your heavenly Father may also forgive your sins." (11:20-26)

Peter remembers hearing Jesus curse the tree the day before. Peter seems surprised that the fig tree has withered to its roots. The withered fig tree represents the temple and serves as a visible sign of the words Jesus spoke the day before about the temple. Quoting Isaiah and Jeremiah, Jesus maintained that worship in the temple had become no more than empty ritual; it is all show and produces no fruit. Jesus teaches his disciples that they must not be like the fig tree. They must have the faith of God. This is the only time the Greek expression *pistin theou* (the faith of God) appears in Mark's gospel. What is God's faith like? It is absolute, consistent, undying, evocative, demanding of all, and confident no matter what happens. Jesus charges Peter and the disciples themselves to have the faith of God.

Jesus gives the disciples an example of what this faith might be able to do: it can move mountains and plant them in the sea. While the example seems to be a hyperbole, like the example about the camel going through a needle's eye just a few days before, Jesus told them that "all things are possible with God" (10:27b). Jesus tells his disciples, and this message is also intended for us, that they are to pray for this gift of faith, a faith that is God's faith, a faith that brings the power to believe and trust in God as Jesus trusts in God. The power of prayer and the power of faith are both one.

Jesus has already instructed them about faith and prayer (for example, "Everything is possible to one who has faith" [Mk 9:23] and certain evils and demons can only be driven out by prayer [Mk 9:28-29]), but Jesus repeats it once again. The disciples are going to have to depend on faith and prayer in the coming days.

Jesus also reminds the disciples—and us—that there is a prerequisite to receiving this gift of faith and prayer. Before we pray, we must forgive "whatever you may hold against anyone." When we have forgiven, then we will be forgiven and God can give us what we need. Sin blocks the power of God from coming into and through us and makes our prayer empty and hollow, as if we were fig trees producing leaves but no figs.

They continue on to Jerusalem, returning to the temple for another encounter with the chief priests, scribes, and elders. Word has obviously spread about what happened the previous day.

> As Jesus was walking in the Temple, the chief priests, the teachers of the Law and the elders came to him and asked, "What authority do you have to act like this? Who gave you authority to do the things you do?"
>
> Jesus said to them, "I will ask you a question, only one, and if you give me answer, then I will tell you what authority I have to act like this. Was John's preaching and baptism a work of God, or was it merely something human? Answer me."
>
> And they kept arguing among themselves, "If we answer that it was a work of God, he will say: 'Why then did you not believe him?'" But neither could they answer before the people that the baptism of John was merely something human, for everyone regarded John as a prophet. So they answered Jesus, "We don't know," and Jesus said to them, "Neither will I tell you what authority I have to act as I do." (11:27-33)

Jesus will continue to speak with the chief priests only if they will take a risk and answer truthfully, but they are not open to him. They are intent only on collecting information to use to attack him. And this is just the beginning of the challenges: group after group will approach him in the temple and try to trip him up to gather ammunition to use against him. (Many of these challenges form the next chapter of Mark.)

But Jesus seems ready for them and does not answer their question; instead, he insists that they must answer his question first. And Jesus' question deals with the source of John the Baptist's authority. John the Baptist called everyone to repent and look for the one who would come after him, but the chief priests and elders did not listen to his words with any intent to obey or change their lives. They did not submit to John's baptism, although Jesus did. Both John and Jesus are prophets who are independent of the religious structure and whose power and authority come directly from God. As the chief priests and other elders *are* the religious structure, they see John and Jesus as direct threats to their power. They set out to devalue and silence them, but, because they are afraid of losing the people's support, they will bide their time and build their case against Jesus.

At the end of Mark 11, we stand in Jerusalem with Jesus and the disciples. Like the members of Mark's community, we are in the company of Jesus and we stand in opposition to a religious authority that is dead at its heart. We must make sure that as church we do not become like that. Forgiveness, prayer, and faith are essential for us to bear fruit for others to eat.

A story from India called "The Tree and the Parrot," which is often told to children, illustrates well what Jesus is asking of his followers and what is being asked of us in these last days of his life.

Once upon a time there was a tree. It was a magnificent tree, ancient and gnarled and towering above the other trees. It was many branched with long, outstretched limbs and a root system spread equally wide across the ground, sticking out here and there as it traveled under the branches. It gave shade in summer, and it kept many of its leaves in winter, affording some protection. It would hang with rich fruit, and the birds loved to come and eat to their heart's content. And small animals would pick up the fallen fruit and carry it off. When the rains came, all manner of creatures buried in its leaves until the rain stopped and the air cleared.

Now there was a parrot that lived in the tree. He'd been born there and it was the only home he'd ever known. He and the tree had become good friends, just sitting together, not needing to talk but just to be there with each other. They remained together in every season. They'd comment on the birds as they came and went, listening to stories from far places as the birds chattered. They endured all sorts of weather. The tree gave of its fruit and the parrot gave back with its presence and conversation.

One day a hunter discovered that the tree was a great place to hunt birds and animals. He shot an arrow with a poisonous tip at a bird. Although he missed the bird, the arrow went deep into the bark of the tree. Over the weeks as the tree took a number of arrows aimed at animals, the tree began to sicken and die. Eventually the leaves started falling off, the bark began to peel, and the limbs and branches dried out and broke easily.

The next season there was little or no fruit, and the birds started spitting it out. The parrot was distressed, but what could it do? The year slowly inched by, and the tree was in terrible shape. No leaves came back, and it looked like a great stick rising black and grey into the sky. Yet the parrot stayed. The others said that he was stupid, that he'd get sick like the tree and die too. But the parrot had loved the tree for as long as he could remember. He couldn't leave it alone when it was dying.

Now the God in heaven looked down one day to see this bright light shining brilliantly in a corner of the world. He hadn't noticed it before, but now it would be impossible not to see it. God sent messengers to see what was the source of this amazing light. They came back with the story of the dying tree and the parrot that refused to leave.

God was pleased. It had been a long time since such light, such goodness and faithfulness has been seen on the earth. God was so heartened that, in fact, God was moved to tears. And so it began to rain upon the earth, and many of the tears dropped directly on the nearly dead tree. The tears of God were healing tears that brought refreshment and life, and the tree began to breathe again, its roots to stir, and its bark to mend. The rain lasted through three days and three nights, and when the sky cleared, the birds and animals and even the other trees couldn't believe what they saw. The tree was taller than ever, vibrant, lush, its leaves every color of green; and the fruit on the tree was wonderfully different from any fruit they'd seen before. The tree also had flowers that bloomed on the top, with some along low branches and moss covering its trunk. It was magnificent.

The parrot was ecstatic with joy, as he danced around in the tree from branch to branch, singing and croaking and sputtering with delight. And God looked down to see the light shimmering and dancing and was pleased. God hadn't wept with joy brought on by one of his creature's faithfulness and friendship in so long. Finally God felt goodness washing into the world again.

Forgiveness, prayer, and faithfulness are what we are to bring to God. The faith of God is the gift we are to ask for, believing that we will receive it and that it shall be ours. Jesus is trying to teach his disciples how to be so faithful and how their faithfulness will delight and please the heart of God once again. God is waiting and watching to see if any of his children will be as faithful as was his beloved son, Jesus, who, in his faith, drew into his circle anyone who would share wealth with others, anyone who would walk the way with him, and anyone who would share his suffering and sorrows.

We can pray a portion of Psalm 118, which is a hymn of thanksgiving. It uses the language of those waiting to welcome the Messiah into his city.

> Open to me the gates of the Just,
> And let me enter to give thanks.
> "This is the Lord's gate,
> Through which the upright enter."
>
> I thank you for having answered me,
> For having rescued me.
> The stone rejected by the builders
> Has become the keystone.
> This was the Lord's doing
> And we marvel at it.
>
> This it the day the Lord has made;
> So let us rejoice and be glad.

Save us, O Lord, deliver us, O Lord!
    Blessed is he who comes in the Lord's name!
We bless you from the house of the Lord.

The Lord is God; may his light shine upon us.

> *With branches, join in procession*
> *Up to the horns of the altar.*

You are my God, and I give you thanks.
You are my God, and I give you praise.
Give thanks to the Lord, for he is good;
His steadfast love endures forever! (Ps 118:19-29)

CHAPTER 8

Marking the Last Days

Mark 12 and 13

> I believe it to be a great mistake to present Christianity as something
> charming and popular with no offense in it. . . . We cannot blink at
> the fact that gentle Jesus meek and mild was so stiff in his opinions
> and so inflammatory in his language that he was thrown out of
> church, stoned, hunted from place to place, and finally gibbeted as a
> firebrand and a public danger. Whatever his peace was, it was not the
> peace of an amiable indifference. (Dorothy Sayers, "A Careless Rage
> for Life," quoted on http://dailydig.bruderhof.org)

IMMEDIATELY AFTER REFUSING to be trapped by the questioning of chief
priests, scribes, and elders, Jesus begins once again to teach. He is aware
of the mounting hostility toward him, but he does not let the challenges
and mean-spiritedness of the Sanhedrin deter him from what he must say.
Jesus again uses a parable, his preferred method of instructing the disciples
and the crowds that follow him. The parable of the tenants makes clear
who he believes he is and what he clearly thinks of those who oppose him.

The parable of the tenants in the vineyard is layered with references
from Isaiah's Song of the Vineyard (5:1-7), a passage that would have been
familiar to his audience. It is helpful to begin with this passage, in which
the vineyard clearly represents Israel.

> Let me sing for my beloved the love song of my beloved about his
> vineyard.
>
> > My beloved had a vineyard
> > on a fertile hillside.
> > He dug it up, cleared the stones,
> > and planted the choicest vines.
> > He built there a watchtower
> > and hewed out a winepress as well.

Then he looked
    for a crop of good grapes,
but it yielded only wild grapes.
Now, inhabitants of Jerusalem and people of Judah,
judge between me and my vineyard.
What more was there to do
that I have not done for my vineyard?
Good grapes was the yield I expected,
why did it yield only sour grapes?

Now I will let you know
what I am going to do
with my vineyard:
I will remove its hedge
and it will be burned;
I will break down its wall
and it will be trampled on.
I will make it a wasteland,
I will neither prune nor hoe it,
and briers and thorns will grow there.
I command the clouds, as well,
not to send rain on it.

The vineyard of Yahweh Sabaoth
is the people of Israel,
and the people of Judah
are his pleasant vine.
He looked for justice,
but found bloodshed;
He looked for righteousness
but heard cries of distress. (Is 5:1-7)

This is a haunting song of lamentation in which God responds to his people with a litany of all that he has done for them. In response, all they have done is to produce wild grapes that no one can eat or use to produce wine. So justice must be done. When God asked for justice, only bloodshed resulted. Isaiah's song proclaims that the problem lies with the people of Israel; their lack of faithfulness and their disobedience to the Law and the covenant have stripped justice from the land.

C. H. Dodd has defined the form of a parable and also described what a parable does to those who hear it.

At its simplest the parable is a metaphor or simile drawn from nature or common life, arresting the hearer by its vividness or strangeness, and leaving the mind in sufficient doubt about its precise application to tease it into active thought. (*The Parables of the Kingdom*, 5)

Hearing the parable, even if the high priests and scribes don't comprehend all of what Jesus is saying about them and about God, they can either listen and be open to change or they can stubbornly refuse to listen and persist in their plans to kill him. There is no middle ground. They have challenged his authority, and now he will use that authority to judge them.

As we hear or read this parable, it is important for us to remember that we are understanding it differently from the people to whom Jesus originally spoke. We are familiar with the theology of the life, death, and resurrection of Jesus. But this theology developed long after the death and resurrection of Jesus and after the movement of the gospel into the Gentile world. While the parable spoke to the religious authorities of the time of Jesus, as it speaks to us today, it was also addressed to the early church of Mark's time. It also describes what had happened by the end of the sixth decade, the destruction of the temple in Jerusalem and the split between the Jewish and the Christian communities.

Using parables, Jesus went on to say, "A man planted a vineyard, put a fence around it, dug a hole for the wine press and built a watch tower. Then he leased the vineyard to tenants and went abroad.

"In due time he sent a servant to receive from the tenants his share of the fruit. But they seized the servant, struck him and sent him back empty-handed. Again the man sent another servant. They also struck him on the head and treated him shamefully. He sent another and they killed him. In the same way they treated many others; some they struck and others they killed. One was still left, his beloved son. And so, last of all, he sent him to the tenants, for he said: 'They will respect my son.'

"But those tenants said to one another: 'This is the one who is to inherit the vineyard. Let's kill him and the property will be ours.' So they seized him and killed him, and threw him out of the vineyard. Now, what will the owner of the vineyard do? He will come and destroy those tenants and give the vineyard to others."

And Jesus added, "Have you not read this text of the Scriptures? *The stone which the builders rejected has become the keystone. This was the Lord's doing; and we marvel at it.*" (12:1-11)

This parable is a theological retelling of the history of Israel that describes all that God has done. If the absentee landlord represents God, then the tenants represent the religious leaders. God sends the prophets (servants) one after another, and throughout history they are rejected, demeaned, exiled, and beaten until the last prophet (likely John the Baptist) is killed. Then God sends his beloved son, Jesus, who is killed and thrown out of the vineyard. (Indeed, Jesus was crucified outside the walls of Jerusalem.) Judgment is then rendered upon the leaders. However, at the end of the parable, Jesus quotes two lines from Psalm 118: Jesus, the beloved son, the stone they have rejected, will become the cornerstone of the new religion, Christianity.

The religious leaders realized that Jesus was speaking of them. Although they wanted to have Jesus arrested, they "were afraid of the crowd." However they will continue to plot to have Jesus killed, not knowing that the death they bring about will be reversed because God will raise Jesus from the dead.

Peter will repeat these same lines from Psalm 118 much later when he is brought before the Sanhedrin for healing a crippled beggar. The leaders begin the interrogation of Peter and the other disciples with the question, "How did you do this? Whose name did you use?" (Acts 4:5-12). With this passage, Mark is trying to provide a sense of perspective for his community. They already know the outcome, and the climate in which they live is similar to the world of conflicts in which Jesus, God's beloved son, lived. They, too, are the beloved children of God, and they are to follow him in life and in death and in resurrection.

The islanders of the South Pacific have a concept called *mana*—a sense of someone's heart, of the essence of a person or thing, a gut feeling. Many traditions make use of this same sense of mana, and it seems that Jesus also makes use of it; he knows when he is approached by those who seek to destroy him. One story of mana from India will give us a sense of how Jesus is dealing with these people and their way of questioning him.

> Once upon a time there was a king, a good king who sought justice for his people and tried to make sure that everyone had the basics of what they needed to survive. He would often go among his people to listen to them and see how they were doing. This made his bodyguards very nervous, but he insisted on doing it.
>
> One day he was out among the people and as he passed through a crowd he had a terrible sense of foreboding, of danger close by. It didn't last long, but it was very, very strong and the king couldn't put it out of his head.
>
> As he continued, he spoke with various people about their work and their families, and, in the course of these conversations, he began to speak with a man who had been standing behind him for a good length of time. He found out that the man was a coffin-maker who was much in demand.
>
> Some feeling within the king told him to investigate this more deeply, so he invited the man to the palace for dinner that evening. The man, who was delighted and honored, came at the appointed time, dressed in his best. He had already begun to plan how he could make use of the king's good favor, how it would affect his business dealings and his prestige in the community and even among his own family.
>
> The dinner was superb and to his surprise only the king and he were dining together. Nervous, he drank a little more than he was used to,

and the food was very rich. As he ate and drank, the king plied him with questions. He started talking very freely, and, as the king continued to draw him out, he spoke of a great quantity of sandalwood that had become available in his area. Because it was very expensive, not many people could afford to buy it for furniture, let alone for their coffins. The man then confessed that when he saw the king earlier that day he suddenly remembered that the kings of the land and their families and close associates were always buried in sandalwood coffins. And he had thought it a coincidence that he was standing right next to the king and that a shipment of sandalwood had just arrived in his neighborhood. If something happened to the king, he could use it to make his coffin and coffins of any others who might be killed with him. He then told the king that he immediately put the thought out of his mind. Such thoughts were not befitting anyone who was a loyal servant of the king.

The king was suddenly relieved. He had learned early on to trust his instincts, his sense of mana, and he knew now what it was he had sensed that morning in the crowd: it had been a definite threat of harm, the intent of violence. However fleeting, its strength had caused a shiver to run down his spine. He knew the source of that feeling from the morning, and he knew that he could continue to rely on it in the future.

He never mentioned any of this to the man, and he didn't rebuke him for his greed or his momentary lapse of thinking that harm to the king could work to his financial gain. Instead, the king sent the man home with gifts and went on with his life, promising himself that he would pay close attention in the future to what he sensed around others.

Likewise, Jesus is attuned to God and to others, sensing and knowing their hearts and minds. He is well aware that these people intend him harm. It is this heightened awareness that gives him additional insight and knowledge to respond to the questions and tests of the religious leaders.

The next group to challenge Jesus includes some of the Pharisees and the Herodians. While they don't get along, they have decided to conspire together against Jesus (see Mk 3:6). They have been biding their time, and now Jesus is on their ground.

They sent to Jesus some Pharisees with members of Herod's party, with the purpose of trapping him in his own words. They came and said to Jesus, "Master, we know that you are true; you are not influenced by anyone, and your answers do not vary according to who is listening to you but you truly teach God's way. Tell us, is it against the Law to pay taxes to Caesar? Should we pay them or not?"

But Jesus saw through their trick and answered, "Why are you testing me? Bring me a silver coin and let me see it." They brought him one and Jesus asked, "Whose head is this, and whose name?" They answered, "Caesar's." Then Jesus said, "Return to Caesar what

is Caesar's and to God what is God's."
And they were greatly astonished. (12:13-17)

While they begin with flattery, they go straight to the question: "Is it against the Law to pay taxes to Caesar? Should we pay them or not?" Many taxes were imposed on the Jewish people; this one was resented most because it was a poll tax that went straight into the imperial treasury. The Zealots and other revolutionary groups refused to pay the tax, while those who worked in collusion with the Romans paid the tax. For the Pharisees, the tax was basically a religious issue, and for the Herodians, it was a political issue. This was a question clearly intended to trap Jesus: Do you serve Caesar or God?

But Jesus is familiar with their ruthlessness and will not fall into their trap. The Roman tax had to be paid with a specific coin, a denarius. On one face of the coin was an image of Tiberius rendered as the son of the god Augustus and the goddess Livia, with an abbreviation of the words "Tiberius Caesar Augustus, Son of the Divine Augustus" inscribed around the image; on the back was the title "Pontifex Maximus." Jews considered the coin an abomination that profaned anyone who possessed it. It is a sacrilege to have it in the temple precincts! Jesus asks them whose image and whose inscription is on the coin, using a precise word for "inscription." Ched Myers describes this situation:

> "Do we pay, or don't we?" (12:15). As far as Jesus is concerned, the question is not his but theirs; he forces them to own up to their collaboration by producing a coin. The image and the inscription this coin bears become the center of the story (12:16). The image alone might have sufficed to settle the matter, since no true Jewish patriot (or Christian) would have used such idolatrous currency. (The revolutionary provisional government in Palestine minted its own coins.)
>
> But Mark is particularly concerned with the inscription, which would have extolled Caesar as the "August and Divine Son." The word "inscription" appears only one other time in Mark: the writ of conviction posted over the cross of Jesus (the divine "Son") at the end of the story, which will read "King of the Jews" (15:26). (*Sojourners* [1987]: 33)

This is a clear-cut choice between rival authorities. A Jewish rabbi I know once said that Jesus would have known of other rabbis who had dealt with this issue. In Genesis we read that we are made in the image and likeness of God: "God created man in his image, in the divine image he created him; male and female he created them" (Gn 1:27). Each person is created singularly, uniquely, reflecting something of God in their person. But when minting coins a ruler makes all the images exactly the same; they are flat representations of himself. When Jesus asks for the coin and poses the question, "Whose image and inscription is this?" they respond with Caesar's name and image. My friend the rabbi said that he could imagine Jesus touching the arm of the man with the coin and saying, "And whose image is this?" and then answering, "Repay to Caesar what belongs to Caesar and to God what belongs to God." The coin belongs to Caesar, but the person, the human being, belongs solely to God. The Pharisees and the Herodians would have been humiliated at being seen through so clearly.

So the next group, the Sadducees, appears. It is as if they are standing in line, waiting their turn at Jesus. The Sadducees, who do not believe in the resurrection of the dead, put a ludicrous situation before Jesus.

> The Sadducees also came to Jesus. Since they claim that there is no resurrection, they questioned him in this way, "Master, in the Scriptures Moses gave us this law: 'If anyone dies and leaves a wife but no children, his brother must take the wife and give her a child who will be considered the child of his deceased brother.' Now, there were seven brothers. The first married a wife, he died without leaving any children. The second took the wife and he, too, died leaving no children. The same thing happened to the third. Finally the seven died leaving no children. Last of all the woman died. Now, in the resurrection, to which of them will she be wife? For the seven had her as wife."
>
> Jesus replied, "You could be wrong in this regard because you understand neither the Scriptures nor the power of God. When they rise from the dead, men and women do not marry but are like the angels in heaven.
>
> Now, about the resurrection of the dead, have you never reflected on the chapter of the burning bush in the book of Moses? God said to him: *I am the God of Abraham, the God of Isaac and the God of Jacob.* Now, he is the God, not of the dead but of the living. You are totally wrong." (12:18-37)

The Sadducees are trivializing belief in the resurrection and mocking Jesus with an improbable example. The custom they describe and practice is called a Levirate marriage. Its intent was to protect a woman should her husband die leaving her without a child to protect her, but it also supported a system in which women were necessary to bear children to secure an inheritance. Jesus demonstrates great control as he refutes their question by using portions of the books of Moses, which they claim to believe in and practice. He accuses them of not knowing their own texts and being misled. Jesus also speaks of the resurrected life, in which men and women will be nothing like they were on earth. Resurrection life is another quality of life altogether, and those who rise are like angels. They rise and live in the power of God. Jesus then deftly quotes from the book of Moses which describes God as the God of Abraham, Isaac and Jacob, leaders of faith who have died. Although they are long buried, God is the God of the living: "You are totally wrong." The implication is that they are ignorant of their own scriptures that state clearly that God is the God of the living. And they are left speechless.

The next interrogator is a teacher of the Law, a scribe who studies interpretations and commentaries on the Law. He comes alone. Mark notes that he has been impressed with Jesus' answers to those who are bent on trapping him with his own words. He treats Jesus with respect as he also poses a simple question.

> A teacher of the Law had been listening to this discussion and admired how Jesus answered them. So he came up and asked him, "Which commandment is the first of all?"
>
> Jesus answered, "The first is: *Hear, Israel! The Lord, our God, is One Lord; and you shall love the Lord, your God, with all your heart, with all your soul, with all your mind and with all your strength.* And after this comes another one: *You shall love your neighbor as yourself.* There is no commandment greater than these two."
>
> The teacher of the Law said to him, "Well spoken, Master; you are right when you say that he is one and there is no other. To love him with all our heart, with all our understanding and with all our strength, and to love our neighbor as ourselves is more important than any burnt offering or sacrifice."
>
> Jesus approved this answer and said, "You are not far from the kingdom of God." But after that, no one dared to ask him any more questions. (12:28-34)

Jesus treats the scribe with respect, teaching him as he would one of his own disciples because he sees that his heart is open. He begins with the *Shema*, found in Deuteronomy 6:4-5, the heart of Judaism's belief in the one God. This was recited by every Jew as part of the morning and evening prayers. Jesus quotes this commandment of undivided and wholehearted love and devotion to God. Loving God with one's heart, soul, mind, and strength demands the complete sacrifice of one's life to God. Nothing is to be excluded or held back from God.

Jesus then links this segment of Deuteronomy with a portion of a verse from the Book of Leviticus: "Do not seek revenge or nurture a grudge against one of your people, but love your neighbor as yourself; I am Yahweh" (Lv 19:18). With this, Jesus makes another judgment against the religious authorities, who have disobeyed this law as well. By bringing these two verses of the Hebrew scriptures together, Jesus creates from the essence of the earlier covenant a unified principle for belief and practice for his disciples and the Christian church. The two laws become one, with no separation. The verse from Deuteronomy could just as easily read: And you are to love your neighbor with all your heart, and all your soul, and all your mind, and all your strength (meaning your resources). Jesus' words are an incredible summary of the Law and theology of the Jewish covenant.

And the scribe responds to Jesus' teaching wholeheartedly, referring to the words of the prophet Hosea (6:6). The practice of loving God and one's neighbor is by far more important than all the ritual offerings or prayers of the temple liturgy.

The man is truly engaged with Jesus in a discussion of the heart and the meaning of the Law. He is a true scribe, who seems to be inviting himself into Jesus' company. Jesus approves fully and says to him: "You are not far from the kingdom of God." Indeed, the kingdom is so close, right there in front of the scribe. What did the scribe do? Did he take that step toward his neighbors in love, toward Jesus, and toward the practices of love that Jesus has been teaching, that one's neighbors include the poor, the lepers, the sick, and the public sinners? Did the scribe begin to practice loving God and loving others with all his heart and soul and mind, and strength (meaning his resources and possessions), in the company of Jesus' followers? We don't know, but the invitation has been extended and heard.

Jesus' proclamation states clearly that love of God and love of others cannot be separated. Indifference to others in need is indifference to God. Because of the incarnation, Jesus becoming one of us, all human beings are one in the sacrament of obedience to God. What we do or don't do for others, we do or don't do for God.

So did the scribe take that step? Will we take that step? We live in a culture, a country and an age that glorifies selfishness, self-sufficiency, greed, and security. Every election year we ask if *we* are better off than we were four years before, but the question we should ask is if the poor are better off than they were four years ago. Then, are fewer prisons being built and filled? Are there fewer executions? Is all of life being respected?" Will the unborn, the youngest in most need of medical care, nutrition, and safety, and the most vulnerable get basic health care, education and support? Will women, especially women of childbearing age and mothers, get what they need, as well as the elderly? Will our decisions be based on the common-good rule rather than the rule of the wealthy and powerful? Will working people receive a living wage this year? Will we remember that we live in a world larger than the United States and that what is good for us is not necessarily good for the rest of the world? Will there be fewer guns and a lessening of violence? Will military budgets be cut? Will whole cities still be bombed? Will we make this step closer to Jesus in belief and practice? An old adage often visible in people's homes sums it up.

> I sought God and him I did not see.
> I sought my soul but it eluded me.
> I sought my neighbor and found all three.

Equally apt is a line from Mark Twain: "One of the nicest things that can happen to a person is to do good by stealth and be found out by accident."

This section ends with the statement: "But after that, no one dared to ask him any more questions." The reactions of those who challenge Jesus range from hostility (12:2) to amazement (12:17) to silence (12:27) to admiration (12:27). How do we feel?

Now Jesus has something to say, provoked by the quality and intent of the questions posed to him. He brings up something that the scribes would have been arguing:

> As Jesus was teaching in the Temple, he said, "The teachers of the Law said that the Messiah is the son of David. How can that be? For David himself, inspired by the Holy Spirit, declared: *The Lord said to my Lord: sit at my right until I put your enemies under your feet.* If David himself calls him Lord, in what way can he be his son?"
>
> Many people came to Jesus and listened to him gladly. (12:35-37)

This fourth question is posed by Jesus himself, and, like a good Jew and rabbi, he provides clues to the answer. Two chapters before, Bartimaeus, the blind beggar, had cried out to Jesus, saying: "Jesus, Son of David, have pity on me." This was an unusual title for Jesus, but one that became common among the early Christians for it was believed that the Messiah would be of David's lineage, and David had been made an adopted son of God: "I will be his father, and he shall be my son" (2 Sm 7:14a). Similarly, in the psalm Jesus just quoted, David refers to the Messiah as "Lord," someone above him in power and nearness to God, who will "sit at [God's] right hand." After the resurrection, the community of Mark will declare openly that Jesus is the Son of God, which is exactly how Mark begins this gospel.

Later in Mark, when Jesus is on trial, he will be questioned directly about this by the high priest:

> The High Priest put a second question to him, "Are you the Christ, the Son of the Blessed One?" Then Jesus answered, "I am, and you will see *the Son of Man seated at the right hand of the Most Powerful and coming with the clouds of heaven around him.*" (14:61b-62)

Mark is already hinting that Jesus is the Son of God, the son of the Blessed One. Jesus is teaching as the son of David and the Son of God, and his teaching is for Jews and Gentiles alike, for all the peoples of the world. The scribes' teachings were limited not only by what they were saying but by how they were saying it. Their lifestyle, their ritual finery, their arrogance, and their appropriation of power and their twisting of the Law for their own gain undercut their teachings. Jesus lays them bare down to the bone.

> As he was teaching, he also said to them, "Beware of those teachers of the Law who enjoy walking around in long robes and being

greeted in the marketplace, and who like to occupy reserved seats in the synagogues and the first places at feast. They even devour the widow's and the orphan's goods while making a show of long prayers. How severe a sentence they will receive!" (12:38-40)

He is not condemning all the scribes, only those whose behavior is insulting to God. If they teach the Law, they must also obey it. The scribe who joined in sincere debate with Jesus was so close to the kingdom of God. Earlier, Jesus had warned his disciples that they must accept his teaching as a child would enter the kingdom of God. How can a scribe, a teacher of the Law, become like a child? They were to teach and practice the single law of love of God and others, especially the poorest of the poor in Jewish society, orphans and widows.

The Widow's Mite

This story of the widow serves as a bridge from the condemnation of the scribes who devour the savings of widows to the next section of the gospel, which ends with the story of Jesus' anointing by a woman in the house of Simon the leper (Mk 14:3-9). The next section will describe the Last Supper and the events that follow. The account of the widow's mite is a further critique of the greed and ostentation of the religious leaders. Because the story is so familiar, we often miss much of its import and insight.

> Jesus sat down opposite the Temple treasury and watched the people dropping money into the treasury box; and many rich people put in large offerings. But a poor widow also came and dropped in two small coins.
> Then Jesus called his disciples and said to them, "Truly I say to you, this poor widow put in more than all those who gave offerings. For all of them gave from their plenty, but she gave from her poverty and put in everything she had, her very living." (12:41-44)

As Jesus sits opposite the treasury, he observes the worshipers putting money in the collection boxes. He is also observing the hearts of the people and judging them rightly. Jesus has just criticized the scribes for stealing from widows and orphans (12:40), and now he uses a poor widow as a model for loving God with all your heart and soul, and mind and resources. Jesus speaks directly to the religious professionals of his time. Here he says that the priests and teachers of the Law who devour the savings of widows and recite long prayers for appearance's sake will receive the harshest sentence. The God of justice is the protector of the poorest and the weakest in society. Those in authority, scribes, teachers, deacons, and priests, must be the servants of all the people. They must use their religious power and affluence and knowledge to ease the suffering of the victims of injustice; if they use religion for their own personal gain, they are worshiping false gods or idols.

Jesus watches as the rich put in large sums and the widow but a tiny pittance. Her two coins probably added up to about one-twelfth of a cent. (Note that although she could have kept one for herself, she gave both.) Jesus then calls his disciples over to show them what she has done. Jesus speaks to them in very formal language, beginning with "Truly" (or "Amen" in other translations) I say to you," which indicates that what he is about to say is of utmost importance. First, he directly criticizes the scribes, and then he teaches his disciples, warning them not to become like the scribes. This widow represents the many who have been taken in by the scribes and reduced to misery and destitution by their offerings to the temple treasury:

> The story does not provide a pious contrast to the conduct of the scribes in the preceding section (as is the customary view); rather it provides a further illustration of the ills of official devotion. Jesus' saying is not a penetrating insight on the measuring of gifts; it is a lament: "Amen, I tell you, she gave more than all the others." Or as we would say, "One could easily fail to notice it, but there is the tragedy of the day—she put in her whole living." She has been taught and encouraged by religious leaders to donate as she does, and Jesus condemns the value system that motivates her action, and he condemns the people who conditioned her to do it. (A. G. Wright, "The Widow's Mites: Praise or Lament?" 262)

Jesus uses the widow as an example of how a disciple or a member of his community should act. He declares that she has contributed more than all of them together, including his own disciples. While the rich gave from their surplus or excess (no skin off their noses, so to speak), she has given from her want, from her "poverty and put in everything she had, her very living."

Jesus says that she is like him! They are to observe her actions and imitate them. She offers sacrifice, virtue, and the practice of poverty for the kingdom as Jesus will give all that he has, even his very life as he offers his body and blood on the cross. She is the image of a disciple, and she is clearly contrasted with the rich young man who cannot bring himself to share his many possessions, and the disciples who are calculating what they have given up and what they're going to receive in return. Her example also contrasts with many of us who give grudgingly, hesitantly, and intermittently to the worship of God and to our "sharing" with the poor. It is in opposition to those of us who use our religious positions to gain our own comfort or livelihood along with status and power within the community rather using our privilege to serve those in our society who are the most destitute.

This portion of scripture demands that we observe our own lives from Jesus' point of view. Are we true followers of Jesus, like this widow? Or are we like the scribes and religious leaders who stand in front to lead the public liturgical and ministerial practices of our religion but who do not practice what they profess to believe or provide an example in their lives.

Although the story refers to the widow's "mite," the mite really was largesse. She risked much in being generous because she gave all that she had in sacrifice. An elderly woman once told me that the value of a gift is not found in its worth but in what it creates as a lack in the giver. After my initial surprise and confusion, it made perfect sense. What we have lost, the lack it creates in us, that is the worth of the gift. The widow and another woman who will lavishly anoint Jesus with perfumed oil (Mk 14:3-9) are worthy of being observed and wondered over and then imitated by us. The true worship of God and the true practice of faithfulness are found in the lives of people like this. They may be unnamed or unknown (except to God) or belittled by others, but they exhibit the marks of a Christian: generosity, sharing from the depths of what they have, accepting the kingdom as children, faithful in public and private. These people, models of discipleship, are truly our "treasure in heaven," whom we can observe and take heart from here on earth.

The Temple, the End, the Signs

Jesus leaves the temple for the last time, and his feelings must include disgust, sadness and sorrow. It is Jesus' body, the body of the crucified and risen Lord, that will form the new temple. At this point, Mark includes a long discourse of Jesus about the destruction of the temple in Jerusalem. These events were probably familiar to the Marcan community because the war began around 66 C.E. and the temple, except for one existing piece of the western wall, was destroyed around 70 C.E. The discourse also includes a description of the end times that will come upon the earth to herald the coming of the Son of Man in judgment and glory. The disciples' praise of the splendor of the temple buildings contrasts sharply with Jesus' praise of the poor widow's generosity.

> As Jesus left the Temple, one of his disciples said, "Look, Master, at the enormous stones and wonderful buildings here!" And Jesus answered, "You see these great buildings? Not one stone will be left upon another, but all will be torn down."
>
> After a while, when Jesus was sitting on the Mount of Olives, facing the Temple, Peter, James, John and Andrew approached him privately and asked, "Tell us when this will be. What sign will be given us before all this happens?"

Then Jesus began to tell them, "Don't let anyone mislead you. Many will come, taking my place, and say: 'I am the one who you are waiting for,' and they will deceive many people.

"When you hear of war and threats of war, don't be troubled; this must occur but the end is not yet. Nation will fight nation and kingdom will oppose kingdom. There will be earthquakes everywhere and famines, too. And these will be like the first pains of childbirth." (13:1-8)

Jesus is acting in a long line of prophets who announced the destruction of the temple. One of these was Micah (742-687 B.C.E.), who cried out for the downfall of the present leaders if they did not repent and with them the temple itself.

Hear this, leaders of the nation of Jacob, rulers of the house of Israel, you who despise justice and pervert what is right, you who build Zion with blood and Jerusalem with crime. Her leaders judge for a bribe, her priests prophesy for money, and yet they rely on Yahweh and say, "Is Yahweh not in our midst? No evil, then, will come upon us." Therefore, because of you, Zion will become a field, Jerusalem will be a heap of ruins and the temple mount a forest with sacred stones. (Mi 3:9-12)

About a hundred years after Micah, Jeremiah castigated the temple leaders.

Tell them: This is what Yahweh says:
"You have not obeyed me and you have failed to walk according to my Law which I have set before you. You have not heeded my servants, the prophets, whom I have persistently sent to you. If you stubbornly close your ears to them, I will treat this House of mine as I treated the sanctuary of Shiloh and let all the nations see that Jerusalem is a cursed city." (Jer 26:4-6)

At the time Mark was writing his gospel, the second restoration of the temple, begun almost a hundred years before, was nearing completion. The restored temple was a magnificent achievement, a building that caused people to look at it in awe. The temple was the center of the worship of Yahweh, and it also represented the people's nationalist hopes for a political messiah who would return Israel to the former glory of the time of David and Solomon. As prophet, Jesus was declaring that the temple had no value and that one day nothing of it would remain.

The very idea that the temple might be destroyed incensed people and caused rage. This was probably the same reaction of the people to the ancient prophets when they spoke about the rubble of people's lives and the inadequacies of their worship of God. But at that time Micah and Jeremiah were addressing—as Jesus is now doing—what the building stood for, a spiritually bankrupt religious monarchy or nation that was an insult to God. In calling for its destruction, they were calling the people and the leaders to restore their covenant with God. True and just worship should be written on hearts and not carved in stone. Israel was never supposed to be like the other nations. Israel was God's people, singularly bound together by the covenant, the Law, the worship of God, and the practice of justice and care for the poor.

Any kind of talk about the destruction of the temple was linked with thoughts about the end of their world and of their hopes as a nation. Thus, when Jesus speaks of the temple being reduced to ruins, with not a stone left upon a stone, the disciples immediately want to know when it will happen and what signs will indicate this coming catastrophe. This particular discourse of Jesus is called *eschatological* because it focuses on the end of the world as we know and experience it. For the disciples, the end of the temple would be synonymous with the end of the world they lived in. *The* cataclysmic event for the entire Jewish community would be the destruction of the temple in Jerusalem.

Until this point, Mark has been propelling Jesus, often at a furious pace, toward the cross. The pace suddenly slows as Jesus sits down on the Mount of Olives, opposite the temple, and speaks of events that will take place after his life and death. Two key events are recounted in Mark 13: the destruction of the temple, which will happen in 70 C.E., and the end of the world, when Jesus will return in glory to judge all the nations as the Son of Man.

Jesus deflects the disciples' question about the timing of the destruction of the temple and, instead, warns the disciples of corruption in their own community. He presents a list of events that will take place, events that happen in every generation and are not to be taken as signs of the end times. These include wars, earthquakes, famine, and nations rising against one another. This is life in the world. In fact, much of what Jesus describes, although often interpreted as apocalyptic (referring to end-time) realities, are not, and are not to be interpreted as such. There were undoubtedly many in Mark's community who were expecting, or hoping, that the end would come soon and that they would witness the coming of Jesus in glory. This discourse of Jesus seeks to alter that thinking and reveal it as wrong. Jesus wants to make sure that his disciples live in the present and continue to preach the gospel, no matter what might happen to them. Jesus emphasizes the coming persecution. As he will be rejected, tortured, and killed, so will the disciples, and so will those who follow. Indeed, Mark's community has already begun to experience persecution.

Be on your guard, for you will be arrested and taken to Jewish courts. You will be beaten in synagogues; and you will stand before governors and kings for my sake to bear witness before them. For the preaching of the Gospel to all nations has to come first.

So when you are arrested and brought to trial, don't worry about what you are to say; for you shall say what will be given you in that hour. It is not you who speak but the Holy Spirit.

Brother will betray brother, even to death, and the father his child. Children will turn against their parents and have them put to death. You will be hated by all for my name's sake, but whoever holds out to the end will be saved. (13:9-13)

The word "apocalypse" means to be "thrown open" or "laid bare," "exposed," or "revealed." Jesus describes a reality for Mark's community: this is the reality of war, the destruction of the temple, and the rigorous persecution of the community. Some scripture scholars maintain that Mark's gospel has two themes: the first is in Mark 1:15 ("This is the time of fulfillment. The kingdom of God is at hand. Repent, and believe in the Gospel"); and the second is the prediction in chapter 13 of the outbreak of war, the destruction of the temple, and the persecution of the Christians. But the chapter also looks forward to the end of time, to the coming of the Son of Man after the days of tribulation. And so Jesus commands his disciples to be on their guard and not to fall prey to the climate of fear, despair, and falsehood that will surround the coming events.

Chapter 13 is filled with phrases of warning: "See that no one deceives you"(v. 5). "Do not be alarmed" (v. 7). "Watch out for yourselves" (v. 9). "[D]o not worry beforehand what you are to say" (v. 11). "[D]o not believe it!" (v. 21). "Be watchful! I have told it all to you beforehand" (v. 23). "Learn a lesson from the fig tree" (v. 28). "Be watchful! Be alert!" (v. 33); and the last line of the chapter, "What I say to you, I say to all: 'Watch!'" (v. 37). As Mark interrupts the rapid pace to the cross with Jesus sitting to talk about the coming days, we need eyes to see and ears to hear the good news of God. It is especially important to see with eyes of faith and to hear with ears attuned to the Spirit to read the signs of the times and to trust that whatever is needed to be faithful in these times of trial will be given to us.

The hinge between the announcement that the disciples will be persecuted (v. 9) and the warning of possible betrayal (v. 12) is this line: "For the preaching of the Gospel to all nations has to come first" (v. 10). This hinge allows movement in two directions. First, it seems to be saying that the preaching of the gospel to all nations results in persecution; and second, it also seems to be saying that persecution is a way to preach the gospel to the nations. This was the experience of the crucifixion and death of Jesus, and so it will be the lot of the disciples.

The verb "to hand over" or "to give over" is key to this section. It appears ten times in Mark's gospel and is always associated with rejection, persecution, torture, betrayal, suffering, or death. In this one section (13:7-10) it appears three times.

They will hand you over to the courts. (v. 9b NAB)

When men take you off into custody, do not worry beforehand about what to say. (v. 11 NAB)

Brother will hand over brother for execution and likewise the father his child; children turn against their parents and have them put to death. (v. 12 NAB)

Helen Graham has described its significance.

> The unit (Mark 13:9-13) seems to be held together by the repetition of a Greek verb, *paradidonai*, which means "to hand over." This verb also appears in the passion narrative (14-15); in two of the three so called passion predictions (9:31; 10:33-34; see 10:45); and in the programmatic transitional summary which begins the first major section of the gospel (1:14-15), which refers to John the Baptist's having been "handed over." The verb is always used, as R. H. Lightfoot has remarked, "with sinister meaning implying the delivery of someone or something good to an evil power." (*You Will Be Handed Over*, 13)

This destiny and lot of the prophets will be the destiny and lot of Jesus the Lord and the destiny and lot of the disciples. This experience of being handed over into the power of others has a long history in Israel, especially in the books of Daniel and Isaiah. Daniel speaks of persecution and trial, writing, "They shall be handed over to him for a year, two years, and a half-year" (Dn 7:25), and "handing over" is found three times in the suffering-servant songs of Isaiah (52:13-53). The text of Isaiah is read in Holy Week to describe Jesus' own passion and death.

What gives the next verses such a grave and harsh edge is the prediction that the persecutions will come from intimacy, from family members: siblings against one another and children betraying their parents. Earlier segments of Mark's gospel have demonstrated again and again that blood ties are not the basis of Jesus' household and that they can be a stumbling block to belief. Here blood ties become even more threatening as they can lead to betrayal and death.

This terrible scene has been offset, however, with the comfort and encouragement that comes from the new family of Jesus (Mk 3:34-35), a family that survives on the word of the Lord and its shared belief and practice. Jesus has just recently assured Peter and the disciples that when they have given up mother, father, brothers and sisters, lands and possessions for his name and the sake of the gospel, they have lost nothing because they will know a new family and life everlasting in the age to come (Mk 10:29-30). And the last sentence in this paragraph on betrayal reiterates that promise of life: "[B]ut whoever holds out to the end will be saved" (Mk 13:13).

Perhaps the strongest lines of comfort and strength appear in this same section, which contains one of Mark's rare allusions to the Holy Spirit and the power it gives believers. "So when you are arrested and brought to trial, don't worry about what you are to say; for you shall say what will be given you in that hour. It is not you who speak but the Holy Spirit" (Mk 13:11). There is startling power in this text about persecution that specifies how the Spirit will work.

> The role of the Holy Spirit here is to provide inspiration for bearing testimony and not primarily to provide strength and consolation in the midst of physical suffering. The passage does not promise a universal outpouring of the spirit, but rather an endowment for a special situation; it is a gift for witness-bearing. The passive expression "will be given you" emphasizes the idea of testimony as something given by God, an idea that is rooted far back in the biblical tradition. (Graham, *You Will Be Handed Over*, 46)

The Spirit is given to help a disciple under duress to testify and, if necessary, hand over his or her life as a martyr, one who is willing to witness to faith, even to death. Mark 13:11 can be read as it is, but also backward, switching the order of the phrases. It is the preaching and the practice, the living of God's word, that bring persecution. While that preaching and practice, becoming the good news of God in the world, result in crucifixion and death, they also break the power of death by the resurrection. This is, indeed, the heart of this rendering of the good news of God according to Mark, and it tells of the experience of Mark's community and of other Christian communities of the first century. "You will be hated by all for my name's sake, but whoever holds out to the end will be saved" (Mk 13:13).

The Gospel of Mark has already hinted at the trials involved in enduring to the end, of dying faithfully alive in the gospel. The parable of the seed is a good example; for the seeds that fell on rocky ground sprouted up quickly, but they didn't develop a root system to sustain them (4:16-17). It doesn't take much to cause them to wither and scatter. Without roots in the community and in practice, the faithful don't last long either. Any kind of persecution, suffering, or discomfort that might arise from their belief in God's word causes them to wilt and let go. Keep in mind that Peter's name means "rock" and that Peter wilts under challenge. Only after the resurrection and his time of preaching and living the life of the Spirit of Jesus in the community will he persevere to the end, later dying a martyr's death in Rome.

Mark's community would be aware of those who endured to the end, for many died horrible deaths, although others gave up their faith in fear and trembling. The latter, the apostates, betrayed the word of Jesus the crucified one and their community, the community into which they had been baptized. Peter is the image of those who did not endure, those who had to learn the hard way what it meant to be faithful to the gospel. Jesus is the model of endurance and perseverance to the end, and he is raised by the Father in the power of the Spirit. This is the model for the disciples and for us: all who believe in Jesus are willing to cling tenaciously to that belief, even unto death. The possibility of capitulating to fear and of failing to live up to one's baptismal vows was a reality for all the disciples and for every community of believers. And it still is today.

Karl Gaspar, a Filipino lay catechist and teacher, was a political detainee in Davao, Philippines. He was arrested and jailed on March 26, 1983. What follows is from his handwritten notes.

When one is faced with the inevitable repercussions of a radical conversion and finds himself being persecuted for his faith commitment, he continues to grapple with fear and helplessness. It is almost a cliché, but he asks: "Why me, Lord?" He asks further: "Is it worth the pain and sleepless nights?" The temptation to give up everything and to succumb to the impact of fear is so great. One becomes afraid and resolves never to put himself in an uncompromising situation again. One even promises never to get involved in the very actions that led him to this ordeal. If one yields to the most human instinct of self-preservation, his trial becomes the reason to give up his discipleship, for the price it demands is so high. . . . Fortunately, there are those who manage to convince themselves that there is no turning back, that a disciple has to move on, even if it means another journey to Calvary. (Karl Gaspar, "Some Reflections" [July 12-15, 1983], p. 3. My thanks to Helen Graham, M.M., for this material.)

The Great Tribulation

Halfway through chapter 13, the discourse moves away from warnings about future persecution. As Jesus was warning his disciples about future persecution, Mark has been warning the followers of Jesus during the 60s and 70s C.E. to hold firm in the face of persecution. Now Jesus speaks of tribulations that cause great distress in Judea, although the exact nature of the threat referred to by Jesus (and Mark) isn't defined. The verses that follow describing other tribulations use prophetic and apocalyptic language, language that today is often difficult to understand. But we must remember, however, that apocalyptic literature isn't as focused on the destruction of all that exists as it is on the restitution and reordering of the powers and structures of the world.

Wars destroy everything. An ancient phrase of Aeschylus, "In war, truth is the first casualty," is oft quoted and has even been applied to the war with Iraq. Although Christians have to reckon with the reality of war, they are not to participate in it. Instead, they are to resist with every bit of faith and strength they can muster. The Roman-Jewish war that took place from 66-70 C.E. would destroy the temple and many of the structures of Judaism. As a result, Judaism would transform itself into a religion based in families and synagogues rather than the temple. The Christians, who resisted fighting with the Jews against the Romans, would be persecuted by the Jews, by the Zealots (a revolutionary group), and by the Romans.

The great tribulation, termed the "idol of the oppressor" or desolating abomination," refers to the absolute destruction of the temple. The apocalyptic vocabulary and images are from the Book of Daniel (chapters 7-12). For Jews, the temple was their world. When it was desecrated, burned, and razed to the ground, their world underwent a cataclysm. Daniel wrote about the destruction of the temple in his time, as Mark is writing about the destruction of the second temple during his time. The images Jesus used to speak about events announcing the coming of the Son of Man and the end of time and of earth would have terrified and broken the hearts and resistance of the Jews. Mark's description of loss and devastation could apply to any war in recent history, including World War II with the bombing of cities like Dresden, Hiroshima, and Nagasaki, and the wars in Afghanistan and Iraq, the Sudan and the Palestinian West Bank, and the loss of the earth itself forever.

> So, when you see the *idol of the oppressor* [in other translations "the abominable and destructive presence" (NAB) and "the desolating sacrilege" (NRSV)] set in the place where it should not be (may the reader understand!), then let those in Judea flee to the mountains. If you are on the housetop, don't come down to take anything with you. If you are in the field, don't turn back to fetch your cloak. How hard it will be then for pregnant women and mothers with babies at the breast! Pray that it may not happen in winter. For this will be a time of distress such as was never known from the beginning when God created the world, until now and is never to be known again. So that if the Lord had not shortened that time, no one would survive; but he decided to shorten it for the sake of some of his chosen.
>
> And if anyone says to you at that time: "Look, here is the Messiah! Look, he is there!"—do not believe it. For false Messiahs and false prophets will arise and perform signs and wonders in order to deceive even God's chosen people, if that were possible. Then be on your guard, I have told you everything ahead of time. (13:14-23)

The horror of war must be resisted by Christians. It has nothing to do with the coming of Christ, even if false messiahs and false prophets say otherwise. Jesus has already warned his disciples to be on their guard and watchful. They (and we) are not to be deceived into being a part of the tribulations and apocalypses that are the wars of the earth (13:5-8). Mark is telling members of his community to flee when these things happen (13:14-19). Christians are to preach the good news of God, and not that of Rome or the United States or Great Britain or Israel or the Arab states or any other national power. Christians are to witness to the gospel and to endure to the very end, relying on the Spirit.

How in the world do we do this? This section of chapter 13 immediately precedes the account of the passion and death of Jesus because this is what we must reckon with when we are baptized and join the household of God. Our belief is rooted solely in Jesus the crucified and risen one and in our love of God and love of our neighbor. We are bound to preach, heal, welcome and include all people, ignoring barriers and walls of hatred. We are to hear the word of God and put it into practice, particularly in our age of greed, hate, nationalism, and war. Where do we begin? Writing in the 1960s, Thomas Merton showed the way.

> The beginning of the fight against hatred, the basic Christian answer to hatred, is not the commandment to love, but what must necessarily come before in order to make the commandment bearable and comprehensible. It is a prior commandment to believe. The root of Christian love is not the will to love, but the faith that one is loved . . . by God although unworthy or rather irrespective of one's worth! (quoted in John R. Donahue, "The Word," *America*, October 28, 2000, p. 31)

Mark uses this passage as Jesus' last warning to his disciples to be vigilant, to not be deceived by the world but to remain faithful. They are to remember always that we and the world belong to God, and in the end God rules everything. Mark's allusions to the destruction of the first temple and his prediction of the destruction of the second temple instruct his readers on the reality of who Jesus is as the Son of Man who will come to judge all nations.

Mark's audience would be familiar with the pagan ruler Antiochus IV Epiphanes, who desecrated the temple in 168 B.C.E. by placing on it an altar to Zeus. The ensuing battles, in which God would stand firm against the "Abominable Idol of the devastator" (Dn 11:31), led to the Maccabean revolt in 167. The temple was again desecrated during the Roman-Jewish war when the Roman army pursued the revolutionaries into the temple and set up their Roman-legion standards.

Mark's references to past and present events also describe future events that will occur before Jesus comes again in glory. Although God, in his mercy, will shorten those end days, Christians must endure faithfully, waiting for the coming vindication. One day—and it may not be any day soon, since more than two thousand years have already passed—there will be a reckoning. All those who did violence and those who remained faithful will know the power of God in the coming of the Son of Man.

> Later on, in those days after that disastrous time, *the sun will grow dark, the moon will not give its light, the stars will fall out of the sky and the whole universe will be shaken.* Then people *will see the Son of Man coming in the clouds* with great power and glory. And he will send the angels to gather his chosen people from the four winds, from the ends of the earth to the ends of the sky. (13:24-27)

This one short text includes many references to earlier biblical texts. These texts attest to the belief that Jews have held throughout their history and to what is now believed by Christians as well that God is God. One day history will be judged, and righteousness will come upon the earth, for the past, the present, and the future all belong to God. We *believe* that the Son of Man, the crucified and risen one, will come in glory and that his power of truth, love, justice, and mercy, and his power to resist evil without violence will be revealed as the power of God. Those who believe and live under that power in the kingdom of God here on earth have nothing to fear on that day or during their lives. The prophets used the language of their day to convey their hope and belief, and they knew as little as we do—nothing! Here are some images of the prophets used by Mark to describe physical signs and the coming of the Son of Man.

> The stars and constellations at night
> will send forth no light, the moon
> will not shine; in the morning the sun
> will be dark as it rises. (Is 13:10—on the destruction of Babylon)

> Before them the earth shakes
> and the heavens tremble,
> the sun and moon grow dark
> and the stars lose their twinkle. (Joel 2:10)

> The sun will darken and the moon turn to blood
> at the approach of the great and dreadful day of God. (Joel 3:4)

One like a son of man came on the clouds of heaven. He faced the One of Great Age and was brought into his presence.

Dominion, honor and kingship were given him, and all the peoples and nations of every language served him. His dominion is eternal and shall never pass away; his kingdom will never be destroyed. (Dn 7:13b-14)

Mark also uses language from the Hebrew scriptures and the prophets to describe the gathering of God's elect from the four corners (13:27). A text in Deuteronomy describes how God will bring back his scattered and dispersed people: "Though you are driven out at the other end of the earth, Yahweh will gather you even from there" (Dt 30:4). Similar words appear in Zechariah; the prophet sees an angel measuring Jerusalem to fit all the people "scattered to the four winds of heaven" (Zec 2:10). Zechariah gives hope to all these people who have been plundered and brutalized by their enemies.

> "Sing and rejoice, O daughter Zion, for I am about to come, I shall dwell among you," says Yahweh.
> "On that day, many nations will join Yahweh and be my people, but my dwelling is among you." The people of Judah will be for Yahweh as his portion in his holy land. He will choose Jerusalem again.
> "Keep still in Yahweh's presence, for he comes, having risen from his holy dwelling." (Zec 2:14-17)

The promise and hope are now extended to those who have believed in him throughout the whole world. The future coming of the Lord (the *parousia*) is something to hang onto in the midst of trials and suffering and martyrdom.

Once again Jesus exhorts his disciples and us to be on our guard. The image of the fig tree, which he had used earlier to instruct his disciples, and to which he now returns was also used by Isaiah.

> The heavens shall be rolled up like a scroll,
>   and all their host shall wither away,
> As the leaf wilts on the vine,
>   or as the fig withers on the tree. (Is 34:4 NAB)

Watch! The Fig Tree

Jesus has already used the withering of the fig tree to speak about the end of the temple. Now he uses the fig tree to speak of the new, of hope in what is coming.

> "Learn a lesson from the fig tree. As soon as its branches become tender and it begins to sprout leaves, you know that summer is near. In the same way, when you see these things happening, know that the time is near, even at the door. Truly, I say to you, this generation will not pass away until all this has happened. Heaven and earth will pass away, but my words will not pass away.
> "But, regarding that Day and that Hour, no one knows when it will come, not even the angels, not even the Son, but only the Father.

"Be alert and watch, for you don't know when the time will come. When a man goes abroad and leaves his home, he puts his servants in charge, giving to each one some responsibility; and he orders the doorkeeper to stay awake. So stay awake, for you don't know when the Lord of the house will come, in the evening or at midnight, when the cock crows or before dawn. If he comes suddenly, do not let him catch you asleep.

"And what I say to you, I say to all: watch." (13:28-37)

Jesus answers the question asked earlier by his disciples ("Tell us when this will be") as he summarizes his last sermon, using "secret" or apocalyptic language. Although there will be tribulations, wars, and all manner of trials in every age, believers must not take them as signs but continue to preach the gospel to all the nations. They are to watch, to be on guard, and not be deceived like others who see the end in every calamity or war.

It is not important for us to know when the final coming of judgment and glory will take place. The angels don't know and even the Son does not know, only the Father. What is crucial is that we live aware and attentive to the word of God and to our world. Despite whatever terrible things happen, we are to watch the fig tree for the signs of tender branches and sprouting leaves and wait for summer to come. The future of the world is holy and is in God's hands. Although Jesus will be handed over, along with many others, we are all in God's hand.

This last short parable telling of the man who goes abroad appears just before Mark moves to the arrest, passion, death, and resurrection of Jesus. The disciples, and readers, have been instructed that persecution will come, that God will come, and that hope will come at any hour of the day or night. Jesus indicates that we are the servants, the slaves of the household of God, and all is now entrusted to us. We each have our work, assigned to us by Jesus, and all of us must remain faithful and watch. The times listed (evening, midnight, at cockcrow, and dawn) correspond to the four watches of the Romans during the night. They also correspond to four critical moments in Jesus' coming passion and death. The first, the evening watch (14:17), is the time of the Last Supper of Jesus with his disciples and friends. The betrayal in the garden takes place around midnight. Peter's denial and bitter weeping comes at the time of the cockcrow (14:66-72), and the Sanhedrin gathers to try Jesus at dawn (15:1).

The last lines remind us that the disciples fell asleep and failed to keep watch in the garden when Jesus asked them to keep watch and pray with him. If they fall asleep in Jesus' presence, how will they learn to stay awake when Jesus is taken from them in death? Will the disciples learn to stay awake with the risen presence of Jesus among them? We must stay awake; we must pray and watch and remain in the presence of Jesus. This is the only way to make it through the days and nights in our world.

A story beloved of the Jewish people speaks eloquently of the building of the temple and the pain and sorrow in living with only a small remnant of the western wall. Although the temple was just a building, it was also the symbol of a people's hopes and the dwelling place of God. Its destruction left a deep, gaping wound in Judaism.

Once upon a time, long ago when David was king, he had trouble sleeping. As long as he was at war, defending his borders and solidifying his kingdom, his sleep was uneasy. At long last, the day came when there was peace, and finally David was able to sleep through the night. He even dreamed. He had magnificent dreams of building God Yahweh a house and in his dreams he was often taken to the heavenly Jerusalem. While everyone knows it is a mirror image of what is on earth, it was present in all its wholeness and freshness and glory. When he awoke from his dreams, he started writing down everything he could remember about his visits to the temple in heaven.

He laid the foundations, knowing that he was not allowed to build the temple because he had killed too many people and plundered the earth. But when his son Solomon grew to be a man, he could build the temple, using David's notes and designs as the basis of the work.

When Solomon became king, he summoned all the people of Israel and declared that everyone would have a part in the building of Yahweh's house. So the people were divided up into four groups, and the lots were cast to see which wall each group would build. The north wall was chosen by the rulers and the princes, and they used fine marble and stones to build it, along with the stairs and pillars of the temple. The southern wall was chosen by the priests and Levites, who would also take care of the Ark of the Covenant and weave the curtains for that area. The merchants chose the east wall, and they spared no expense in the stone and materials and also provided the oil in the lamps that would always burn. The western wall was the last one to be chosen, and this would be built by the poor of Jerusalem. They would also make the temple's curtains, and the masses of poor people were to pray daily for the work of building the temple.

Everyone set to work because they wanted to see its completion in their lifetime. The merchants sold their jewelry and then paid workers to put up their wall. It went up first and was magnificent. The leaders and princes sold property to buy materials and pay workers, and their wall was finished soon after the first one. The priests talked people into building their walls, with promises of prayers and special gifts from God.

Now the only wall not completed was the western wall, the wall of the poor. They worked every day at their jobs as servants, slaves, and hired hands, and they could work on the wall only after finishing their daily work, so it was taking a long time. But they rushed home from work each day, hastily ate their meal, as though remembering the

Passover, and then everyone began work on the temple as the sun fell. Husbands and wives and children, all worked together on their wall and the curtains of the temple. Finally the temple was completed, and no one had ever seen anything as beautiful. It was a fitting building for the dwelling place of God.

Whenever the poor would visit the temple, they would take their children and grandchildren and bring them to a particular piece of the wall saying, "Look here, these are the stones we made. I was with your grandfather when we laid these stones." The women would take their children by the hand and lift a piece of the great curtains in the temple, run their hands over the fine, even stitches and embroidery and say, "Look, this is your mother's work. Look at what grandmother made." It was their temple, their gift, the work of their hands offered to God.

But in the times that followed, the temple was destroyed, and only the western wall remained. They said that the angels had saved the western wall because they couldn't bear to let all that love, that devotion, hard work, and worship be destroyed. They stood in the midst of the battle and the fire with their wings spread protectively over the wall. Built by the poor, it was the most precious of all in the eyes of God.

Today a piece of that wall still stands. It is called the Wailing Wall, and people come from all over the world to pray there, placing small pieces of paper with their petitions on them into the cracks between the stones. They say that sometimes if you come very early in the morning the stones are wet with dew and the sun glistens on the wall, making it dance and sparkle as though it were studded with diamonds and jewels. But those who know who made that wall and also know the heart of God know that the wall was weeping during the night, for the wall remembers the glory of the temple and its beauty before God. Even now, when you stand before that wall, the power of faith and hope and love breathes out at you; and the presence of God, the presence of sorrow and of peace, is there. (Howard Schwartz and many other rabbis tell this story.)

For us Christians, the new temple is the body of Christ, the people of God themselves, all the peoples of the entire world. Perhaps the best prayer for this new temple is the prayer that Jesus himself taught to us, the Our Father. As we pray it, we remember that as we stand with Jesus before the passion and death, we need to reach out to one another and to God for support and strength.

CHAPTER 9

The Passion of Jesus

Mark 14 and 15

AS CHAPTER 14 BEGINS, it is two days before the feast of the Passover and Unleavened Bread. The first verse, a chilling warning of what is to come, announces that a group of religious leaders is still intent on arresting Jesus and putting him to death (14:1). The days of Passover were at the center of Jewish religious rituals, hopes, and even nationalistic aspirations, as the feast was a commemoration of what Yahweh had done for the people in bringing them out of slavery in Egypt and freeing them to live in covenant as the people of God in the Promised Land. Large crowds gathered in Jerusalem for the festival, and the religious leaders were accountable to Rome for keeping order. Whatever was to be done would have to be in secret so that the Jews would not call down the wrath of the Roman army and invite retaliation against the people or the temple.

The word "arrest" will appear four times in this section, an indication of the determination of the leaders to condemn Jesus and put him to death. By its repetition, Mark also creates a sense of foreboding and hostility as the plan of the chief priests and scribes unfolds. This sense of foreboding continues when Jesus' reveals at the Last Supper that Judas will collaborate with them and later that Peter will also betray him. The narrative culminates in the dramatic scene in the garden of Gethsemane where Jesus is finally arrested, and more and more people are drawn into the process that will lead to Jesus' trial.

This entire section is referred to as "the passion" of Jesus. Its Latin root means "to suffer, to endure, to bear, to pass through," and it can also mean "intense emotion or feeling, ardent devotion, and a commitment to" something. Indeed, Jesus' passion encompasses all those meanings. For more than two thousand years, Christians have celebrated the passion and death of Jesus during Holy Week, a solemn time that focuses on suffering and endurance. It recalls a time of violence, hatred, and killing that has been described by Bishop Thomas Gumbleton as follows.

184

I know that many of you have heard me quote a couple of sentences from a book called *The New Testament Without Illusions* by scripture scholar John McKenzie. The sentences that I have quoted are: "If Jesus did not reject violence for any reason whatsoever, then we know nothing about Jesus." In other words, it is so clear in the Scriptures that if we can't say that about Jesus Christ we may as well say nothing about Jesus.

The other sentence, John McKenzie goes on to challenge us, is: "Jesus taught us how to die, not how to kill." I admit, the first time I read those sentences quite a few years ago, I was really stunned because I had not truly accepted the fact that Jesus rejected *all* violence and expected his followers to do the same, reject violence. Jesus taught us how to die loving and forgiving even the ones putting you to death, not how to kill.

Maybe many of us are still surprised to hear that Jesus rejected all violence and wanted his followers to do the same and that the first Christian community for hundreds of years rejected violence, refused to kill in war or in any other way.

But the reason we'd be surprised or find it difficult to accept this reality about Jesus is that we never really listened carefully to what Jesus said and we never watched with real understanding how he acted. Today's scriptures are totally clear in declaring this truth about Jesus. ("Palm Sunday Sermon," April 13, 2003 [see Peace Pulpit: Homilies at http://www.NCRonline.org])

These words were spoken after the reading of the passion on Palm Sunday and we should keep them in our hearts and minds as we study and reflect upon Mark's account of the passion. It is detailed and intense in its focus. It demands that those who read it take responsibility for where they stand in relation to Jesus. Later in his sermon Bishop Gumbleton quoted Dr. Martin Luther King, Jr., who said, "We will surpass your capacity to afflict us with sufferings with our capacity to endure sufferings." This is the way of the cross, the way of Jesus, the way of life without violence. It is the way of truth and integrity for all Christian followers of the crucified and risen one. It is only in this complete and wholehearted rejection of violence that we can understand Jesus and come to the peace offered by his life and resurrection.

It is also important to note that these last chapters (14:1-16:8) can stand alone or can be read as an interpretation of the rest of Mark's account of Jesus Christ, Son of God. Each of the previous stories can be read in light of this final story of confrontation and the proclamation of the good news of God. Many of the previous stories have hinted at this culmination, which describes endurance and betrayal and then Jesus' trial, torture, and execution.

All this begins with a story at a meal, and midway through the chapter another story of a meal will interrupt the building tension surrounding Jesus. As the story of Jesus' passion and death is being told, it will be consciously interrupted and interpreted. This story would have been told many times and also experienced by the community of Mark as it lived through its own time of passion and death in the first century, liturgically, catechetically, and in actual death based on hope in the resurrection.

The first story tells of an unknown woman who recognizes who Jesus is and what lies ahead. She senses that he is going to die soon, even as she realizes his disciples do not. This story ends the segment that began with the account of the widow's mite. It is a moment of witness and confirmation of Jesus that falls in between the treachery of the leaders and the betrayal of Judas, one of his own disciples.

> Jesus was in Bethany in the house of Simon the leper. As he was reclining at dinner, a woman entered carrying a precious jar of expensive perfume made of pure nard. She broke the jar and poured the perfumed oil on Jesus' head. Then some of them became angry and said, "What a useless waste of perfume. It could have been sold for more than three hundred silver coins and the money given to the poor." And they criticized her.
>
> But Jesus said, "Let her alone; why are you troubling her? What she has just done for me is a very charitable work. At any time you can help the poor, for you always have them with you, but you will not have me forever. This woman has done what was hers to do, she has anointed my body beforehand for my burial. Truly, I say to you, wherever the Good News is proclaimed, and this will be throughout the world, what she has done will be told in praise of her." (14:3-9)

Jesus is in the house of Simon the leper. Other guests would likely be present, seated in tables radiating outward around an open space. There would be room at the back for others to come and listen, to watch and take home whatever food was left over. So the woman's action is quite public. What she does is unusual and extravagant: she pours the nard, which cost an entire year's wages, on Jesus' head. It would have run down his hair and beard, his neck, shoulders and down the rest of his body if he was seated or reclining at a table, as was the custom.

This extravagant act brings a vicious and loud reaction from some. Readers are not told who speaks of it as a waste of good perfumed oil. This is an insult to Jesus as well as of her gesture. Jesus defends her and acknowledges what she has done and why. It is anticipated mercy and service tendered to him for his coming death and burial. Jesus' response to her, which mentions his burial, must have been a shock to the guests at this meal. She is attentive to him; they are not. She is filled with tender regard for him; they are not. She is one of the few people who has done "a good thing" for Jesus, and he will not let it go unappreciated or belittled by others. His powerful praise of her links her to him for all time: "Wherever the Good News is proclaimed throughout the world, what she has done will be told in her memory" (14:9 NAB). This woman has accepted his invitation to be with him on his way of the cross. None of his disciples came close to her devotion and her will to love and to follow him, even unto death and burial.

People often say that this unnamed woman anointed Jesus as priest, prophet, and king, but Jesus' own words contradict that. He acknowledges that she has anointed his body for burial, a body that will first be tortured, beaten, and nailed to a cross. Seeking to ease his passion and death, she will accompany him on the way, and no one is to object to her actions.

This passage has also been used to insist callously that money spent on worship is more important than money spent on the poor. This, however, is an impossible conclusion. Jesus is the poor; he is the poorest man in that house. He faces a sentence of death and will be betrayed and abandoned by his own followers and friends. He will face torture before his body will be stretched out and nailed to a wooden cross where he will hang until he dies.

When Jesus, as a just and righteous Jew, quotes from the scriptures about the poor, he is not pushing the poor aside but rather acknowledging what Jews are supposed are to do, especially in the year before the jubilee when all debts of the poor are canceled.

> When you give anything, give it willingly, and Yahweh, your God, will bless you for this in all your work and in all that you undertake.
>
> The poor will not disappear from this land. Therefore I give you this commandment: you must be open-handed to your brother, to the needy and to the poor in your land. (Dt 15:10-11)

Jesus is saying that what they want to do for him, they should do for the poor. Mercy is their sign of devotion. When was the last time that any of us has spent an entire year's wages on corporal works of mercy for the poor? She will be remembered always as aligned with Jesus. In Hebrew the word "remember" means to "put back together as it was originally," or "to re-member the body of Christ." Memory is practiced best in imitation and obedience. The story of this unnamed woman appears just before the passion account, in seeming opposition to Judas and all those who fled, betrayed Jesus, or actually participated in his suffering and death, and all those who stood and watched and did nothing. She shows care for him and provides some measure of what Jesus needs as he goes to face his death alone. She is the alternative, the one held up for veneration.

The care and the understanding the woman has shown toward Jesus is echoed in this brief story of two old friends.

Two peasants, Ivan and Boris, the closest of friends for years, were sitting in a tavern one evening, drinking, telling stories, and remembering all they had shared together. Ivan, who had started drinking before Boris and was a bit ahead of him in that regard, turned abruptly to his friend, interrupted him, and said, "Do you love me?"

Boris answered quickly in the affirmative, "Of course I love you." But Ivan persisted, slurring a bit, "Do you really love me?" Boris was a little put out and replied, "Of course. You know me. We've been to hell and back together. You know that I love you."

Ivan was still not satisfied. "Do you love me? Do you love me?" Again and again, Boris said, "Yes, yes, yes. I do, I do." Soon Ivan was crying, and Boris also began crying in response to his friend. Ivan spoke once again, gulping through his tears: "If you really loved me, you'd know what was wrong with me and why I feel so terrible!" All that Boris could do at that point was to wrap his arms around his old friend and hold him. And it was enough.

The intimate ritual the woman performed for Jesus was an act of honor. She truly knew the heart of Jesus. Have we ever responded with such love to the word of God, to the person of Jesus, to the poor and those facing suffering and death?

The next segment, which is noted briefly, identifies Judas as the betrayer. In sharp contrast with the actions of the woman who has just anointed Jesus, recognizing that his prophetic words reveal him to be the anointed of God, Judas rejects any notion of Jesus' suffering and death.

> Then Judas Iscariot, one of the Twelve, went off to the chief priests in order to betray Jesus to them. On hearing him they were excited and promised to give him money. So Judas started planning the best way to hand him over to them. (14:10-11)

The deed is set in motion. The text alludes to what has already taken place during Jesus' last visit to the temple. He has driven out the money changers, who buy and sell commodities in God's dwelling place. Now the body of Jesus, God's dwelling place and the new temple, is going to be bought and sold on the open market like any other commodity. Mark presents another sharp—and chilling—contrast. While Judas, the disciple, is handing Jesus over for money, the woman, also a disciple, is "wasting" a year's wages on perfumed oil to anoint him.

While Jews are arriving in Jerusalem and making preparations for the feast of Passover, Jesus directs his disciples to make ready for his Passover. While the story of Jesus' trial, suffering, and death will include many others in addition to the disciples, the focus, the hub of the wheel that holds it all together, is Jesus' person and will and his obedience to God in passing through death into life to become the new covenant and the new opening to life.

The preparations sound a lot like those for Jesus' entry into Jerusalem, when he also sent two disciples ahead into the city. Those preparations echo the liturgical rituals for Passion Sunday and Palm Sunday in the Christian community. Images of the liturgical cycle abound in the text. It is the feast of the Unleavened Bread, when Jews sacrificed lambs in the temple and people ate of the Passover lamb, in memory of their liberation from the slavery of Egypt to freedom as the people of God. The man who will show the two disciples the room they are to use for the Passover meal is carrying a water jar, representing baptism. Jesus is relying on the hospitality of others in order to celebrate the feast with his disciples, which is what he has enjoined them to do when they go out to preach the gospel. And this Passover meal will pass over into the ritual of the Eucharist, in which the faithful share the body and blood of Christ.

The evening begins with a sense of ritual quiet and reflection on what has gone before. This quickly changes as Jesus announces in the presence of his disciples, chosen to be with him from the beginning, that one of them will betray him.

> When it was evening, Jesus arrived with the Twelve. While they were at table eating, Jesus said, "Truly, I tell you, one of you will betray me, *one who shares my meal.*" They were deeply distressed at hearing this and asked him, one after the other, "You don't mean me, do you?" And Jesus answered, "It is one of you Twelve, one who dips his bread in the dish with me. The Son of Man is going as the Scriptures say he will. But alas for that man by whom the Son of Man is betrayed; better for him if he had never been born." (14:17-21)

Jesus speaks first and makes clear what is going to happen. This diversion from the ancient ritual disoriented the disciples and caused great distress. Mark's account does not name the betrayer, and although we know it was Judas, the disciples do not. They all dip their bread in the common dish and eat with him. And while Judas will hand Jesus over, all of them will betray him in some manner, some will do so vehemently and some will run away in fear.

Mark's own community has also known betrayals by those who have shared the Eucharistic meal. And Jesus has warned disciples about all those who might betray them in the future: religious authorities, political powers, and their own blood relatives and friends (13:9-14). We must all remember that these words did not describe only Judas; they were also directed at each of us.

Jesus' words of accusation are immediately offset by the rituals of Passover, what we now call the Last Supper or the Lord's Supper. In Mark's account, it appears that Judas has remained to receive this gift of intimacy and presence given to all the disciples, whether faithful or deceitful. The account is so short and packed with what for us are familiar parts of the liturgy that we can almost hear Jesus' voice chanting the words aloud.

While they were eating, Jesus took bread, blessed and broke it, and gave it to them. And he said, "Take this, it is my body." Then he took a cup and after he had given thanks, passed it to them and they all drank from it. And he said, "This is my blood, the blood of the Covenant, which is to be poured out for many. Truly, I say to you, I will not taste the fruit of the vine again until the day I drink the new wine in the Kingdom of God."

After singing psalms of praise, they went out to the Hill of Olives. (14:22-26)

This is one of the earliest accounts of the celebration of the Lord's Supper (although Paul also repeats the words of the ritual formula in 1 Corinthians). For Jesus and the disciples, the blessing and the giving and receiving of the bread and the cup take place within the context of a meal. This was likely the liturgical practice within Mark's own community as well.

Jesus' words are so familiar because they form almost word for word the first part of the Eucharistic ritual. "Jesus took bread, blessed and broke it, and gave it to them. And he said, "Take this, it is my body" (14:22). For us who live in a society where bread is no longer the "staff of life" as it once was in cultures where it was the staple of their diet, we often don't appreciate the full meaning of this simple gesture. Once when I was visiting Israel, I stayed with an Armenian Christian family. While we were eating one afternoon we talked about what bread meant to them. Because there were no utensils, I was learning the art of eating with bread. The thin pita bread was torn off in strips and used to pick up whatever you wanted to eat. The main dishes could only be taken by dipping bread in the food and eating it with the bread. There was lots of laughter as people constantly leaned back and forth to scoop up the food and eat. One of the children said that bread wasn't just a food, it was *the* necessary food. People had to have bread in order to eat anything else.

I had never thought of bread in that way but realized immediately that this is what Jesus was saying! This bread, his word and life, his body and presence, is the only way we can truly eat. Sharing the bread, the word, and the body is also the only way to one another. Whenever I hear the words of the Eucharist or go to liturgy, I remember that family meal. This is the covenant Jesus is giving to us.

Jesus continues with the taking of the cup. Again, the words are very familiar. After blessing the cup, he addresses them. There is a gravity, almost a heaviness to his words when he said that he will not drink of the fruit of the vine until he drinks of it in the kingdom of God. Jesus' imminent suffering and death hover around the table as he links the breaking of the bread and the sharing of the cup with his passion.

At this point, for the second time Jesus alters the Passover ritual (the first change was his announcement of the coming betrayal). Tradition said that each drank from his or her own cup, but now they will all drink from the one cup. When they have all shared the cup, Jesus tells them what they have done, what they have been initiated into: "This is my blood, the blood of the Covenant, which is to be poured out for many" (14:24). Jesus offers to them his blood, his life, as his last gift. Although Jesus is offering them a new covenant, the disciples would have been remembering and thinking about Moses and the covenant story in Exodus.

> Moses came and told the people all the words of Yahweh and his laws. The people replied with one voice: "Everything that Yahweh has said, we shall do."
>
> Moses wrote down all the words of Yahweh, then rose early in the morning and built an altar at the foot of the mountain with twelve raised stones for the twelve tribes of Israel.
>
> He then sent young men from among the sons of Israel to offer burnt offerings and sacrifice bullocks as peace offerings to Yahweh.
>
> And Moses took half the blood and put it in basins; and with the other half of the blood he sprinkled the altar.
>
> He then took the Book of the Covenant and read it in the hearing of the people. They said, "All that Yahweh said we shall do and obey."
>
> Moses then took the blood and sprinkled it on the people saying, "Here is the blood of the covenant that Yahweh has made with you in accordance with all these words." (Ex 24:3-8)

The disciples, including Judas, all drank from the cup that Jesus offered. Earlier, when James and John had asked for seats of honor in Jesus' kingdom, Jesus had asked if they would be able to "drink the cup that I drink or be baptized with the baptism with which I am baptized" (Mk 10:38). Although they said yes, and have now ritually taken the cup to drink, they are still far from extending their lives to others in service, in love, and in submission to the words of Jesus.

The verbs used by Mark reveal that the ritual of this meal will take place literally in Jesus' body and life, and that it must be internalized in all who follow him and belong to his community. He takes, he blesses, he breaks, he shares and gives, and he speaks. He takes his life, blesses God for it, and then his life will be taken from him. He will be broken open, and he will share his life, giving it away, just as he says in the formal offering to them this night. We could say that he takes his life up to lay it down for others. Theologian Dennis Hamm reflected on what Jesus has done for the disciples and for us at this Lord's Supper.

> Now they are quite literally given Jesus' cup to share. Continuing to be his disciples will entail a full giving of self somehow like his. Such laying down of one's life—in a loving service that may or may not include martyrdom—is the life-blood of the covenant community

called the body of Christ. Jesus' giving of his blood provides not only the model but the source of this new covenant life. . . . Sharing in the sacramental body and blood entails behaving as one body by donating the gift of life to one another. ("The Word," *America*, May 24, 1997)

Jesus is explaining to the disciples that his death is a gift, a sacrifice, something that is made holy by giving it over to God. His way is the worship of God. Jesus will lead them to a new model, as Moses led the people in the sacrifice and the shedding of blood for the covenant in the wilderness. They are now to pour out their lives in obedience to the teaching that has been given them, as the blood of the animals was poured out before the Lord in the temple. Jesus' own life will be taken and his blood poured out so that all might be liberated and made holy, just as Moses led the Hebrews into freedom and liberation. His death, though horrible, will be holy. His life will be violently wrested from him, and yet he will give it over, as he has given it every moment, now and always.

Just as Israel shared in the liberation and deliverance from evil by celebrating the Passover each year, now those who follow Jesus, including Mark's community, share in the liberation and deliverance from evil and from death itself by celebrating this supper together. Those who share in this cup will share in giving their lives over and over again. Jesus had told them earlier that "The Son of Man has not come to be served but to serve—to give his life in ransom for the many" (Mk 10:45 NAB). Reality is revealed by the ritual: taking the cup (taking hold of one's life), he gave thanks (we give thanks with our lives) and gave it to them (sharing our lives and resources in love and service to one another). This is *our* covenant proclaimed, prayed, offered to God, and made holy.

Do the disciples know what is happening? They probably do not, but Mark's community does. They read the text of the passion, as we do, knowing of Jesus' death and resurrection. Like the members of Mark's community, we also read it as disciples who face the passion in our own lives and communities, in our own history. By our baptisms we have been initiated into this new covenant, which is recognized not by the sacrifice of animals but by the way in which we offer of our lives to one another, in sacrifice with Jesus and in service to others. Our offering should be daily, a daily denying of ourselves, handing over our bodies, our resources, our will and time, our passionate devotion and obedience to those most in need of the good news of God. There is no limit to what we can do to give life to others. We must make a daily commitment to picking up our cross and walking with Jesus.

Do we know what is happening? Perhaps, but perhaps not, since most of us know very little of persecution and suffering and betrayal, except on a personal or individual level and usually because of decisions we have made rather than because of the harsh demands of others.

A story from the time of the Vietnam War tells of the great pain and suffering of the Vietnamese people. It has been told by Vietnamese and also by Army veterans struggling with memories of what they did and what happened to them during the long years of the war.

There was an orphanage on the edge of a village, and the village took a lot of heavy artillery fire on a daily basis for weeks on end. The American forces stationed nearby had visited the village and the orphanage often before the bombing had started, bringing medical supplies and food for the children and the staff. One afternoon the orphanage took direct hits, and a number of the children were badly wounded. As soon as word reached the camp, Navy doctors and nurses ran to the orphanage to see what they could do for the injured children.

The scene was one of chaos, with children stunned and in shock, some severely injured and others scraped and bruised, with superficial cuts and bleeding. But one girl, about nine or ten and in desperate need, was still losing a great deal of blood. They went to work on her immediately while the other children were gathered together to be treated according to the severity of their wounds.

The girl needed an immediate transfusion. A donor was needed, preferably one of the children, because he or she would be a better match than someone who was either American or French. With their poor and limited Vietnamese and French the doctors and nurses tried to ask the children if they would be willing to give their blood to save the little girl who was hurt so badly. The children understood but were afraid, having never given blood or even seen anyone give blood to someone else. They stood there shaking and crying or just numb and unresponsive. The medical team begged and pleaded, and finally one little boy stepped forward, nodding that he would give his blood. He was also about ten.

The team moved quickly, inserting the needle and quickly testing to see if his blood would be compatible with hers. They sat him down just inches away from the little girl's body and the transfusion began. He was ashen and shaking, but he intently watched the little girl's face to see if the new blood was helping her. Soon he was crying and then sobbing silently. The nurse asked him his name and if it hurt, and then she held his head in his lap, trying to comfort him and allay his fears at what was happening. But they couldn't stop his crying, and it was obvious that they couldn't deal with his growing fear.

Just then a Vietnamese woman from the village arrived, and she started to talk to the boy and sing to him, trying to soothe his fear. As she began to rock him back and forth, he started to calm down. They went back and forth in Vietnamese, and she also asked questions of the doctors in French and English, then turned back to the boy. By now, the boy was quiet and smiling and watching the little girl intently for signs that she was going to live. The doctor asked the woman what had been the problem, telling her that he was grateful that she had comforted him. She looked at the doctors and nurses and soldiers all gathered around and said, "He thought he was dying because she got his blood and his life." They were shocked. A doctor asked, "Then why did he do it?" She turned to the little boy and asked him. The little boy looked at the doctor and said, "She's my friend. I had to help her."

Through Jesus' life, death, and resurrection we become the friends of God. This friendship with God can only be intimately expressed and shared by giving our lifeblood, the sustenance of our lives, the bread of justice, hope, peace, and nourishment to others, as Jesus has shared himself with us. This third meal that Jesus shares with his disciples goes beyond loaves and fish to include his own flesh and blood, food that will satisfy everyone. Mark "sandwiches" this story of the Lord's Supper in between two stories of betrayal, that of Judas and the later betrayal of the disciples. Although the disciples are loud in their commitment to Jesus and drink from the cup, they, like us, are not worthy or faithful. Yet they are all loved, as we are all loved and offered the cup at Eucharist. Jesus ate with sinners and the unworthy. His mercy and forgiveness were and still are the great marks of his ministry and practice.

Peter's Denial and the Agony in the Garden

We are told that when the supper concluded, they sang a hymn of praise and went out to the Mount of Olives. As the arrest and passion of Jesus draw nearer, the tension grows. Jesus attempts to explain what is going to happen to him, using words of the prophet Zechariah, and he also warns Peter of his coming betrayal of Jesus.

> Jesus then said to them: "Your faith in me will be shaken, for Scripture has it,
>> 'I will strike the shepherd,
>>   and the sheep will be dispersed.'
> But after I am raised up, I will go to Galilee ahead of you." Peter said to him, "Even though all are shaken in faith, it will not be that way with me." Jesus answered, "I give you my assurance, this very night before the cock crows twice, you will deny me three times." But Peter kept reasserting vehemently, "Even if I have to die with you, I will not deny you." They all said the same. (14:27-31 NAB)

Jesus' words to them repeat what he has already warned them about, and he links that warning to the events that are now taking place and to events that will occur in the future. Note that Jesus has already used the image of himself as a shepherd whose heart was moved to pity for the sheep on the shoreline with no one to lead them (Mk 6:34). Then Jesus warns the disciples once more that their faith in him will be shaken. Perhaps a better translation of this text would be that they will be "scandalized" in Jesus and desert him. The Greek verb *skandalisthēsesthe* can mean "to be an obstacle" or "to cause offense to." This night Jesus will cause offense to all of us, and we will stumble over the passion, the cross, and death of the Lord. Jesus used the same word in the parable of the seed that fell on rocky ground; when tribulation and trials came, it dried up and became "scandalized," as were the people of Nazareth who couldn't accept his wisdom and understanding or the healing acts he did elsewhere.

Peter cannot bear to hear himself described along with all the others as a deserter who will be so shaken that he will deny Jesus, and he states clearly that he will stay true. In response, Jesus describes very precisely Peter's betrayal three times over: three times Peter will deny Jesus, and this will happen before the cock has crowed twice. Peter seems unaware of the fragile reality of his faith and of his willingness to practice what Jesus is preaching. Each time I read this passage in which Jesus corrects Peter, who will be the leader of the church after the coming of the Spirit, I am reminded of Catherine of Siena, who spent a good part of her life correcting the popes of her day. She spoke very bluntly to one pope:

> There are three things God requires of you. The first is to reform the church—to pull up the bad herbs by the roots, that is to say, the bad pastors and governors who poison and corrupt the garden. . . . Be a man. Father, arise! No negligence! Do God's will and mine! (quoted by Paulo Evaristo Arns, "From Hope to Hope," a homily reflection in *National Catholic Reporter*, April 4, 2003, p. 11)

Once again Peter and the others have paid attention to only part of what Jesus is saying and miss the crucial line: "But after I am raised up, I will go to Galilee ahead of you." This line is crucial. A young man appearing at the tomb in a white robe will pronounce it again in the final lines of Mark's gospel as part of the proclamation of the resurrection. Perhaps the disciples are too closely involved with Jesus and their own sense of being chosen and faithful to be able to absorb what is about to take place.

At nightfall they walk to a place that Jesus frequented to pray. As Jesus starts to pull away from the disciples, he takes with him only Peter, James, and John; and they will disappoint him by falling asleep while he prays. When the crowd comes to arrest him, Jesus will be praying alone before God, his Father, and he will be alone as he faces the coming ordeal of the trial and his passion. Now Jesus prays and invites Peter, James, and John to pray with him.

They came to a place which was called Gethsemane and Jesus said to his disciples, "Sit here while I pray."

But he took Peter, James and John along with him, and becoming filled with fear and distress, he said to them, "My soul is full of sorrow, even to death. Remain here and stay awake."

Then he went a little further on and fell to the ground, praying that if possible this hour might pass him by. Jesus said, "Abba [Daddy], all things are possible for you; take this cup away from me. Yet not what I want, but what you want."

Then he came and found them asleep and said to Peter, "Simon, are you sleeping? Couldn't you stay awake for one hour? Keep watch and pray, all of you, so that you may not slip into temptation. The spirit indeed is eager but human nature is weak. And going away he prayed saying the same words. When he came back to the disciples, he found them asleep again; they could not keep their eyes open, and they did not know what to say to him.

When he came back the third time, he said, "You can sleep on now and take your rest! It is all over, the time has come; the Son of Man is now given into the hands of sinners. Get up, let us go. Look: the one betraying me is right here." (14:32-42)

They are in the garden of Gethsemane (the name means olive press), and Jesus withdraws to pray. He is deeply troubled and distressed—words that were used before when Jesus told the crowds that if they wished to be his disciples they must begin by denying themselves and pick up their crosses and come after him. It was the crowd that was deeply troubled and distressed (8:34). The words *ekthambeisthai* and *adēmonein* will appear again after the crucifixion when the women who enter the tomb cannot find Jesus' body and instead see the young man seated off to the side, who speaks to them of the crucified Jesus. Peter, James, and John are supposed to remain behind and be watchful, as Jesus exhorted them, but their prayer drifts and they fall asleep.

Jesus begins to pray to his Father about the cup he took up at the supper and offered to all of us. It is the cup of his passion, his suffering and death. Knowing that anything is possible, he asks his God, his Father, if this cup can be passed up or refused. Jesus puts aside his own desires and strives to learn the will and the word of his Father. When his prayer is finished, he takes the cup to drink. It is not possible to refuse. He has lived obedient to the kingdom and the word of God the Father, and it is the Father's will that he die. In taking the cup and drinking from it, he will share with us his close and intimate relationship with God, the one he calls Abba, Father. He will be the ransom for all peoples. He will break the power of death by handing his own life over to the Father in love. His dying will be a gift of thanksgiving, as his life has always been, to God the Father.

The Garden

"Was I sleeping, while the others suffered?" Samuel Beckett

The disciples' failure to share in Jesus' prayer or his passion makes me think of this line from Samuel Beckett's well-known play *Waiting for Godot*. They reject Jesus by escaping into the numbness and unawareness of sleep. Jesus turns to face what is coming. He returns three separate times to find that his disciples are still asleep. They are not praying with him or watching. They are not on their guard. They are unaware of what is about to happen. The first time Jesus goes back to check on the disciples, he asks Peter: "Simon, are you sleeping? Couldn't you stay awake for one hour?" ("Simon" was Peter's name before he met Jesus, before he was called as a disciple and apostle.) They have forgotten Jesus' warning in the parable of the man who left his household telling his servants to stay alert and his gatekeeper to be on watch. That parable ends with the warning "If he comes suddenly, do not let him catch you asleep" (Mk 13:36). The disciples, who Jesus appointed gatekeepers and watchmen, cannot bear to listen to Jesus, even though time after time he tells them that they must watch and stay on guard. During Jesus' passion, they will react to moments in his suffering and faithfulness in the midst of torture and lies, and execution, but they will not share in it.

And what about us, we who are his disciples today? When the hour comes, as it has countless times in the past, have we resorted to sleep in order to ignore the reality of oppression, injustice, violence, or the pain of others? Have we refused to see oppression and confrontation because we prefer "our" Jesus, a Jesus who doesn't make hard demands, to the Jesus of the gospels who expects us to stand up for truth and the inclusion of all people and to stand against suffering and exclusion? If we do not pray for help in facing the harsh realities of denying ourselves and in actively taking up the cross, then when the moment comes, we will fail. This is what the pastor and prophet Martin Luther King, Jr., wrote.

> You may be 38 years old, as I happened to be. And one day, some great opportunity stands before you and calls you to stand up for some great principle, some great issue, some great cause. And you refuse to do it because you are afraid. . . . You refuse to do it because you want to live longer . . . you're afraid that you will lose your job, or you are afraid that you will be criticized or that you will lose your popularity, or you're afraid that somebody will stab you, or shoot at you or bomb your house; so you refuse to take a stand. Well, you may go on and live until you are 90, but you're just as dead at 38 as you would be at 90. And the cessation of breathing in your life is but the belated announcement of an earlier death of the Spirit.

Martin Luther King's words may seem overly harsh, yet such is the truth during a time of crisis, the hour when good and evil face off, the time when we are laid bare, despite our words and protestations to the contrary. This is the moment for Jesus' disciples and for each of us. Whom do we align ourselves with in the world? The ones close to the crucified one, the despised of the earth, those thought by others to be expendable? Are we aligned with the poor who are without food and sustenance in the face of violence, and with the sheep who have no shepherd? Are we with those who are caught in the machinations of others? How many times have they pleaded with us to be with them when they fell into the hands of vengeance, of heartless systems of law and brutal punishment? How many times have the poor and excluded of our world asked for our presence in their pain? But we sleep, with our own dreams, our own avenues of escape.

The Arrest and Betrayal

Now the events start to move very quickly, as Jesus is passed from one group to the next and finally handed over to the Romans for crucifixion. Jesus' betrayer is at hand, but the kingdom of God is at hand as well! The hour has come when the Son of Man will be handed over. Although this moment appears to be the result of the conspiracy between Judas and the chief priests and the scribes and elders who seek to eliminate Jesus for personal, political, or religious reasons, that is not really the case. This moment is the "time of fulfillment" that Mark referred to in his first chapter. "The time has come; the kingdom of God is at hand. Change your ways and believe the Good News" (1:14). This is God's moment of hope and of saving grace and liberation.

> While Jesus was still speaking, Judas, one of the Twelve, came up. With him was a crowd armed with swords and clubs, who had been sent by the chief priests, the teachers of the Law and the elders. The traitor had arranged a signal for them, "The one I kiss, he is the man. Arrest him and take him away under guard."
> So, when he came, he went directly to Jesus calling, "Master! Master!" and kissed him. Then they seized Jesus and arrested him. One of the bystanders drew his sword and struck out at the High Priest's servant, cutting off his ear.
> Jesus turned to them saying, "So you have set out against a robber! Did you need swords and clubs to arrest me? Day after day I was among you teaching in the Temple and you did not arrest me. But let the Scriptures be fulfilled." Then they all deserted him and fled.
> A young man covered by nothing but a linen cloth followed Jesus. As they took hold of him, he left the cloth in their hands and fled away naked. (14:43-52)

We are all familiar with the kiss that betrays Jesus. This isn't the kiss that was often a greeting between disciple and master; instead it is a sign of intimacy that is twisted into hypocrisy and deceit. Because this event is so familiar, we sometimes miss the stories of two men that appear immediately after. The first man grabs a sword and cuts off the ear of the high priest's servant, and the second is seized and then runs away like the disciples. Mark uses symbols quite carefully, so these two men are inserted in the text for a reason. They appear to illustrate ways of responding to the arrest of Jesus: one responded with violence and the other ran away in fear.

The second person, the young man wearing a linen cloth, is described in the same way as the young man clothed in a white linen garment who appears in the tomb in the resurrection account. Mark is connecting the white robe of baptism with new life through resurrection. Even though we may have been baptized and entered the death and rising of Jesus in the initiation rituals, each of us is still capable of picking up the sword in fear to harm others or of running away in fear and leaving our baptismal commitments behind us.

Members of Mark's community would be familiar with both responses, as are Christians today. Perhaps it is Mark himself who is there in the garden, for the text mentions more than once that there were followers besides the Twelve who were with Jesus. If so, Mark is acknowledging his own sin, that he has also missed the mark of being faithful. There is an old tradition that the Passover ritual took place at the house of John Mark's mother, Mary (see Acts 12:12), and that John Mark is the writer of the gospel. Mark could have been following the disciples when the ritual was completed and they left to pray.

The trial before the Sanhedrin, which takes place that same night, must have been hastily convened. The verdict is decided beforehand, and witnesses have been secured who will testify to the verdict. This is the reverse of what a trial is supposed to do: a trial is intended to draw out the truth of a matter, not to act on a predetermined verdict. When the religious authorities try to collect evidence to convict Jesus, the witnesses present conflicting stories. They talk about Jesus' intent to destroy the temple and then rebuild it again in three days' time, but they stumble over their own distortions of the words. But this is preliminary to the moment of reckoning when the high priest will demand that Jesus answer and incriminate himself. Jesus bides his time. He will speak the truth about who he is, in his time and in his own way. Although his declaration will be stunning and pure, the religious leaders will choose not to understand him.

The High Priest then stood up in the midst of them and asked Jesus, "Have you no answer at all? What is this evidence against you?" But Jesus was silent and made no reply.

The High Priest put a second question to him, "Are you the Christ, the Son of the Blessed One?" Then Jesus answered, "I am, and you will see *the Son of Man seated at the right hand of the Most Power-ful and coming with the clouds of heaven around him.*" The High Priest tore his clothes to show his horror and said, "What more evidence do we need? You have just heard his blasphemous words. What is your decision?" And they all condemned Jesus saying, "He must die."

Some of them began to spit on Jesus and, blindfolding him, they struck him saying, "Play the prophet!" And the guards set upon him with blows. (14:60-65)

"You are my Son, the Beloved, the One I have chosen" were the words heard at Jesus' baptism by John in the Jordan River. Mark's text has been moving steadily toward this moment. The high priest is trying to condemn Jesus on the basis of his identity. Jesus' initial silence, which links him to the suffering servant of Isaiah, is eloquent. During Holy Week we hear this text from Isaiah.

> He was harshly treated,
> but unresisting and silent, he humbly submitted.
> Like a lamb led to the slaughter
> or a sheep before the shearer
> he did not open his mouth.
> He was taken away to detention and judgment—
> what an unthinkable fate!
> He was cut off from the land of the living,
> stricken for his people's sin. (53:7-8)

When Jesus does answer, he uses words and phrases that are statements of belief in Mark's own community thirty to forty years after the trial and the death and resurrection of Jesus. Mark uses this text to preach to his community rather than to incriminate the high priest or to condemn some of the leaders of the Jews for their treatment of Jesus.

The high priest had the responsibility of maintaining order during the Jewish feasts. The high priest at this time was a man named Joseph Caiaphas. He had been the high priest for seventeen years, so he and Pilate would have had many dealings with each other. Whether this was an actual trial or a preliminary questioning of Jesus before some of the religious authorities before bringing him to Pilate, Mark is using the construct of the trial so that Jesus can confess who he is in a definitive way for the Marcan community.

The entire text of Mark's gospel is moving toward this moment when Jesus announces clearly to the religious and political figures of his day who he is. Up to this point, Jesus has silenced everyone who has cried out in recognition of him, whether they were demons or spirits or even his own followers. Sadly, all have been lacking in any deep understanding of the real meaning of this "anointed one," the Christ, the Son of Man, and the beloved Son of God. They have not understood his singularly unique relationship with God the Father or the intimacy and power that they share. Now the time is here for telling the truth, for stating without a doubt clearly why Jesus is in the world. This moment is the axis and source of power and meaning.

In a most remarkable book, *Christ on Trial*, Rowan Williams, the archbishop of Canterbury, writes of the trials of Jesus as precise confessions of truth "when it is spoken by a captive under sentence of death" (p. 7) or spoken at the point where "God comes in" or where "God becomes manifest" (p. 12). He explains why Jesus' self-disclosure is placed here in response to the high priest.

> Jesus breaks his silence at this moment in the trial because only now can what he says be heard. There is little or no danger that we shall now mistake what he means, that we shall confidently describe him in words that reflect our own aspirations. He is who he is, and we can do nothing but let our imagination and our language be reshaped by him—if, that is, we have ears to hear, if we are not already determined to abide by the standards of the insane world that has brought him to trial. ("Mark: Voices at Midnight," in *Christ on Trial*, 7-8)

A few pages later, Archbishop Williams makes it utterly clear who Jesus is and what his life, his trial, and death are all about—the heart of the message of the Gospel of Mark.

> So it is that Mark's Jesus at his trial becomes a revelation of where God is: God is simply that which makes it natural and necessary to act against insanity and violence. God is the reality that, simply by being what it is (or who it is), establishes that violence cannot fill up the whole space of the world. . . .
>
> The Son of the Blessed One is indeed the silent prisoner; the condemned human form is what God will show as he comes in glory. The reality—or could we say—the "worthwhileness" of God is not in the promise of safety, the possibility of escape from the world; there is only the recognition here and now of God's glory in the freedom that appears when the insane violence of the world meets immoveable resistance. (*Christ on Trial*, 12-13)

In a real sense, Jesus' words are God's verdict passed on our world of violence, injustice, and evil. It is we and our world that stand convicted by Jesus' silence, by his life and words, and now as he faces death. Jesus is the beloved Son of the Father, the Blessed One of God, the Messiah and king spoken of by the prophets. But Jesus is also the Son of Man crucified. Although his murder was technically legal according to Roman law, it was grossly unjust and unmerited in the courts of the world. It is this Son of Man who will come in glory to judge the nations and all people of the world with justice. He is God incarnate.

In response to the high priest's second question, "Are you the Christ, the Son of the Blessed One?" Jesus announces "I am" (*ego eimi*), using the name for God from Exodus 3:14 ("I AM WHO AM"). Given this name, we must wonder who is standing before whom, who is judging and who is being judged. Jesus continues, "and you will see *the Son of Man seated at the right hand of the Most Powerful and coming with the clouds of heaven around him.*" These are clearly intimations of the resurrection and the judgment that is coming to bear upon our words and lives.

The high priest takes Jesus' self-disclosure as more than enough evidence to move on to the next phase. Dramatically, he stands and cries out and rends his garments. Throughout the gospel, Mark often uses clothing as symbols, sometimes of baptism or healing or of recognition of Jesus. In tearing his garments, the high priest seemingly destroys his identity and unwittingly declares the end of the temple and its ritual. By voiding his power and the rituals of the temple, he is making way for the new temple of God in the presence of Jesus, the new sacrifice that makes all holy, and the new covenant that is the hope of the world.

The religious leaders begin to treat Jesus as many Jews treated the prophets throughout history: they spit on him, blindfold him, and strike him. Truly, Jesus is the prophet of God, the word of God made flesh, God incarnate among us. Unfortunately, this kind of violence is often the reaction of powers on earth that are not rooted in the good news of God. They turn from forgiveness, peace, mercy, inclusion, and healing.

Mark situates Jesus' trial within the story of Peter's trial. As the procession moves to the court of the high priest's house, Peter follows at a safe distance and then waits, but he doesn't escape scrutiny. Peter, whom Jesus addressed as Simon when he slept in Gethsemane, is now confronted and questioned as was his master, Jesus. Simon Peter rushes to answer, to deny, to distance himself further and further from Jesus by his language and protests. In fear, he ends up cursing and swearing that he is not bound to Jesus and is not part of his company, that he has nothing to do with the man. Simon reveals his lack of faithfulness to Jesus, his fear, his cowardice, and his callousness.

> While Peter was below in the courtyard, one of the High Priest's servant-girls came by. Noticing Peter beside the fire, she looked straight at him and said, "You also were with Jesus, the Nazarene." But he denied it, "I don't know or understand what you are talking about." And he went out through the gateway.
>
> The servant-girl saw him there and told the bystanders, "This man is one of them." But Peter denied it again. After a little while those standing by said to Peter, "Of course you are one of them; you are a

Galilean, aren't you?" And Peter began to justify himself with curses and oaths, "I don't know the man you are talking about."

Just then a cock crowed a second time and Peter remembered what Jesus had said to him, "Before the cock crows twice you will deny me three times." And he broke down and wept. (14:66-72)

While Jesus is being confronted with the religious authorities, Peter is being questioned by a maid in the high priest's house and by some bystanders. Even though his questioners have no power or authority to harm him, Peter denies any association with Jesus, steadily growing more testy and brutal. His denial is as fervent as his earlier pledge to Jesus that he would die rather than disown him. The Peter of Mark's gospel is the Peter of the early church. In spite of his denial of Jesus, he became the leader of the fledging and struggling communities of faith. This portrayal of Simon Peter is a warning that Mark holds up to his own people who have turned their back on their baptismal promises and vows in fear or cowardice. They must pray and be willing to deny themselves to remain faithful.

The last line is this account reads simply, "And Peter broke down and wept." With these words, Peter disappears from the passion account. He will not participate but will hear the rest of the account of Jesus' trial and crucifixion as a member of the community that has fled. Peter also represents the part of the church that must weep, ask for forgiveness and mercy, and once again recommit itself to Jesus as Lord and God. Jesus is now alone, except for God, his Abba, his beloved and revered Father.

With these sad words, the immediate preface to Jesus' torture and execution comes to an end. The violence will escalate and become ever more brutal, inhuman, and murderous. Jesus will die, but only after becoming the victim of Roman torture and power. Mark is contrasting the power of God with the powers of the world, its governments and military, economic, political, and religious structures that cause people to become part of the crowds that blindly participate in that power.

An ancient Buddhist story calls us to choose where we stand, whom we will follow, and which God rules our lives, our bodies, and souls. It's called "Buddha and the Bandit."

> Once upon a time Buddha was on his way to a village on the other side of the mountains to teach, to beg, and to call more disciples to follow his way. He intended to take a shortcut over the mountain pass to save time. But immediately the people and his friends said, "No, don't go that way. The pass is filled with bandits lying in wait for you and if they find you don't have money or jewels then they will kill you brutally!"
>
> But Buddha couldn't be bothered with such warnings, and he continued on his way. Well, no sooner had he climbed high into the pass when

a notorious bandit appeared, bearing down on him with sword in hand and shouting, "Your money or your life!" Buddha looked up at the man astride his horse, pulled out his pockets—empty! And he said, "I guess it's my life, since I have no money." As the man moved toward him, sword in motion, Buddha's words stopped him in his tracks: "You know the rules. If you take my life, then you must at least grant me a last wish!" The man stopped. "All right. What do you want? Make it quick, old man."

The Buddha said, "Well, my wish is simple and has two parts. First, see that great tree over there and the limb that extends far out over the path? Cut it off!" The bandit grinned and in seconds the limb lay on the ground. "All right, old man. What is the second part?" Buddha turned toward him and said very quietly and steadily, "Now put it back on again."

The bandit was speechless and then started laughing uproariously. "You are the stupidest man I've ever met! No one can put a limb back on a tree after it's been cut off! Insane! You're idiotic." But the Buddha looked at him and said, "I am not the one who is stupid. You are. Anyone can destroy. Any child without knowledge can cut things up. Anyone can maim, kill, mutilate, and undo reality. It takes no power or intelligence whatsoever."

The bandit was caught off guard. Buddha continued, "What takes power, real power, is to be able to heal, to bring life, to restore, to stand in the breach, to undo the evil and the destruction that you've done in the past. That takes real power, imagination, and creativity. What you've done takes nothing at all. Anyone can do what you've done." They eyed each other for a long time.

Then, they say, the notorious bandit got down off his horse, laid his sword at the Buddha's feet, knelt in respect before him, and humbly asked, "Teach me that kind of power." They say that it was the bandit who became one of his most loyal followers and carried the Buddha's legacy and teaching to others after his death.

This is the choice laid before us in Mark's gospel and every time we participate in the ritual of the passion of Jesus in Holy Week. This choice also lay before Mark's church. Do we follow the insane and violent powers of the world, of evil, of killing and the diminishment of life, or do we follow the power of Jesus, denying ourselves, picking up our cross, and serving others and remaining truthful and faithful to our Lord handed over to others? The choice does not get any easier.

Jesus' Death by Crucifixion

When morning comes, the chief priests, elders, and scribes of the Sanhedrin hold a council. Then they "put Jesus in chains, led him away and handed him over to Pilate" (15:1b). With this one short sentence, Jesus is on his way to crucifixion. When Pilate questions him, Jesus keeps his silence. Pilate listens to the accusations of the chief priests, but Jesus does not defend himself against his own people.

Pilate's first question is, "Are you the king of the Jews?" At the time of Jesus (and this is also true today), it was impossible to separate the political and religious implications of public actions. Religious acts of Jews and Romans had political implications, and, similarly, political acts of Romans and Jews had religious implications. One either belonged to God and was held accountable for the practice of that creed, or one belonged to the Roman culture of the era and used religion, or any other segment of society, to further the ends of a government, business, or social enterprise.

For Christians at the time of Mark and for the next few hundred years, their religious system and the ruling political systems stood clearly in opposition to each other. From the time of Constantine forward (313 C.E.), religion served the reach and the domination of the empire. It demanded total obedience and put to death anyone who breached the power and authority of its realm or called into question its integrity. And as Christianity spread geographically outward from its center, it became distorted and directly contradictory of Jesus' good news of God to the poor of the world.

The Christians at the time of Mark had to deal with the brutal occupation of Rome. Mark takes pains to make sure that no one in Rome can accuse Jesus of nationalistic intent or aspirations as messiah. Mark makes clear that Jesus and his followers are not interested in the overthrow of Rome, militarily or politically. The kingdom they refer to is altogether different; it is a new form of living. It is in opposition to all that Rome stands for, but it does not confront Rome. This is the kingdom of God, the Father of Jesus. Jesus' community worships God alone and not the emperor or the government. God alone, the God of the living "I am," is the object of reverence and worship.

The trial before the Sanhedrin and the trial before Pilate are both concerned with revealing who Jesus is, to the Jewish authorities and also to the Roman ones. Jesus' response to Pilate's question, "Are you the king of the Jews?" is simple: "You say so." Pilate is not as interested in who Jesus is as he is about whether or not Jesus may be a threat to the social order at a volatile time when crowds are easily roused to chaos and violence. He is already accused of being a messiah, a title that has political and nationalistic overtones to the masses of people crowding into the city for the ritual of Passover.

Mark depicts Pilate as a mediocre man, watchful of public reactions to his decrees. He seems aware that Jesus has been brought before him because of conflicts internal to the Jews, whom he despises. Pilate turns to the crowd to let them decide the fate of Jesus, seemingly not caring himself what happens. In reality, Pilate and Rome were brutal beyond imagining to Jews and Christians alike; both groups endured massive persecution and death at the hands of Rome. By exploiting the custom of allowing the crowd to seek release of a prisoner during the festival, Pilate manipulates the situation to his benefit. His appeal to the crowd is a political maneuver that appeases the crowd and reinforces the power of Rome over life and death.

In Mark's account, Pilate, the crowd, and the chief priests are apparently working together to get what they want done. However, believers reading the gospel know that these events are taking place to fulfill the scriptures through Jesus' freely given obedience to God, his beloved Father. He is a human being, and as he lives, he will die. All of us stand together, participating to some degree in the violence, injustice, and evil against Jesus and one another. We are all sinners, involved in the continuing passion and death of Jesus in the world. When we hear how Jesus is condemned, we must realize that we are part of that reality in the world today.

> At every Passover festival, Pilate used to free any prisoner the people asked for. Now there was a man called Barabbas, jailed with the rioters who had committed murder in the uprising. When the crowd went up to ask Pilate the usual favor, he said to them, "Do you want me to set free the King of the Jews?" For he realized that the chief priests had handed Jesus over to him out of envy. But the chief priests stirred up the crowd to ask instead for the release of Barabbas. Pilate replied, "And what shall I do with the man you call King of the Jews?" The crowd shouted back, "Crucify him!" Pilate asked, "What evil has he done?" But they shouted the louder, "Crucify him!"
>
> As Pilate wanted to please the people, he freed Barabbas and after the flogging of Jesus had him handed over to be crucified. (15:6-15)

Pilate appears to have no personal grudge or vendetta against Jesus; he plays out his role politically, deciding what might be astute or acceptable in dealing with the crowd. He has used sarcasm from the beginning in referring to Jesus as the "King of the Jews." He mocks the crowd as he mocked the Sanhedrin, using a religious term even when he has absolute power over them; he can refuse to allow the Jews to enter the temple or practice their religion.

It is not clear that the crowd even knows that Jesus is the "King of the Jews," because there is no mention of his name in the shouting back and forth between Pilate and the crowd. It is the crowd that first shouts out "Crucify him!" Until now Mark has referred often and in detail to Jesus' passion and death, and he has presented Jesus telling his disciples that they must pick up their cross, but now it is the crowd that demands a crucifixion, a form of execution reserved for non-Romans. And, as was the custom, Pilate orders that Jesus be flogged, a preliminary torture to break the will and resistance of criminals who were to be crucified.

We must remember that the members of Mark's community lived during the time of the Roman Empire and that they were persecuted and murdered. Jesus of Nazareth was condemned to death by a Roman governor and executed by the standard form of torture and death that Romans reserved for those they conquered. Although the crowds and even the chief priests of the Jews may have had a hand in it, it is Rome that killed Jesus. His death resulted from political reasons rather than religious ones.

Joseph O'Hanlon has cited a description of Pilate recorded by a Jewish scholar who was a contemporary of Pilate.

> A Jewish scholar, Philo Judaeus, who lived in the Egyptian city of Alexandria and was a contemporary of Pilate, had occasion to write to the emperor Gaius (Caligula) in 40 C.E. when the latter proposed to have a statue of himself erected in the Temple in Jerusalem, a proposal which would have led to widespread revolt had Gaius had his way. He was, however, conveniently assassinated. Philo's letter refers to Pilate and recalls "the briberies, the insults, the robberies, the outrages and wanton injuries, the executions without trial constantly repeated, the ceaseless and supremely grievous cruelty" which marked the prefect's time of office in Palestine. Indeed, Pilate was removed from his post because of the many summary executions he carried out. He was not a man who knew how to make terror serve political circumspection. (*Mark My Words*, 290)

Jesus was treated brutally, as were all those condemned to death. According to Mark, Jesus was treated shamelessly both in the court of the high priest's house and in the court of the Roman procurator. Both accounts tell how the suffering servant, the just one, beloved of God and innocent of any wrongdoing, acted when he was seized and manhandled. We hear many of these echoes and lamentations during Passiontide.

> I gave my back to those who beat me,
>   my cheeks to those who plucked my beard;
> My face I did not shield
>   from buffets and spitting.

> The Lord GOD is my help,
>   therefore I am not disgraced;
> I have set my face like flint,
>   knowing that I shall not be put to shame. (Is 50:6-7 NAB)

> There was in him no stately bearing to make us look at him,
>   nor appearance that would attract us to him.
> He was spurned and avoided by men,
>   a man of suffering, accustomed to infirmity,

> One of those from whom men hide their faces,
>   spurned, and we held him in no esteem. (Is 53:2b-3 NAB)

> With the rod they strike on the cheek the ruler of Israel.
>   (Mi 4:14b NAB)

For Mark and the early church, Jesus, the crucified one, was the suffering servant, who was condemned and tortured because he was obedient to the word of God in a world that rejected God's power and presence in Jesus.

Jesus is mocked by the cohort, humiliated, clothed in purple, and crowned with a wreath roughly constructed of thorn branches. A cohort would have comprised anywhere from two hundred to six hundred men, so probably those who were not on duty were given the task of breaking the prisoner before the actual execution began. They kneel in mock homage and insult him. The insults escalate into torture as they scourge Jesus and then reclothe him in his own garments and lead him out to crucify him. Similar executions would have been carried out thousands of times as part of the brutal Roman occupation.

For Mark, Jesus' way of the cross began in chapter 8 when Jesus first began to speak in Caesarea Philippi of his coming passion and death. He sought to prepare his disciples for what is happening now by teaching them about what life as his follower would mean. Mark's account of the actual way to the cross and the crucifixion is very brief and focuses on those who observe, witness, or participate in it rather than on the details of the horror that Jesus experienced.

The very first person we meet is Simon, a Cyrenian who is remembered for having carried the cross of Jesus. Even his children, Alexander and Rufus, are named, which indicates that this family was known to Mark's community. Again, Mark appears to be directing this telling of the flogging and crucifixion of Jesus to members of his own community as they walk the way of Jesus.

Mark makes no mention of the actual way of the cross or the nailing of Jesus to the crossbeam, but he does note that two robbers were crucified with him. Mark also pays attention to those who stand below the cross and read the inscription over Jesus' head or jeer at him.

> When they had led him to the place called Golgotha, which means *the Skull*, they offered him wine mixed with myrrh, but he would not take it. Then they nailed him to the cross and divided his clothes among themselves, casting lots to decide what each should take.

> It was about nine o'clock in the morning when they crucified him. The statement of his offense was displayed above his head and it read, "The King of the Jews." They also crucified two robbers with him, one on his right and one on his left.

> People passing by laughed at him, shook their head and jeered, "Aha! So you are able to tear down the Temple and build it up again in three days. Now save yourself and come down from the cross!"

In the same way the chief priests and the teachers of the Law mocked him, saying to one another, "the man who saved others cannot save himself. Let's see the Messiah, the king of Israel, come down from his cross and then we will believe in him." Even the men who were crucified with Jesus insulted him. (15:22-32)

In Mark's account, Jesus suffers alone. At the time, no one recognizes this tortured and torn man as the beloved of the Father, the Son of Man. They sarcastically call him "Messiah" to demean him and all that he stands for, even mocking how he has healed others. The religious leaders now address him with a religious title, the "King of Israel," a title they had objected to earlier. In this pathetic rendering of Jesus bearing his pain alone, even those condemned with him heap abuse on him. Again, we are reminded of lines from the Hebrew scriptures: "All who see me make a jest of me; they sneer and shake their heads" (Ps 22:8).

Mark's Jesus is revealed in his isolation, pain, and suffering and finally in his death. Only those who believe, those who follow Jesus in picking up their crosses can see him for who he is, the crucified one revealed in love. With the crowd, we are left standing before the cross to ask ourselves what we are doing. Do we join in the mockery or do we listen to those in pain? Even if we cannot alleviate their pain, do we hear them and take their words to heart?

Several years ago, Elie Weisel spoke about the need to listen to others.

I always try to listen to the victim. In other words, if I remain silent, I may help my own soul but, because I do not help other people, I poison my soul. Indifference means there is a kind of apathy that sets in and you no longer appreciate beauty, friendship, goodness, or anything. So therefore, do not be insensitive. Be sensitive, only sensitive. Of course it hurts. Sensitivity is painful. So what? Think of those that you have to be sensitive to. Their pain is greater than yours. (Personal notes from a talk given in New York)

Jesus' way of the cross and crucifixion form a school in which we are to learn sensitivity to the pain and suffering of others, especially those who are innocent or caught in the cracks of evil or deemed expendable by those with power. We are not to dwell on our own sufferings. If they are a consequence of our faithfulness, then they are bound to Jesus' own cross and death. As we walk the way, we are to seek to carry another's cross, as Simon of Cyrene was privileged to do for Jesus. This is our place.

The Death of Jesus

Just as Mark's account of the crucifixion is brief, so is his account of Jesus' actual dying and death. The practice of crucifixion would be terrifyingly familiar to Mark's own community, who would have witnessed it and experienced it all too often. The upright beams of the crosses were left in place just outside the city so that everyone could see them as they passed by. For non-Romans, they were a stark reminder of the tyranny and power under which they lived. Those condemned to death carried their own cross beams. They weren't dragged, as is often depicted by artists, but were roped across the shoulders of those to be executed, as a slave would be yoked to carry water or building materials. The person to be executed was stripped naked and nailed to the cross beam, which was then lifted up and put in place. Then the feet were nailed to the upright beam and the long wait began. Mark gives a time frame: the nailing to the cross was at nine in the morning; darkness fell over the land at noon and lasted until three o'clock, when Jesus died. This text bears ancient echoes of the words of the prophet Amos.

> Yahweh says, "On that day I will make the sun go down at noon and darken the earth in broad daylight.
> I will turn your festivals into mourning and all your singing in to wailing. . . . I will make them mourn as for an only son and bring their day to a bitter end." (8:9-10)

Jesus does not drink of the myrrh and wine that is offered. The only cup he will drink from is the one he offered his disciples the night before, the cup of blessing, which is the cup of baptism and the cup of pain and bitterness that saves. The soldiers take his clothes, attempting to strip away his dignity as son, his identity, and his truth. Jesus will pray once more on the cross before he dies. He cries out to God; this time, however, he will not call God Father, as he did with such intimacy the night before, but simply God, *Eloi*, the Aramaic word for God that was used when in need, in necessity, in pain and terror.

> [A]nd at three o'clock Jesus cried out in a loud voice, "*Eloi, Eloi, lamma sabachthani?*" which means "My God, my God, why have you deserted me?" As soon as they heard these words, some of the bystanders said, "Listen! He is calling for Elijah." And one of them went quickly to fill a sponge with bitter wine and, putting it on a reed, gave him to drink, saying, "Now let's see whether Elijah comes to take him down."
> But Jesus uttered a loud cry and gave up his spirit. (15:34-37)

Jesus' cry to God, "My God, my God," even at the end, avows that Jesus belongs to God alone. It is also the opening line of Psalm 22 and is followed by "Why are you so far from me, from the sound of my groaning?" This is prayer of anguish and lament, of pain and loss, of hanging on for dear life, of hanging in death, knowing you will die. You will not be rescued as others have been. From very early in the tradition of the church, Psalm 22 has been used to describe Jesus in his pain. While the emphasis is on the person's horrible suffering, a refrain is repeated in which this person reaches out again and again to God for help. At the end, the sufferer praises God to the ends of the earth for the deliverance God has brought: "For dominion belongs to the Lord and he reigns over the nations." In a sense, this psalm could serve as a preface to the Gospel of Mark; it demonstrates how Christians should pray in the midst of persecution, relying on Jesus' faithfulness as they seek to remain faithful.

Jesus dies crying out. There are no last words, only his last cry and breath. As John the Baptist cried out in a loud voice to herald Jesus' coming after him, now Jesus cries out as he lets go of life. And, finally, recognition of who Jesus is appears on the lips of someone who witnessed his passion and death.

> But Jesus uttered a loud cry and gave up his spirit. And immediately the curtain which enclosed the Temple sanctuary was torn in two from top to bottom.
> The captain [in some translations, centurion] who was standing in front of him saw how Jesus died and heard the cry he gave; and he said, "Truly, this man was the Son of God." (15:37-39)

These are the words with which Mark began his account of the life and death of Jesus: "This is the beginning of the Good News of Jesus Christ, the Son of God" (1:1). This moment of Jesus' death is the beginning of the good news of God. It is now a reality. And recognition comes from a Roman, a Gentile centurion who participated in the death and was a witness to it. For Mark's community in Rome, the words of the Roman centurion are a moment of confession. The community members stand facing the cross of Jesus, witnessing to his passion and death in their belief, practices, rituals, and by laying down their own lives. They also recognize Jesus, and they take his words to heart, seeking to live in faithfulness and commitment to the cross. This is the way we are to live and to die, crying out "My God, my God!" and abandoning ourselves with Jesus into the heart of God.

As Jesus gives up his spirit, Mark announces that the veil of the temple was torn in two. The old covenant was rent. The sanctuary that was built by the human hands of the people of God is now broken. And there is now a new temple, the body of Jesus, all the people of God. The new temple is not an edifice or building, but all human flesh. From now on the Holy of Holies can be found in the bodies of all the people of the earth. Now nothing separates any human being from the presence of God. All can pray to God as one, as the beloved children of God with Jesus, in the power of the Spirit. The revelation that had been proclaimed is now being seen and heard.

At this point Mark calls our attention to other people who will be a link between Jesus' death and his resurrection.

> There were also some women watching from a distance; among them were Mary Magdalene, Mary the mother of James the younger and Joses, and Salome, who had followed Jesus when he was in Galilee and saw to his needs. There were also others who had come up with him to Jerusalem. (15:40-41)

It should be noted that throughout the gospel Peter, James, and John form an inner band of disciples within the Twelve. Similarly, it seems that these three women also form an inner circle of the followers of Jesus. Like Peter, who followed at a distance in the court of the high priest, these women are watching from a distance the execution of Jesus. Like Peter and the other men, they have been with Jesus from the beginning and have ministered to him. Some of these women will come to the tomb when the sabbath is over to anoint his body for burial, and in their mission of mercy, they will receive the proclamation of resurrection.

But now, as the day ends and the sabbath is fast coming upon them, the last things, the burial and the closing of the tomb, must be completed. Mark tells us that another disciple steps forward to stand up for his faith. He approaches Pilate to ask for the body of the Lord.

> It was now evening and as it was Preparation Day, that is the day before the Sabbath, Joseph of Arimathea boldly went to Pilate and asked for the body of Jesus. Joseph was a respected member of the Council who was himself waiting for the kingdom of God.
>
> Pilate was surprised that Jesus should have died so soon; so he summoned the captain and inquired if Jesus was already dead. After hearing the captain, he let Joseph have the body.
>
> Joseph took it down and wrapped it in the linen sheet he had bought. He laid the body in a tomb which had been cut out of the rock and rolled a stone across the entrance to the tomb. Now Mary of Magdala and Mary the mother of Joses took note of where the body had been laid. (15:42-47)

Joseph of Arimathea, who, as a respected member of the Sanhedrin, has much to lose, is emboldened to go to Pilate to claim Jesus' body. In doing so, he is also identifying himself as a follower of Jesus. This is what the death of Jesus calls us all to do. We are to come forward and declare Jesus' claim on us through our baptism into the death and resurrection of the Lord. Joseph, who has not been mentioned before, is a righteous Jew who is practicing the law found in the Book of Deuteronomy, which reads: "If a man, guilty of any crime that deserves death, has been put to death by hanging him on a tree, this body must not remain hanging there through the night. But you shall bury him on the same day because the hanged man is a curse of God" (21:22-23). He obeys the law and also honors the sabbath of God. And the same centurion who confessed Jesus as the Son of God now tells Pilate that Jesus is already dead. Jesus' death has brought out the courage and latent belief of some witnesses who can now begin to see with the eyes of faith. The corpse is then interred.

The women, beginning with the mother-in-law of Simon Peter, have ministered to Jesus from the beginning. Unfortunately, this is not something that has ever been said of the male disciples. But here a man, Joseph of Arimathea, performs the corporal works of mercy for Jesus in death. The passion began with another work of mercy—the anointing of Jesus by a woman in the house of Simon the leper—and now it ends with the burial of Jesus by Joseph of Arimathea. The Christian community, in Mark's and in our time, needs to be reminded that this is what our God wants: mercy. This is what Jesus preached when he called sinners to follow him. Here is what Dorothy Day had to say about mercy.

If I did not believe, if I did not make what is called an act of faith (and each act of faith increases our faith, and our capacity for faith), if I did not have faith that the works of mercy do lighten the sum total of suffering in the world, so that those who are suffering on both sides of this ghastly struggle somehow mysteriously find their pain lifted and some balm of consolation poured on their wounds, if I did not believe these things, the problem of evil would indeed be overwhelming. (from "On Pilgrimage," quoted on "Your Daily Dig" website at http://dailydig.bruderhof.org)

In searching for a story that would reflect God's love for all that he has made, I remembered one from Taiwan about a man named Wu Feng, who lived in the 1700s.

He was appointed the visitor-delegate of the Manchurian emperor to islands in the Straits of Taiwan. The people who lived there were a primitive and barbaric people, and Wu Feng spent decades attempting to bring some semblance of law, justice, and structure to the islands. He became friends with the leader, and as they spoke often, many things improved.

But every year they brutally sacrificed one of their finest men or women, hoping to attract the attention of their gods so they could ask for good weather when they fished and were out on the ocean in the coming year. The custom was rigidly enforced. The names of all the people were collected, and the lot was drawn and one person was executed, chopped up, and thrown into the sea to appease the gods.

No matter what Wu Feng did and no matter how much he argued, the leader would not relent. He held to the practice partly out of fear of the old gods and partly in stubbornly maintaining the power he had over the people. Year after year Wu Feng pleaded, bribed, threatened, cajoled, screamed, cried out, but all to no avail. Year after year someone was murdered and given over in sacrifice.

Finally, after more than twenty-five years had passed, Wu Feng went to the leader before the annual grisly ritual and declared: "This year, if you are going to kill anyone, kill me." The leader was appalled. Not only had he grown fond of Wu Feng, he was also afraid that if he killed him, the people who sent him would come down on the island and destroy everyone. But Wu Feng was adamant. "Kill me and no one else." It was only when the leader was faced with this personal demand and the offering of Wu Feng's life that the killing stopped and the ritual was forever discarded.

So it is with the death of Jesus. God has clearly proclaimed to humankind that the killing must stop, and any rituals that involve death, violence, humiliation, or the diminishment of human beings must be discarded forever. The followers of Jesus must faithfully refuse to kill, to be soldiers, to participate in the destruction of creation and the human race, to pay homage to any government or nation that extends its power by killing, by war, by bombs, or pre-emptive strikes. Disciples of Jesus must find the courage to refuse to bend or collude with any structure or group that discriminates, executes, destroys, or takes the life of others. They must speak out on behalf of victims and steadfastly stand with them, if only in silent witness. They must seek to share their pain and to be in communion with them. Otherwise, like the rest of Jesus' followers, including Peter, James, and John, we too betray our Lord; we flee in faithlessness and add to the pain and isolation of the suffering and crucified people of God still among us. Our prayer must be: Lord, have mercy on us, for we are sinners. Amen.

CHAPTER 10

The Resurrection—"Go!"

I was born in the morning of the world
so I know how morning looks.
Morning looks like people look
like a sea waiting for ships
like a cornfield waiting for corn.
Morning looks like any strong beautiful wanting.
There is your morning, my morning, everybody's morning.
—Carl Sandburg

IT IS ALMOST UNIVERSALLY BELIEVED by scholars that the original ending of Mark consisted of only the first eight verses of chapter 16. The empty tomb is the first proclamation that Jesus is alive. It is thought that the additional endings were added because at the time of the early church people had trouble dealing with the abruptness of Mark's handling of the resurrection and what it portended for the community of believers. They wanted more of an explanation, more to work with, more to go on. Yet the original ending is as finely crafted as the rest of Mark's gospel. It is a proclamation of the good news that should be read, both then and now, with the inspiration of the Spirit. I recall a saying of Carolyn Heilbrun that "Power consists in deciding which story shall be told."

The first story, the story of the resurrection, brought heart, courage, and hope to Mark's community in Rome as they faced their own internal struggles, suffering, and death by persecution at the whim and at the hands of the Roman Empire. This resurrection story asks many questions, including what difference the death and resurrection of Jesus makes for the daily lives of those who follow after him in faithfulness? What does the empty tomb say about the power of Jesus' words and life? What does the raising of Jesus say about the power of God in contrast to other powers that profess to believe in a god, yet more often than not, act as though they themselves are gods? What does the dying and rising of Jesus mean for all those who find themselves at odds with the powers of the world or with the leaders of their own religious groups? How are Christians, followers of the crucified and risen Lord, to live the resurrection now, at our time and in our place

215

in the world? These questions put to us by Mark's gospel are foundational. Mark was apparently trying to get his own community to reflect upon them throughout the gospel; like the members of his community, we must answer for ourselves.

Here is what is thought to be the original ending. It is marked by a stark simplicity and the use of phrases that have appeared before in the gospel.

> When the sabbath was over, Mary of Magdala, Mary, the mother of James, and Salome bought spices so that they might go and anoint the body. And very early in the morning on the first day of the week, just after sunrise, they came to the tomb.
>
> They were saying to one another, "Who will roll back the stone for us from the entrance to the tomb?" but as they looked up, they noticed that the stone had already been rolled away. It was a very big stone.
>
> As they entered the tomb, they saw a young man in a white robe seated on the right, and they were amazed. But he said to them, "Don't be alarmed; you are looking for Jesus of Nazareth who was crucified; he has been raised and is not here. This is, however, the place where they laid him. Now go and tell his disciples and Peter: Jesus is going ahead of you to Galilee; you will see him there just as he told you." The women went out and fled from the tomb, for terror and amazement had seized them. And they were so afraid that they said nothing to anyone. (16:1-8)

Rowan Williams says that "Mark is at his most enigmatic here, leaving us with the silent terror of the women at the tomb, not with a triumphant vindication." He considers the meaning of Jesus' resurrection for all of us.

> The resurrection comes across as radically unexpected, almost disconnected with what has gone before. It is as if the resurrection is like the moment of revelation at the trial; it is what it is; it is the bare fact that the life of Jesus is not contained or swallowed up by the way of this world; not even by the "natural" ways of death and corruption. The freedom revealed at the trial becomes materially visible in the empty tomb—yet, as Mark's Gospel ends, we are told nothing of what this might mean in any concrete sense. As has sometimes been said, the *reader* is the "lost ending" of Mark. We have to discover for ourselves what difference is made by this life, this death and this disorienting mystery after the crucifixion. (*Christ on Trial*, 17)

We must never take our eyes off Jesus of Nazareth, the crucified one who has been raised and is not "here," as the young man at the tomb explains to the frightened women. Whatever the resurrection is, it is not easily rendered in words, explained, or lived. We have been introduced to

Jesus and seen him through the eyes of believers and unbelievers alike, within and outside his own community, Jew and Gentile, women and men, righteously religious, sinners and unclean. And we have been relentlessly exposed to disciples who, along with his family, his people, the leaders and authorities of his own religion, and those who give allegiance to the Roman Empire, reject him. Mark's steady focus on Jesus calls the attention of his stubborn and faithless followers back to Jesus' words, his life and death and now his resurrection. Rowan Williams sums it all up:

> Nonetheless, it is here, in Jesus crucified and in the struggling and failing community, that the coming of the Human One in glory is made visible in the world. . . .
>
> [T]he gospel remains the gospel of the crucified, asking of us an attention to the reality that is before us and within us here and now, a reality that will be scandalous and painful. Pascal's stark assertion that "Jesus will be in agony until the end of the world" is much in the spirit of Mark; and it is not an observation about the deplorable state of unbelievers, but an exhortation to believers to keep awake—awake to their own inability to stay in the almost unbearable present moment where Jesus is—rather than look for an unreal future or past to run to. (*Christ on Trial*, 19-20)

Most of us don't like things to be left hanging. Mark was intent on preaching the gospel so his community would hear it and take it to heart in the same way that Jesus taught his disciples. They were to remain with Jesus through his passion and death, and they were not to avoid the empty tomb. It wasn't enough to hear the words; they had to live them. And so it is with us. We must hear and believe and then, in the style of Mark, immediately enter the empty tomb to hear the proclamation of belief in the risen Lord. Then, with the frightened and bewildered women, we are to run from the tomb into the world in obedience. The young man at the tomb told the women that they were to announce to the disciples and Peter that Jesus was not in the tomb. He was not dead. The disciples were to go to Galilee and they would see him there, just as he had told them before his death. Each generation that hears the gospel must do the same: Go!

The women had risen early in the morning after the sabbath to go to the tomb to anoint the body of Jesus. However, because Mark's account of Jesus' passion and death began with an unnamed woman disciple anointing Jesus' body for burial, it was not necessary. It had already been done. Did the women going to the tomb know of that earlier anointing at the house of Simon the leper? Could Salome, the last woman named in the group going to the tomb, have been the one who honored him earlier? It seems fitting to think it is so.

All the gospel accounts note that Jesus' resurrection happened on "the first day of the week," a good time for new revelation. Eugene LaVerdiere once gave a homily about this first day of the week. He said that the words shouldn't really be translated as "the first day of the week" but instead as "Day one, or the first day," a reference to the first day of creation in Genesis 1:5. The resurrection ushers in the new creation. This is the beginning of life as the hold of death is broken forever. God created light on the first day, and now light appears as a person, Jesus the Christ, the Son of God alive forever. This is the day of baptism, of rising to new life after being buried in the tomb with Christ. It is baptism that sows the seeds of resurrection in our bodies. We return to the first sentence of Mark, "This is the beginning of the Good News of Jesus Christ, the Son of God." Our lives in God begin today as the gospel takes root in our own bodies.

The urgency and immediacy of Mark's account urge us to proclaim the gospel in our lives and world, to run from the tomb and announce to one another that Jesus goes before us. Despite their fear and trembling, the women obey, although clearly they do not understand what the resurrection means. The disciples are blind: the men didn't see what was happening during the passion and death of Jesus and now the women don't understand the raising of Jesus. Nonetheless, all are invited to believe and to proclaim the gospel.

As they leave the tomb, the text says that they "said nothing to anyone." They certainly wouldn't have announced their news to anyone who was part of the conspiracy to kill Jesus or to anyone who would turn them over to the Jewish leadership or to the Romans. No, they would first speak to those of their own community.

And the disciples went home to Galilee, back to where it all started, where Jesus first appeared walking along the sea, watching them fish and calling them to follow him. Although Jesus is identified before his baptism as coming from Nazareth, "a town of Galilee" (1:9), and his temptation in the desert is briefly mentioned (1:13), Mark's account of Jesus' life really begins after the arrest of John, when "Jesus went into Galilee preaching the Good News of God" (1:14). Other translations may read "Jesus appeared in Galilee," which makes the meaning clear. It is time to begin at the very beginning and walk the way again, this time in light of the passion, death, and resurrection of Jesus. It is time to see what we did not want to see, to heed what we first ignored, to take to heart what we rejected and, with others, to walk and talk our way through our fears. It is time to practice more and more what Jesus called us to when he cried out, "This is the time of fulfillment. The reign of God is at hand! Reform your lives and believe in the gospel!" (1:15 NAB). It is time to renew our baptismal promises and to once again walk the liturgical year as believers struggling to be faithful to the word and the body of Jesus, prophet, beloved Son of God, Son of Man, the crucified and risen Lord.

As we turn back to the tomb, we hear the women speak only of the stone and its size. They wonder about who will roll it away for them, and the stone is described as being very large. Eugene LaVerdiere points out the significance of this within the context of the baptismal life of Mark's community.

> In terms of Mark's story of the passion-resurrection, the stone was a baptismal symbol, blocking the way for someone to effectively be buried with Christ. The passion was a story not just of Jesus dying but of the challenge for the disciples to die with Christ. So also Jesus' burial and the visit to the tomb was not just a story of Jesus being buried, but of the challenge for the disciples to be buried with Christ. In this, the stone is a symbol for everything that blocks the way. It may be different for each, but for everyone it is a very large stone. (*The Beginning of the Gospel*, 2:320)

While the Gospel of Matthew explains who removed the stone, Mark does not. Some people think it was rolled back by the young man in the tomb, who would have been an angel or a messenger of God. Perhaps, instead, Mark wants us to struggle with what we perceive as huge stones or obstacles to our believing in Jesus the crucified or to serving as his disciples, subject to grace, to God's power, and the Spirit. If Jesus can bind the strong man (Mk 3:27), certainly no stone is impossible to move with the word of the gospel, the support of the community, and the power of the crucified and risen Lord among us.

With the removal of the stone, the three women simply walk into the tomb. Now they are baptized. They have accompanied Jesus from the beginning and ministered to him, and they are now ready for baptism, even though they still do not understand the full meaning of what is happening to them. Lao Tzu once said, "The room is valuable not because of the walls, but the emptiness within." The tomb is empty, and its emptiness screams silently and cannot be ignored. This entire text is a preparation for baptism as well as postbaptismal teaching. It will be entered into and reflected upon by community members year after year, ever deepening their level of insight and acceptance of what is demanded in baptism. The translation of the New American Bible recounts that they were "amazed," but the fuller meaning of the Greek used here is that they were "deeply disturbed and troubled," an expression that has appeared earlier in Mark's text.

The young man who appears before them is dressed in a white garment, a linen garment like that worn by the young man on the night Jesus was arrested in the garden, and like the shroud in which Jesus was wrapped for burial. He sits at the right side of the tomb, as Jesus will sit at the right hand of the Father. Christians are buried with Christ in the tomb, and then from the waters of baptism they rise with Christ in glory. Everyone baptized into Christ is given a white garment as a symbol of this new life, of their privileged relationship to God the Father, with Jesus, in the power of the Spirit. The young man is not Jesus in disguise, and not even an angel, although he represents the memory of the words Jesus spoke before dying. Many believe that Mark has placed himself in the text as the young man, proclaiming for all time that he seeks to be faithful to the gospel by writing and living the text. Now, he is in the tomb, proclaiming faithfully the words of Jesus. He does not run away, as he once did.

The young man tells the three women to go and tell the disciples and Peter to go to Galilee, where they will see Jesus. On the way, as they talk, they will walk once again with Jesus of Nazareth, listening to him speak of mercy and forgiveness. The name of Peter, usually referred to first, is now mentioned after the disciples. He no longer appears as the leader but as one who is loosely connected to them. Peter is in need of mercy.

The disciples need to revisit the gospel and see themselves as they were—more often than not as failures, deserters, those who followed at a safe distance, or those who don't see and don't hear and don't understand. They had missed so much—the loaves, the Son of Man, the call to the cross, the identity of Jesus—that can be recognized only with eyes of faith, with prayer and by sharing the bread and cup together, and by facing Jesus crucified.

All the disciples failed: they failed Jesus, they failed in their baptismal vows, and some failed miserably when they stood before the powers of the Roman Empire. Peter failed when he stood before a servant girl and casual bystanders. Mark, who may have been the young man on that last fatal night, failed and ran as the other disciples fled in fear. The women failed by watching from a safe distance while Jesus died and by their terror.

Although all of us fail as well, we are all saved in the death and resurrection of Jesus. We are all called to remember again and again the unbelievable mercy of God in Jesus and the power of the Spirit that can be touched through prayer and acts of belief. We can touch God's mercy by sharing the bread and the cup and especially by a life of service to the least, to those in need of freedom, healing, and acceptance and the gospel of God. The gospel will never fail, for it is Jesus' word and presence among us. It is given to sustain us on Jesus' way, all the way to the cross and resurrection.

We are not left alone. Jesus is here, and we have only to turn, to repent, to listen to the gospel and pray "Lord, help my unbelief" to see Jesus, the beloved Son of God and the suffering Son of Man, standing with all the shattered and broken of the earth. Following Jesus is not impossible. Nothing is impossible if we believe that Jesus is who the Gospel of Mark proclaims him to be: Jesus, Son of God, crucified and risen, savior, and the one who walks with us along the way.

Although the way is not impossible, we always seem to need help, to go back to the beginning. Jesus' words to us are, "Begin by denying yourself, picking up your cross and then come after me along the way." We are novices at denying ourselves. In *The Way of Man* Martin Buber describes a place to begin.

Once they told Rabbi Pinhas of the great misery among the needy. He listened, sunk in grief. Then he raised his head. "Let us draw God into the world," he cried, "and all need will be quenched." God's grace consists precisely in this, that he wants to let himself be won by humanity, that he places himself, so to speak, into human hands. God wants to come to his world, but he wants to come to it through men and women. This is the mystery of our existence, the superhuman chance of humankind. (quoted from http://dailydig.bruderhof.org)

Jewish rabbis, who can still speak to the mystery of who Jesus is as the suffering servant and model for those who follow him, are sharp in their demand to choose and to commit to a practice that includes everyone. This is not easy.

The greatest task of our time is to help our fellow human beings out of the pit. God will return to us when we are willing to let Him in— into our banks and factories, into our Congress and clubs, into our homes and theatres. For God is everywhere or nowhere, the father of all people or of none, concerned about everything or nothing. Only in His presence shall we learn that the glory of humankind is not in its will to power but in its power of compassion. We will reflect either the image of God's presence or that of a beast. There can be no neutrality. (Abraham Joshua Heschel, "The Mark of Cain," http://daily-dig.bruderhof.org)

The last chapter of Mark is the third and last call to discipleship. We have been called to follow Jesus in the tradition of the prophets and to catch people for the good news of God—all people. And we have been called to face the cross and the passion of Jesus' power, which is without violence and based on the truth of a God of mercy and compassion; and now we are called again to believe in and stake our lives on the death and resurrection of Jesus as an abiding reality in the world. We are called to mercy, to go and return to walking the way of Jesus, drawing others into the company of believers who walk the way in justice and in peace together with the crucified and risen one. This last call and the last lines of Mark fall like a stone, sinking into the sea; they have the heavy sound of the stone grinding as it is rolled away from the entrance to the tomb. Is that all there is? Of course not! This is the beauty and the ingeniousness of the text.

The young man who proclaims the gospel of resurrection in the tomb summons Mark's community to remember their baptisms and to stake their lives on their commitment. He cries out, "You need not be amazed! You are looking for Jesus of Nazareth, the one who was crucified. He has been raised up; he is not here. See the place where they laid him. Go now and tell his disciples and Peter, 'He is going ahead of you to Galilee, where you will see him as he told you'" (16:6b-7 NAB). These words remind us that we must be intent on seeking Jesus, a Jewish human being born in Nazareth, a man limited by time, family, geography, culture, language, and religious creed who is the crucified one of the earth. This Jesus is the suffering servant of Isaiah who is obedient to God and tender to all those who suffer innocently and at the hands of others. And this is Jesus, the Son of Man whose just judgments over all the nations and peoples of the earth are born of and tempered by the pain and torture that he experienced in his own body. This is the compassionate God who exposes the murderers among us and holds close to him the masses of humanity who suffer at the hands of others. This is Jesus Christ, the Son of God who wants no sacrifices but instead desires mercy that is extended to others in need. The words of St. Bonaventure scratch our consciences and call us to change our lives and hearts: "O human heart, you are harder than any hardness of rocks, if at the recollection of such great expiation you are not struck with terror, nor moved with compassion, nor shattered with compunction nor softened with devoted love."

And, more recently, a prayer of John Paul II cries out to us to take heed of the crucified and risen one's own living, dying, and rising as a model for our way to dwell in the world.

> On my knees I beg you to turn away from the paths of violence and return to the ways of peace. You may claim to seek justice. I too believe in justice and seek justice. But violence only delays the day of justice. Violence destroys the work of justice.

In some ways, this last call to conversion—to live the resurrection life now—is harder than facing the cross and following Jesus to his death and rising. It is a call to live in hope and to defy death at every moment by aligning ourselves with the force for good, by making peace, by reconciling, by being a merciful balm for all the world's children. Now political domination, slavery, collusion between religious faiths or organizations and nations and the military must be resisted and denounced. State-sanctioned destruction of human beings or countries or natural resources or cultures cannot be allowed. Such destruction takes place without even seeing or knowing the human faces of those who cry out against it.

There was the equivalent of a warrant out for Jesus' arrest. He was named as a terrorist and executed summarily as one. Watching was a crowd whipped into a convenient frenzy that served the tactics and intent of both state and religious authorities. There was no recourse to justice. To follow this Jesus, the Holy One of God, is to resist with all one's heart and soul, mind and flesh, and power and resources any state or nation that relies on lies, violence, military might, and political domination. Jesus' death in the first century makes demands on believers today.

> Jesus died, then, not only as rebel in an imperial and politicized context. He also died as a blasphemer in the eyes of the religious estab-

lishment. The way of the executed God entails being not only on the underside of imperial power but also on the downside of established religious leaders who work in concert with the imperial hegemony. Rome did have its own imperial theology that often put it into conflict with the theology of Jewish priestly elites, but those elites also often stood ready to build their respectability and power through connections with imperial Rome.

The way of the executed God, which entails locating oneself among the alienated or among movements of diverse people consigned to an underclass, will often entail loss of religious respectability. Especially if one lives and organizes or participates in movements among such as these, religious power in an imperial milieu will consider you to be one without respect, without power. To follow the executed God today is to let die the god of religious respectability. We cannot serve the executed God and the god of religious respectability. (Mark Lewis Taylor, "The Executed God," 5)

This third call to conversion summons us to return to the intensity of our first commitments. Sooner or later we must choose, as did the disciples. And, amazingly, they did! It was belief in the reality and power of the resurrection of Jesus that drew them to stand before the world and all its powers and declare themselves as followers of the crucified and risen one who promised to live under no sign of power but the sign of the cross. The Gospel of Mark is written for those who said yes, were baptized, and then said no from fear or insecurity or reluctance to deny themselves. Then they wanted desperately to unsay the words and return to the body of Christ.

Mark's gospel ends hanging, and so it affords every reader, every listener, the chance to undo what has been done, to take back their words and actions. It gives each of us the chance to repair any damage to the community and to renew our commitment to the crucified and risen one. Here we come to terms with how we have we missed the mark of what it means to be a Christian, a Catholic, a follower of Jesus of Nazareth, the crucified one, raised from the dead.

Other Endings Telling of Other Appearances of Jesus

Attempts to extend the Gospel of Mark by adding on to the original ending offer glimpses of traditions that were available to the early Christian communities or to those who prayed the Gospel of Mark and felt moved to add to the text. The first two, beginning with Mark 16:9, are short renderings of stories that appear later and are more fully formed in the other gospels. They tell of an appearance of Jesus to Mary Magdalene, who tells the disciples but is not believed (16:9-11). Perhaps this is a piece of what transpires in Luke's account of the women at the empty tomb (Luke 24), or it may be connected to the more extensive story of Mary of Magdala in John's gospel. In the latter account, Mary does not enter the tomb. Thinking that someone has stolen the body of Jesus, she runs to Peter and the disciple that Jesus loves, and she tells them. They, in turn, run to see the empty tomb themselves (John 20).

Then Jesus makes a second appearance to two disciples along the way (16:12-13). This is perhaps an allusion to the long story in Luke 24 of the disciples on the way to Emmaus.

The account of a third appearance differs a bit from later accounts of the resurrection.

> Later Jesus showed himself to the Eleven while they were at table. He reproached them for their unbelief and stubbornness in refusing to believe those who had seen him after he had risen.
>
> Then he told them, "Go out to the whole world and proclaim the Good News to all creation. The one who believes and is baptized will be saved; the one who refuses to believe will be condemned. Signs like these will accompany those who have believed: in my Name they will cast out demons and speak new languages; they will pick up snakes and, if they drink anything poisonous, they will be unharmed. They will lay their hands on the sick and they will be healed."
>
> So then, after speaking to them, the Lord Jesus was taken up into heaven and took his place at the right hand of God. The Eleven went forth and preached everywhere, while the Lord worked with them and confirmed the message by the signs which accompanied them. (16:14-20 CCB)

The language and tone of this text differ from the rest of Mark's gospel. It is in the genre of a summary, a general accounting of what happened in the community of believers long after the resurrection. The resurrection, which is now part of the tradition, forms the background for what is happening in the church. This text has elements that note new developments in the community, such as praying for those who are sick (Letter of James), preaching the gospel to the whole world and baptizing (Matthew 28), and a description of the signs accompanying the followers of Jesus (Acts).

There are also odd inclusions: references to picking up serpents and drinking poison without being harmed. While something like this might have happened once, such practices were certainly not considered routine or normative. And the account of Jesus' appearance in Galilee while the eleven are at table does not appear in the other gospels.

All in all, this text, added on to the original, seems a feeble attempt to provide a conclusion, to complete the story line as one would do for any story. But this is a gospel, not an ordinary story. It is the good news let loose in the world, and there is no ending that is precise or verifiable. The story continues even today as we seek the crucified one on all the continents of the earth, far removed from Galilee.

The text above (Mk 16:14-20) is called the "longer ending." There is also a short text referred to as the "shorter ending," which in some early versions of Mark follows the first eight verses of this chapter; in this way, it would complete the story. If the "shorter ending" were added after verse 3, the complete text would read:

> They made their way out and fled from the tomb bewildered and trembling; and because of their great fear, they said nothing to anyone. (16:8 NAB)

> [They promptly reported to Peter and his companions all that had been announced to them. Later on it was through them that Jesus himself sent out from east to west the sacred and immortal proclamation of eternal salvation.] (The Shorter Ending NAB)

An attentive reader sees immediately that it is impossible to simply end the text with this shorter ending, tying up all the loose ends. Mark's text is intent on discipleship, on our starting on the way with Jesus in the company of other believers, and struggling once again to come to belief in Jesus, the crucified and risen one. Discipleship cannot be found in a few lines about an imperishable proclamation of eternal salvation. It must be integrated into our daily lives, both liturgically and in practice with others, as we face violence, persecution, and moral decisions and care for the poorest of the body of Christ with mercy and forgiveness, service and companionship.

The Gospel of Mark demands our attentiveness and practice with others. There is a dynamic, an energy in the Gospel of Mark that must be "caught," swallowed, and digested. This is found in the word "Go!" or in the adage "Don't just stand there, do something!" Go! Walk and talk your way through your fear, and become the community of believers, the body of Christ in the world, calling others to hope and to new life in Christ.

This is Mark's birth canal and the birth pangs of his community, a community born in the waters of baptism, dying and being buried in the tomb with Jesus, called forth by the power of the word of God in the scriptures and then drawn forth from the tomb. Finally, this community was clothed in white garments and sent to proclaim the good news of God in a hostile world where the Roman Empire sought to dominate and subordinate all peoples.

It is also our birth pangs in a world that calls itself Christian culturally and historically but does not consistently worship the Trinity in justice, peace, mercy, and truth. It is a summons to life here and now that is echoed in the words of Mahler's Symphony no. 2 (*Resurrection*): "Forget thy trembling! Prepare thyself for life! . . . With wings that I have earned in the struggle of love, I shall fly upwards to the light no eye has reached. . . . And in dying, I shall live!"

The word of God in Jesus as told by Mark is contemporary good news that demands that we face the way of Jesus, the way of the cross, the way of mercy and peace-making, and the bringing of justice for all. We are to stand "on our mark," the sign of the cross, sign ourselves with its power alone, and then "get set" to face those who will persecute us or refuse to listen to the words of Jesus that call for forgiveness, no violence, reconciling of enemies, and inclusion of all. Then we are to "go" out into our world, to our nations, to our homes, our places of work, study, and commerce and seek the face of the Lord among us. And we will see him, as he has promised, if we remember all of his words and take them to heart.

A story by Rabindranath Tagore of India, which I call "God in Exile," tells where we are to go, where our God waits for us today.

Once upon a time there was a king who wanted to be remembered and praised to heaven for his accomplishments. He wanted his name on the lips of those who wrote the histories. And so he began to build a temple. It was lavish, huge, and decorated down to the finest detail. It consumed most of his working days and his dreams at night.

But there was a prophet in his kingdom who would walk the groves of trees and the roads preaching to the people and crying for justice, for food and clothing, for medicine and care, for education for all the people. The people flocked to hear his stories and his teachings.

The king thought to himself, "As soon as the temple is complete, then I can gather the people there and they can worship in my temple and not in the roads and groves scattered all over."

The temple was duly dedicated with myriads of priests and attendants, with incense, fruit, flowers, offerings, and rituals of blessings. But the prophet never came to the temple, and so very few of the people would come. Finally, annoyed, the king knew he had to get the prophet to come to the temple if he ever wanted the people to worship there.

The king found him in one of the groves, sitting in the dirt with hundreds of people sitting, standing, and listening to his every word. After long hours, he approached him and asked him why he did not come to the temple and draw the people there to worship. The prophet looked at him and said, "That is your temple, not the temple where God dwells."

The king was furious. "What do you mean?" The prophet looked at him and spoke again so that all could hear his words. "While you were building that temple, over years, even decades, you neglected your people and your kingdom. In fact, you harmed them with your decisions to put all your resources into that building. There were floods and famine, devastations of the land that left people with nothing. The people sought entrance to your temple as high ground, as safety. They begged for food, but you barred the doors to the temple grounds and ignored their cries and desperate pleas. You wasted gold in all your adornments and ceilings of the temple while your people went naked and their children died needlessly. That is your temple, not God's, and I will never set foot within its boundaries."

Sputtering and spitting, the king could barely control himself. "You—you, get out of my kingdom and never return. You will be arrested if you do." The prophet arose, looked at the king and calmly said, "I go from your kingdom gladly, but I will not leave the people. I go from your kingdom gladly, rejoicing in my exile, for my God left long ago, and now dwells in exile, among the people, wherever they are, and that is where I shall dwell." And he walked away and disappeared from the king's sight, moving into the crowd.

Mark's Jesus disappeared into Galilee, back among the people, exiled among the poor and the rejected, in the company of his disciples, the community of believers. They are found in every grove and on every road where people walk and talk their way through their fears and grief and care for one another with the tenderness born of crucifixion and death and the strength born of resurrection life in baptism. Jesus the crucified and risen Lord waits for us, observing us as we go about our lives, calling us once more to follow him, to repent, and believe in the good news of God. He invites us to walk in his company, all the way to the cross and the empty tomb and the life of resurrection.

The members of Mark's community struggled to live their belief. At times they fell and failed, as we all do, and yet they rose again to stand faithful, even in a world that refused to believe and among those who sought to return to the Way. In *Perelandra*, C. S. Lewis describes the power that Mark's community and our communities can gain from Jesus Christ, Son of God and Son of Man.

> Beneath everything is a vast emptiness, a longing: incompletion. The world bleeds.
>
> But into that gaping wound has come the music of the spheres, the harmony. It rings so deep, so true; it swells through the pain. It answers the long heart-rending sighs with a word beyond and above—yet within—all words. It sings of hope. It will not be gainsaid.

That music ends Mark's gospel. It is the pause, the emptiness as solid as the emptiness of the tomb. It is the future that beckons us out of the tomb and back into the world, where God still is and dwells among us. It is hard music and also music that comforts. It is soothing music yet music that evokes and demands allegiance. It is healing music and music that stands between the forces of death and those who choose life.

This chapter, and this book, will end with a poem by a dear friend, Catherine de Vinck. She writes of responding to death and resurrection in an act and a statement of belief much like that of Mark's own community.

> "I am in agony till the end of the world."
> Spread-eagled, in torment
> he of the long suffering
> hangs in the void.
> The cathedral of his body breaks open
> the walls crack, the bones stick
> through the flesh at the wrists.
>
> "If I walk into the fields
> look! Those slain by the sword;
> if I go into the city
> look! Those consumed by hunger."
>
> Thin as a thread, death passes
> through the eye of the needle
> enters the long avenue of the blood
> aims at the central place, the heart;
> Death streams, cold, implacable
> invading the house, flooding the rooms
> carrying the body violently
> into millennia of stones.
>
> Auschwitz, Treblinka, Hiroshima
> Mi-Lai, Kosovo, Rwanda, Sierra Leone;
> Ethiopia, a million dead of starvation
> the Sudan, children crucified;
> Guernica, Dresden, Jerusalem, New York
> and further down Troy buried in the sand;
> past and present jumbled, stacked
> into a huge smoldering heap.
>
> What happens next in the sealed chamber?
> What images, what words can be retrieved
> sifted from the ashes? Out of centuries of pain
> out of the darkest shadows, light rises
> in molten heat and the world catches fire.
> Over disorder and conflict
> over relentless affliction a Face, immensely alive, appears:

all-seeing eyes, ears listening
to the smallest whimper
lips deep-speaking in a silence
beyond speech: the language, incommunicable
bound in sacredness to every life
to the movements of air and water
earth and flame until time
released from its toil, stops
its spiraling speed.

Bibliography

On the Gospel of Mark

Achtemeier, Paul, Daniel Harrington, Robert Karris, George MacRae, and Donald Senior, eds. *Invitation to the Gospels*. Mahwah, N.J.: Paulist Press, 2004.

Beck, Robert. *Nonviolent Story: Narrative Conflict Resolution in the Gospel of Mark*. Maryknoll, N.Y.: Orbis Books, 1996.

Belo, Fernando. *A Materialist Reading of the Gospel of Mark*. Maryknoll, N.Y.: Orbis Books, 1984.

Crotty, Robert, and Ernie Smith. *Voices from the Edge: Mark's Gospel in Our World*. Dublin: Gill & Macmillan; Victoria, Australia: Collins Dove, 1994.

Graham, Helen. *You Will Be Handed Over: The Persecution Prediction in Mark 13:9-13*. Vol. 7. Nagliliyab. Quezon City, Philippines: Claretian Publications, 1987.

Hamerton-Kelly, Robert G. *The Gospel of the Sacred: Poetics of Violence in Mark*. Minneapolis: Fortress Press, 1994.

Harrington, Wilfrid J., O.P. *Mark: Realistic Theologian: The Jesus of Mark*. Dublin: Columba Press, 1996.

Hendrickx, Herman. *A Key to the Gospel of Mark*. Quezon City, Philippines: Claretian Publications, 1993.

———. *The Parables of Jesus: Studies in the Synoptic Gospels*. Manila: St. Paul Publications, 1990.

———. *The Passion Narratives of the Synoptic Gospels*. Manila: St. Paul Publications, 1989.

———. *The Resurrection Narratives of the Synoptic Gospels*. Manila: St. Paul Publications, 1988.

Kelber, Werner. *The Kingdom in Mark: A New Place and a New Time*. Philadelphia: Fortress Press, 1974.

———, ed. *The Passion in Mark: Studies on Mark 14-16*. Philadelphia: Fortress Press, 1976.

Kinukawa, Hisako. *Women and Jesus in Mark: A Japanese Feminist Perspective*. Maryknoll, N.Y.: Orbis Books, 1994.

LaVerdiere, Eugene. *The Beginning of the Gospel: Introducing the Gospel According to Mark*. 2 vols. Collegeville, Minn.: Liturgical Press, 1999.

Martini, Carlo M. *The Spiritual Journey of the Apostles: Growth in the Gospel of Mark*. Boston: St. Paul, 1991.

McBride, Denis. *The Gospel of Mark: A Reflective Commentary*. Dublin: Dominican Publications, 1996.

McFadyen, Phillip. *Open Door on Mark*. London: Triangle Books, 1997.

Moloney, Francis J. *The Gospel of Mark: A Commentary.* Peabody, Mass.: Hendrickson Publishers, 2002.

Myers, Ched. *Binding the Strong Man: A Political Reading of Mark's Story of Jesus.* Maryknoll, N.Y.: Orbis Books, 1988.

———. *Who Will Roll Away the Stone? Discipleship Queries for First World Christians.* Maryknoll, N.Y.: Orbis Books, 1994.

Myers, Ched, Marie Dennis, Joseph Nangle, O.F.M., Cynthia Moe-Lobeda, and Stuart Taylor. *"Say to This Mountain": Mark's Story of Discipleship.* Maryknoll, N.Y.: Orbis Books, 1996.

Newheart, Michael Willett. *"My Name Is Legion": The Story and the Soul of the Gerasene Demoniac.* Collegeville, Minn.: Liturgical Press, 2004.

O'Hanlon, Joseph. *Mark My Words.* London/Kildare, Ireland: St. Paul's Publications, 1994.

Painter, John. *Mark's Gospel: Worlds in Conflict.* New York: Routledge, 1997.

Reiser, William. *Jesus in Solidarity with His People: A Theologian Looks at Mark.* Collegeville, Minn.: Liturgical Press, 2000.

Senior, Donald, C.P. *The Passion of Jesus in the Gospel of Mark.* Collegeville, Minn.: Liturgical Press, 1984.

Trainor, Michael F. *The Quest for Home: The Household in Mark's Community.* Collegeville, Minn.: Liturgical Press, 2001.

Williams, Rowan. *Christ on Trial: How the Gospels Unsettle Our Judgement.* Grand Rapids, Mich.: Eerdmans, 2000.

General and Historical

Berrigan, Philip. "Exorcising the Demons." *The Other Side* 30 (September-October 1994): 16-21.

Carroll, James. *Constantine's Sword: The Church and the Jews (A History).* New York: Houghton Mifflin, 2001.

Casey, Michael. *Fully Human, Fully Divine: An Interactive Christology.* St. Louis: Liguori Publications, 2004.

Crowe, Jerome. *From Jerusalem to Antioch: The Gospel across Cultures.* Collegeville, Minn.: Liturgical Press, 1997.

Dodd, C. H. *The Parables of the Kingdom.* New York: Charles Scribner's Sons, 1961.

Dunn, James, Daniel Harrington, Elizabeth Johnson, John Meier, and E. P. Sanders. *Jesus: A Colloquium in the Holy Land.* Edited by Doris Donnelly. New York: Continuum, 2001.

Ehrman, Bart D. *Lost Scriptures: Books That Did Not Make It into the New Testament.* New York: Oxford University Press, 2003.

Freyne, Sean. *Texts, Contexts and Cultures: Essays on Biblical Topics.* Dublin: Veritas Publications, 2002.

Larsen, Ronald, ed. *A Potter's Companion: Imagination, Originality, and Craft.* South Paris, Me.: Park Street Press, 1992.

Needleman, Jacob. *Lost Christianity: A Journey of Rediscovery.* New York: Penguin Books, 1980.

Neusner, Jacob. *Judaism in the Beginning of Christianity.* Philadelphia: Fortress Press, 1984.

———. *Judaism When Christianity Began: A Survey of Belief and Practice.* Louisville: Westminster John Knox Press, 2002.

Pilch, John J. *The Cultural World of Jesus, Sunday by Sunday, Cycle B.* Collegeville, Minn.: Liturgical Press, 1996.

Rhodes, Daniel. "Legends of Ahimsa." *Studio Potter* 3, no. 2 (Winter 1974/75).

Rotelle, John, O.S.A., ed. *Meditations on the Sunday Gospels, Year B.* Hyde Park, N.Y.: New City Press, 1996.

Taylor, Justin. *Where Did Christianity Come From?* Collegeville, Minn.: Liturgical Press, 2001.

Taylor, Mark Lewis. "The Executed God." *Radical Grace* (January-February 2004).

Wiesel, Elie. *Souls on Fire: Portraits and Legends of Hasidic Masters.* New York: Random House, 1973.

Wright, A. G. "The Widow's Mites: Praise or Lament? A Matter of Context." *Catholic Biblical Quarterly* 44 (1982).

Wylen, Stephen M. *The Jews in the Time of Jesus: An Introduction.* Mahwah, N.J.: Paulist Press, 1996.